THE CONIURACION OF LUCIUS SERGIUS CATELINA

EARLY ENGLISH TEXT SOCIETY
O.S. 366

2025

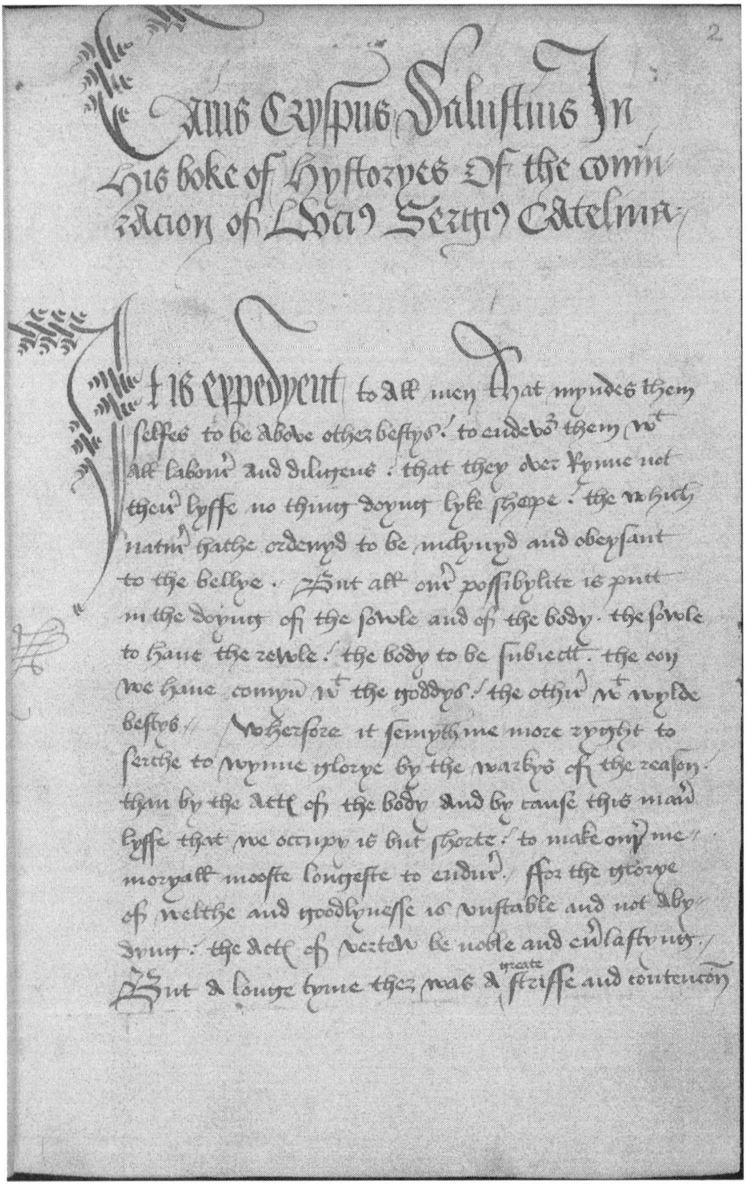

2

Caius Crispus Salustius In
his boke of hystoryes Of the conju-
racion of Lucii Sergii Catelina.

It is expedyent to all men that myndes them
selfes to be above other bestys! to endevor them wt
all labour and diligens: that they ouer Renne not
their lyffe no thing doyng lyke shepe. the which
natur hathe ordeynyd to be inclynyd and obeysant
to the bellye. But all our possibylite is putt
in the doyng of the sowle and of the body. the sowle
to haue the rewle! the body to be subiect. the con
we haue comyn wt the goddys! the other wt wylde
bestys. Wherfore it semyth me more ryght to
serche to wynne glorye by the warkys of the reason.
than by the act of the body And by cause this man
lyffe that we occupy is but shorte! to make our me-
morye all moste longeste to endur. For the glorye
of welthe and goodlynesse is unstable and not aby-
dinge: the act of vertew be noble and endurynge.
But a longe tyme ther was a greate striffe and contencion

Cambridge University Library, MS Nn.3.6, f. 2r

THE CONIURACION OF LUCIUS SERGIUS CATELINA

AN EARLY TUDOR TRANSLATION OF SALLUST'S *BELLUM CATILINAE*

EDITED BY

JOHN COLLEY

Published for
THE EARLY ENGLISH TEXT SOCIETY
by the
OXFORD UNIVERSITY PRESS
2025

OXFORD
UNIVERSITY PRESS

Great Clarendon Street, Oxford, OX2 6DP,
United Kingdom

Oxford University Press is a department of the University of Oxford.
It furthers the University's objective of excellence in research, scholarship,
and education by publishing worldwide. Oxford is a registered trade mark of
Oxford University Press in the UK and in certain other countries

First edition published in 2025

Impression: 1

British Library Cataloguing in Publication Data
Data available

ISBN 978–0–19–897638–7

Typeset by John Waś, Oxford

Printed on acid-free paper
and bound by
CPI Group (UK) Ltd, Croydon, CR0 4YY

MIX
Paper | Supporting responsible forestry
FSC® C013604
FSC
www.fsc.org

ACKNOWLEDGEMENTS

My work on this edition is chiefly indebted to two individuals. Daniel Wakelin, my *Doktorvater*, first introduced me to *The Coniuracion* in 2019. This edition was initially conceived as a joint venture, but Dan—with characteristic generosity—offered me the chance to work on it solo, as my first post-doctoral project. Dan nonetheless remained on call throughout, offering help along the way. I'm deeply grateful to him for being such an inspirational and immensely supportive supervisor, both during and after the doctorate. My second debt is to Richard Beadle, my *Doktorgroßvater*, who spent hours helping me get to grips with the manuscript and the text's language. I'm especially grateful to Richard for inducting me in the ways of the *Linguistic Atlas of Late Mediaeval English*. Richard's warmth and generosity are reflective more widely of the support I've been fortunate to receive at St John's College, Cambridge, which has offered an ideal environment for bringing this project to completion.

Many other debts have also been racked up. Also at St John's, Orietta Da Rold offered incisive advice at several key moments. Jacob Currie generously advised on some knottier aspects of Latin and collation, as well as offering advice more generally. Many useful suggestions were also incorporated thanks to the diligence and extreme generosity of Richard Dance and an anonymous reader; my thanks also to other members of the Council of the Early English Text Society for their feedback and to Bonnie Blackburn for seeing the book through production. Among colleagues at Cambridge, I'm further grateful to James Freeman and Michael D. Reeve for responding generously to requests for help. In Oxford, I'm grateful to Cosima Gillhammer, Diarmaid MacCulloch, and Daniel Sawyer for their help at various stages, and especially to Jane Griffiths for supervising my first work on MS Nn.3.6 in 2020. Further afield, thanks are due to Cecilia Sideri and Charles Tolkien-Gillett for their help, and to Robert Ulery and especially Patricia Osmond for their correspondence and for sharing unpublished work.

Also in need of thanks are the many librarians who have made this edition possible. I'm grateful in particular to Carlotta Barranu (Eton College), Jean-François Brio (Orléans), Angel Cossigny and Angela Petyt-Whittaker (John Rylands), Sarah Dege and Dietlind Willer (Göttingen), Bethany Hall, Harriet Patrick, and Julian Reid (Corpus Christi College, Oxford), Briony Harding (St Andrews), Nathalie Herin and Mathilde

Pays (Roanne), Lynley Anne Herbert (Walters Art Museum), Elena Leith (Ushaw College), Kathryn McKee, Adam Crothers, and Lynsey Darby (St John's College, Cambridge), and Stephen Willis (Edinburgh). Thanks are also due to librarians at the Cambridge University Library, British Library, and Bodleian Libraries for their support.

J.W.S.C.

February 2025

CONTENTS

LIST OF ILLUSTRATIONS

PLATES

FIGURE

ABBREVIATIONS

EDITIONS OF AND COMMENTARIES ON THE *BELLUM CATILINAE*

Asc	Jodocus Badius Ascensius, commentary on the *Bellum Catilinae* in Sallust, *Opera* (Paris, 1504), *USTC* 182604
Loeb	Sallust, *The War with Catiline; The War with Jugurtha*, trans. J. C. Rolfe, rev. John T. Ramsey, Loeb Classical Library, 116 (Cambridge, MA, 2013)
McGushin	P. McGushin, *'Bellum Catilinae': A Commentary* (Leiden, 1977)
Sal	C. Sallustius Crispus, *Catilina; Iugurtha; Historiarum fragmenta selecta; Appendix Sallustiana*, ed. L. D. Reynolds, Oxford Classical Texts (Oxford, 1991)
Ramsey	*Sallust's 'Bellum Catilinae'*, ed. and comm. John T. Ramsey, 2nd edn. (Oxford, 2007)
Val	Lorenzo Valla (attrib.), commentary on the *Bellum Catilinae* in Sallust, *Opera* (Venice, 1491), *ISTC* is00076000, *USTC* 991411

References to individual early printed Sallust editions are given by date in boldface type; the editions in question are listed in the Appendix.

OTHER ABBREVIATIONS

BC	*Bellum Catilinae*
BJ	*Bellum Iugurthinum*
BL	London, British Library
BodL	Oxford, Bodleian Library
CBMLC	*Corpus of British Medieval Library Catalogues*, gen. ed. †Richard Sharpe, Teresa Webber, 16 vols. to date (London, 1990–)
Con	*The Coniuracion*
CUL	Cambridge, University Library
EETS	Early English Text Society
ES	extra series
OS	original series
SS	supplementary series
ISTC	*Incunabula Short Title Catalogue*, https://data.cerl.org/istc
JRL	Manchester, John Rylands University Library
MED	*Middle English Dictionary*, ed. Robert E. Lewis et al., http://quod.lib.umich.edu/m/middle-english-dictionary

ODNB	*Oxford Dictionary of National Biography*, ed. H. C. G. Matthew, Brian Harrison, and Lawrence Goldman (Oxford, 2004), https://www.oxforddnb.com
scr.	scribe/scribal
USTC	*Universal Short Title Catalogue*, ed. Andrew Pettegree and Graeme Kemp (St Andrews, 2017–), https://www.ustc.ac.uk

INTRODUCTION

At some point in the early to mid-1490s, Sallust's *Bellum Catilinae* was translated from Latin into English. G. Sallustius Crispus (86–35 BCE) was a sometime soldier and politician who turned to history writing after retiring from public life. He was an eyewitness to the turbulent events that he describes and analyses in the *Bellum Catilinae*. Central to this text's narrative is the conspiracy of the Roman patrician Catiline to overthrow the Roman Republic in 63 BCE. The history also considers the conditions in Rome that precipitated Catiline's plot, how the conspiracy was foiled with the help of the orator and statesman Cicero (who was consul in the year that the conspiracy emerged), and why many of the conspirators were executed despite being Roman citizens and therefore supposedly immune to such punishment. Sallust's account is deeply moralizing and notable for its scathing portrayal of Catiline. Catiline and his followers are even said to have sealed their confederacy with a blood oath, though Sallust also casts doubt on this rumour. The text ends with Catiline's death, when he and the remainder of his allies were defeated by a Roman army at the Battle of Pistoia in 62 BCE. Catiline's actions seared the imaginations of his contemporaries and subsequent generations. His name became a byword for a conspirator throughout the Middle Ages and beyond.[1]

The anonymous translation edited here, *The Coniuracion of Lucius Sergius Catelina*, survives in just one manuscript and has attracted only fleeting critical attention. The translation itself remains entirely unstudied, going unmentioned in existing scholarship on Sallust's reception.[2] The critical neglect can partly be chalked up to the translation's apparently limited circulation in its day: as noted, only one witness survives, and the translation is neither cited nor alluded to by any other premodern

[1] For more about Sallust's history and the conspiracy, see e.g. Barbara Levick, *Catiline* (London, 2015); D. H. Berry, *Cicero's 'Catilinarians'* (Oxford, 2020); William W. Batstone and Andrew Feldherr (eds.), *Sallust*, Oxford Readings in Classical Studies (Oxford, 2020).

[2] For references to the manuscript, see Margaret Connolly, *Manuscripts in the University Library, Cambridge (Dd–Oo)*, Index of Middle English Prose, 19 (Cambridge, 2009), 340; Jeffrey Todd Knight, *Bound to Read: Compilations, Collections, and the Making of Renaissance Literature* (Philadelphia, PA, 2013), 21–53, which supersedes Knight, 'Fast Bind, Fast Find: The History of the Book and the Modern Collection', *Criticism*, 51 (2009), 79–104; David McKitterick, *Cambridge University Library, a History: The Eighteenth and Nineteenth Centuries* (Cambridge, 1986), 218; Daniel Wakelin, 'Classical and Humanist Translations', in Julia Boffey and A. S. G. Edwards (eds.), *A Companion to Fifteenth-Century English Poetry* (Cambridge, 2013), 171–85 at 172.

writer. But *The Coniuracion* nevertheless deserves our attention. The text is historically significant, pre-dating by over a century what has long been assumed the first translation of the *Bellum Catilinae* into English—that was by the playwright and poet Thomas Heywood, in 1608. Our translation also precedes by several decades what has long been considered the first ever translation of a Roman history into English, Alexander Barclay's version of Sallust's *Bellum Iugurthinum* (1522). *The Coniuracion* moreover stands out as one of the earliest instances of a vernacular humanist translation that was made directly from its classical Latin source. Recovering *The Coniuracion* from its present obscurity, this edition sheds new light on Sallust's reception, translation culture, and the influence of the *studia humanitatis* in early Tudor England.

MANUSCRIPT

Cambridge, University Library, MS Nn.3.6

Binding

Quarter brown morocco over pink mottled board, by W. H. Smith & Son, Ltd, London, Oct. 1959. 260×180 mm. Remnants of an earlier CUL binding on the front pastedown.

Foliation and Flyleaves

The manuscript consists of ff. i–ii+45+iii–iv, foliated in pencil. Folios i–ii at the front and iii–iv at the rear are modern paper.

Materials

The manuscript is paper, measuring 250×168 mm (as trimmed), sourced from two different paper stocks. Folios 1–44 are from the same stock, with one watermark persistent throughout and positioned between two vertical chainlines, 32 mm apart. The watermark is like Lombardic **D**, about 13 mm tall and about 20 mm from the extensions on the left-hand side of the **D** to the right-hand widest point of the curve. The watermark is striking for its position, always near the fore-edge, positioned between 32 mm and 36 mm from the right-hand side of the **D** to the fore-edge as now trimmed, and between 110 mm and 115 mm from the bottom of the **D** to the bottom edge of the leaf as now trimmed. The watermark is always oriented as though legible from the recto. The watermark is a match with Briquet 8130, which is attested in south-western France in 1493.[3]

Folio 45b is from a different paper stock, with vertical chainlines 23 mm apart and a watermark of a cuffed hand with a five-petalled flower extending from the middle finger. A lifeline extends from the base of the watermark's thumb to a z-shaped ornament above the cuff, which contains the letters 'R B'. The thumb and part of the cuff cross a chainline. The watermark is 79 mm from the top of the flower to the bottom of the cuff and 25 mm wide at its widest point. This watermark resembles Briquet 11377–11385: the closest comparanda are nos. 11379 (Wassenaar, Belgium, 1552), 11380 (Osnabrück, 1552; Bruges, 1552), 11381 (Clervaux, Luxembourg, 1552; Metz, 1552), 11382 (Varenguebec, 1547), 11383 (Neubourg, 1537; Hamburg, 1545–6), 11384 (Lisieux, 1557), and 11385 (Neubourg, 1536).[4] This leaf is probably from a mid-sixteenth-century binding (see Provenance).

Collation

1^{12} 2^{10} 3^{12} 4^{13} (wants 11, 12; 13 is a singleton). Each new quire is marked in pencil by the librarian H. L. Pink (1902–88) with an Indo-Arabic numeral, positioned at the bottom right-hand corner of each quire's first leaf. Pink also adds a '+' sign at the bottom right-hand corner of the recto at the middle of each quire. There are no catchwords. There is visible sewing in the middle of the third and fourth quires. Paper guards have been added to reinforce the first two leaves of the fourth and final quire (ff. 35, 36), since the corresponding half of each of these bifolia is now wanting. The guard on f. 35 is probably conjugate with the singleton (f. 45b). The guard on f. 36 must also be attached to this new forty-fifth leaf (see Fig. 1). These guards were probably added as part of a mid-sixteenth-century binding (see Provenance). What originally existed as the fourth quire's penultimate leaf (f. 45a) presumably contained the rest of the translation, which ends abruptly at the foot of f. 44^{v}. Almost two hundred words of Latin are missing, from 'cohortem praetoriam in medios' (*BC* 60.5) to the end.

[3] C. M. Briquet, *Les Filigranes: Dictionnaire historique des marques du papier dès leur apparition vers 1282 jusqu'en 1600*, 4 vols. (Paris, 1907), iii. 440. No similar variants have yet been catalogued at <https://www.wasserzeichen-online.de> or <https://www.memoryofpaper.eu/BernsteinPortal> [accessed Oct. 2024].

[4] Briquet, *Les Filigranes*, iii. 574.

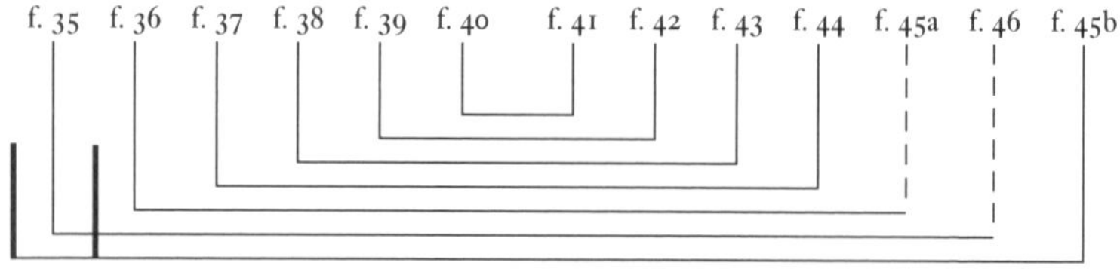

KEY: thicker line=guard; dashed line=leaf wanting

FIG. 1. MS Nn. 3.6, quire 4

Scribe and Script

The manuscript is written neatly by a single anonymous scribe. The script is predominantly a cursive early Tudor secretary, whose common features include single-compartment **a**, flat-topped **g** (often with a coat-hanger descender), z-shaped **r**, **h** with an angular shoulder in the ascender, and crescent-shaped **c**. Occasionally the scribe also uses single-compartment **d** with a straight ascender. These features appear alongside Anglicana features such as two-compartment **a**, boxy **h** with a straight ascender, two-compartment **d** with a looped ascender, and long **r**. The latter is used more than occasionally—nearly eighty times—but still far less frequently than short **r** and z-shaped **r** (the latter most frequently of all). There is one clear instance of dotted **y** ('doyng', 41). The blend of secretary and Anglicana features supports a copying date around the turn of the sixteenth century; this is consistent with the date of the main paper stock. An earlier rather than later date is also suggested by the scribe's apparent nervousness about the newer secretary forms: he once retouches minuscule z-shaped **r** into majuscule **r**, twice retouches one- into two-compartment looped **d**, and at least four times retouches one- into two-compartment **a**.[5] Similar fussiness over allographs is witnessed in other late fifteenth-century manuscripts.[6]

The script is often ornate, too. Some ascenders are extravagantly flourished into the upper margins of each page; these are sometimes partially lost due to trimming. Horizontal strokes are used to cross double **l**, many instances of **h**, and sometimes double **t**. Short **r** is flourished in all but one instance, and always when it appears at the end of a word. A separate engrossed script with more calligraphic feet and protrusions is also used for most proper nouns and titles (e.g. 'consul'). Two words in the manuscript are underlined ('*cohortes veterane*'), probably because they were meant to have been executed in this engrossed script.[7] A separate, cal-

5 See, respectively, 734; 155, 734; 208, 411, 1019, 1032.

6 See e.g. William Worcester, *'The Boke of Noblesse' and the English Texts from Its Codicil*, ed. Catherine Nall and Daniel Wakelin, EETS os 362 (Oxford, 2023), p. xxvi.

7 1665. For another late 15th-c. example where underlining indicates that a different grade

ligraphically impressive display script is used for initial letters of new sections of text. These display-script letters seem to have been executed by the same scribe who was responsible for copying the rest of the manuscript.

Corrections

There are over 170 corrections, most of which involve writing new text. All appear to be in the same hand of the scribe who was responsible for copying the main text. The corrections are executed neatly, sometimes almost imperceptibly. More than a third involve overwriting existing letters. Roughly a quarter involve erasure and rewriting over the top. Almost thirty involve crossing or blacking out, often with the purpose of correcting eyeskip errors. There are twenty-five insertions of text above, between, to the side of, or below lines. Supralinear and interlinear additions are usually marked with a caret. There are only a handful of relatively minor errors that the scribe has failed to correct; these include dittography, dropped letters, and the transposition of letters within words. At least one preposition, one conjunction, and one article are also erroneously omitted. (See further under Revision.)

Language and Dialect

Much of the manuscript's language is the south-eastern and metropolitan late Middle English that was dominant in English literary writing around the turn of the sixteenth century. A date of around this time is further suggested by the scribe's occasional use of etymological spellings, such as 'adventure' (with medial **d**), 'advises' (also with medial **d**), and 'people' (with medial **o**). These spellings reflect a modern, classicizing influence on older Middle English words.[8] Note, however, that equivalent etymological spellings are not used for words including *authority*, *corpses*, *debt*, *doubt*, and *soldiers*.

More significantly, two regional layers of language can also be identified in the manuscript with the aid of the revised, electronic version of the *Linguistic Atlas of Late Mediaeval English* (*eLALME*).[9] The *Atlas* only extends

of script should have been used, see *A Late-Medieval History of the Ancient and Biblical World*, ed. Cosima Clara Gillhammer, 2 vols., Middle English Texts, 63–4 (Heidelberg, 2022), ii, p. lxxv.

[8] See further Vivian Salmon, 'Orthography and Punctuation', in Roger Lass (ed.), *The Cambridge History of the English Language*, iii: *1476–1776* (Cambridge, 2000), 13–55 at 27–8.

[9] Angus McIntosh et al., *An Electronic Version of A Linguistic Atlas of Late Mediaeval English* (Edinburgh, 2013), http://www.lel.ed.ac.uk/ihd/elalme/elalme.html [accessed Oct. 2024].

to 1450, which is several decades before our manuscript was copied. Nevertheless, the database still suggests which forms in MS Nn.3.6 are unusual and where they originated.

One layer of language reflects forms from north of the Humber. These include 'warke' and 'warkys' (44, 877, 1318), **-ys** for the third person plural present indicative ('encressys', 1598), and **-s** as a third person singular present indicative inflection ('lays', 1667). The scribe also occasionally uses some northern forms from Old Norse, including 'fro' for *from* (up to 1100), 'felawe' and 'felawys' for *fellow* (629, 1383), and 'ware' as present tense third person singular and plural, both indicative and subjunctive (up to 581). Dot maps in *eLALME* show that these forms were widely attested in Norfolk, the north Midlands, and the North. The scribe's frequent use of 'awne' may further suggest a northern layer of language, but could also just reflect the writing of Londoners around the turn of the sixteenth century.[10] Meanwhile, a second, more prominent layer of language reflects forms common to East Anglia. The scribe often lowers the front vowel [ɪ] to [ɛ] (e.g. 'leve', 'levid', 'prevy', 'mesery', 'wheche'), **d** is frequently used for **th** (e.g. 'oder', 'eyder', 'fader', 'ferder', 'farder', 'thedyr', 'togader', 'whedyr', 'hyder'), the prefix **on-** sometimes replaces **un-** (e.g. 'onlyke', 'onharnessid'), and **w** and **v** are interchanged (e.g. 'wolgare', 'wouted', 'bevayling').

These layers of language combine to create a *Mischsprache*, a mixed form of language that appears uniquely in one text. *Mischsprachen* come about when a scribe neither consistently 'translates' unfamiliar forms to his own usage nor consistently copies verbatim from his exemplar. In Margaret Laing's terms, this kind of scribe is a 'Mixer'.[11] *eLALME* indicates that *The Coniuracion*'s northern and East Anglian forms could overlap in Norfolk, which makes one of two hypotheses plausible. First, the East Anglian and northern forms could be relicts that 'show through' forms in the scribe's exemplar, which perhaps came from around Norfolk: perhaps our scribe usually erased these forms by imposing the metropolitan or south-eastern forms with which he was more familiar.[12]

[10] e.g. 'awne' appears throughout the letters of Thomas More: see M. L. Samuels, 'Spelling and Dialect in the Late and Post-Middle English Periods', in Michael Benskin and M. L. Samuels (eds.), *So meny people longages and tonges: Philological Essays in Scots and Mediaeval English Presented to Angus McIntosh* (Edinburgh, 1981), 43–54 at 50.

[11] Margaret Laing, 'Multidimensionality: Time, Space and Stratigraphy in Historical Dialectology', in Marina Dossena and Roger Lass (eds.), *Methods and Data in English Historical Dialectology* (Bern, 2004), 49–96 at 52; see also Margaret Laing and Roger Lass, 'Early Middle English Dialectology: Problems and Prospects', in Ans van Kemenade and Bettelou Los (eds.), *The Handbook of the History of English* (Chichester, 2006), 417–51 at 424.

[12] On relicts and show-throughs, see Michael Benskin and Margaret Laing, 'Transla-

The second possibility is that our scribe was trained in or lived around Norfolk. If so, he may occasionally have translated his exemplar's metropolitan and south-eastern forms into the East Anglian and northern forms with which he was more familiar. There are two reasons for preferring this second hypothesis. First, East Anglian and northern forms (except 'ware') do not decrease in frequency across the manuscript: that decrease could have happened in the work of a south-eastern scribe who increasingly 'translated' a more northerly exemplar into his preferred usage, as he became more familiar with that exemplar.[13] Second, there are instances where the scribe retouches more northerly or East Anglian forms—namely, 'opon' and 'onto'—as the semantically identical but orthographically distinct forms 'vpon' and 'vnto'.[14] The best explanation for these corrections is that the East Anglian forms were part of the scribe's active repertoire, which he wrote on autopilot before correcting to the forms given in his exemplar. It may also be relevant that the scribe knew y-shaped thorn, but only uses it once and as part of a correction.[15] Perhaps this form was also part of the scribe's active repertoire, then, and something that he suppressed elsewhere.

Since nothing is known about the manuscript's circulation before the mid-sixteenth century, these suggestions about the scribe's background can only be advanced tentatively. The fact that the text's language is a *Mischsprache* nevertheless confirms two things, however. First, MS Nn.3.6 cannot contain the first ever written text of *The Coniuracion*, even if the only preceding version may have been the translator's first draft. Second, and relatedly, the scribe of MS Nn.3.6 was not *The Coniuracion*'s translator. Future research could perhaps identify the scribe from the idiosyncratic form 'emonxte' (i.e. 'among'), which appears throughout. The closest analogue known to this editor is 'amonx' in the *Book of Margery Kempe*.[16]

tions and *Mischsprachen* in Middle English Manuscripts', in Benskin and Samuels (eds.), *So meny people longages and tonges*, 55–106. On linguistic 'translation', see e.g. Jeremy J. Smith, 'Tradition and Innovation in South-West-Midland Middle English', in Felicity Riddy (ed.), *Regionalism in Late Medieval Manuscripts and Texts: Essays Celebrating the Publication of 'A Linguistic Atlas of Late Mediaeval English'* (Cambridge, 1991), 53–65.

[13] See further Benskin and Laing, 'Translations and *Mischsprachen*', 87.

[14] 1169, 1224.

[15] 191.

[16] *The Book of Margery Kempe*, ed. Barry Windeatt (Cambridge, 2000), line 2754. My thanks to Richard Beadle for this observation.

Punctuation

The manuscript is punctuated with virgules, *punctūs*, *punctūs elevati*, and curls. Punctuation often appears between main clauses and subordinate clauses, as in modern German. Double virgules (//) are common, especially before indentations within a line; these may have been intended to signal the addition of paraphs. Sets of round brackets are used three times.[17] Deictic *punctūs* flank some proper nouns and numerals. A small '//' sign signals runovers of words across the end of a line.

Layout

Each folio's frame is ruled palely in ink, now sometimes too faded to be seen. The ruling is guided by pricking in each folio's top and bottom corners. The size of the ruled text block varies between 194–200 mm tall and 117–23 mm wide. Individual lines are not ruled. The text is presented in a single column, with no sidenotes. There is no title or incipit on f. 1^r, but a heading in engrossed script on f. 2^r separates the translator's preface from the main body of the translation. The text is not divided into chapters, but untitled sections are marked by horizontal blanks which are equivalent to between one and five written lines of text. There are more horizontal blanks around the middle of the manuscript, perhaps because the scribe became less concerned about expending paper at this stage of copying. New sections of text are also marked in three other ways. First, indentations are sometimes left in the middle of a line before the start of a new passage, often with a '//' or '// ~' sign in the indentation. Second, new passages are sometimes delayed to the start of a new line. Third, new passages sometimes start on a new line of text and begin with calligraphic display-script majuscules. The first or first few words at the start of new sections are sometimes also engrossed. On pages without any horizontal blanks there are between twenty-six and thirty lines of text, with a median and mode of twenty-eight. The writing becomes visibly more cramped towards the feet of ff. 35^r, 36^r, and 39^r, probably because the scribe became more concerned again about running out of paper. Three rectos contain a word or short phrase that appears below the bottom of the ruled text block and which is highlighted with a paraph: once the intention was to include text retrospectively, and twice so that the verso could begin cleanly with a new section of text.[18]

[17] 6–7, 55–6, 342–3. [18] 1670; 466–7, 735.

Annotation

The word 'horse', now partially erased, appears in the gutter of f. 13^r in a mid-Tudor hand, opposite 'horsemen of Spayne' in the main text.[19] The remains of a manicule, mostly lost to trimming, are visible in the left-hand margin of f. 23^v. Other presumably sixteenth-century annotations have probably also been lost to trimming, as for example at the top left of f. 15^v.

Provenance

The front pastedown has a Royal Library bookplate, which suggests that the manuscript was one of the many bequeathed to the Crown by Bishop John Moore (1646–1714) and which entered the Cambridge University Library in 1715.[20] The manuscript, indeed, is listed as no. 688 in a 1698 catalogue of Moore's manuscripts, which confirms his ownership of the book by that date.[21] MS Nn.3.6 is subsequently listed as C.IV.4 in the University Library's mid-eighteenth-century old class catalogue.[22] The manuscript is further described in this catalogue as the last item in a *Sammelband* that also included three early printed books. The same information is recorded in William Pugh's late-eighteenth-century AB catalogue of Cambridge University Library manuscripts, in which C.IV.4 becomes AB 10.54.[23] The manuscript was disbound from the printed items in the nineteenth century and renumbered as MS Nn.3.6. A subsequent and unpublished description of the manuscript by M. R. James (1862–1936) treats it as a discrete item, not bound with other books.[24] The three early printed books from the *Sammelband* also survive and are, in their original order:

(1) Cambridge, University Library, Sel.3.265: William Caxton, *Myrrour of the worlde* (London: Laurence Andrewe, 1527?), *STC* 24764;

19 453–4.

20 Brian North Lee, *British Royal Bookplates and Ex-Libris of Related Families* (Aldershot, 1992), no. 73. On the movement of Moore's books after his death, see McKitterick, *Cambridge University Library*, 87–152.

21 Edward Bernard, *Catalogi librorum manuscriptorum angliæ et hiberniæ*, 2 vols. (London, 1697–8), ii. 394: 'A Translation of Salust *de Bello Catilinario*, in old English'. In this Introduction's transcriptions from early printed books and manuscripts other than MS Nn.3.6, original word division, punctuation, and spelling are maintained; all contractions and abbreviations are silently expanded and superscript letters are silently lowered.

22 CUL, MS Oo.7.57, f. 23^v: 'M.S. "Caius Cryspus Salustius In His boke of Hystoryes Of the coniuracion of Lvcius Sergius Catelina." being a translation of Sallusts Catilinarian war into English. Imperf. at the end.'

23 Cambridge University Archives, ULIB 7/3/28, pp. 292–3.

24 See Cambridge University Archives, ULIB 7/3/74/65.

(2) Cambridge, University Library, Inc.3.F.6.2[3396]: William Caxton, *The veray trew history of the valiaunt knight Iason* (Antwerp: Gerard Leeu, 2 June 1492), *ISTC* il00112100, *STC* 15384; and
(3) Cambridge, University Library, Inc.3.J.1.1[3491]: Anthony Woodville, *Cordiale quattuor novissimorum* (Westminster: William Caxton, 24 March 1479), *ISTC* ic00907000, *STC* 5758.

All three books have annotations, though they are especially numerous in the second and third items. Particularly telling is the subtraction of '1492' from '1562' on f. 1^{r} of the *Sammelband*'s third item. In the *Sammelband*, this folio would have faced the last page of the second item (Inc.3.F.6.2[3396]), which states that book's date of publication as 1492. '1562' is therefore probably the year in which this annotation was made, and indicates that the second and third books—and, in all likelihood, all four books—had been bound together in the *Sammelband* by this date.[25] Meanwhile, the publication of the *Sammelband*'s first item around 1527 provides a *terminus a quo* for the *Sammelband*'s creation. The resulting *c.*1527–62 window for the *Sammelband*'s creation is consistent with the hypothesis that f. 45b is part of a sixteenth-century binding (see Materials). To complicate matters, though, the *Sammelband* probably also spent time in a wooden binding before the addition of f. 45b: this is suggested by the worming both at the start of the *Sammelband*'s first item and at ff. 42–4 of MS Nn.3.6, and by the absence of wormhole damage on f. 45b. So, perhaps it was during a sixteenth-century rebinding process that the final two leaves of the manuscript's fourth quire were lost or damaged, necessitating the addition of f. 45b to reinforce the damaged quire. Alternatively, maybe the loss of the final quire's two leaves was the reason for rebinding in the first place.

The annotations to the printed books also include names. In particular, the title page of the copy of Caxton's *History of Jason* is signed 'Thomas Warley', 'Hanricum coldwell', and 'Iohannas Warley'. This title page also contains the note, 'Master vmfray at the syne of the harpe In chep syde goldsmyth owys thys boke T warley testator', which probably refers to a mid-Tudor shop at the sign of the harp on Goldsmiths' Row, Cheapside (and which continued to exist into the seventeenth century).[26] Later in

[25] Similar subtractions that include the year in which the annotation was made are also found in other early English books: see e.g. the subtraction of '1400' from '1656' in a 1602 edition of Chaucer's *Workes*, as discussed in Devani Singh, *Chaucer's Early Modern Readers: Reception in Print and Manuscript* (Cambridge, 2023), 1. Singh gives another example of a similar subtraction at p. 1 n. 2.

[26] See *The Register of the Goldsmiths' Company: Deeds and Documents, c.1190 to c.1666*,

the same book we also find the note 'Per me thomas fote goolld smyth off London'.[27] The final page has the names 'Thomam vmfray' (next to a version spelled 'vmfrey'), 'T. Warley', 'Iohn Gones', and 'hanrycum Coldewell'.

These names suggest that Inc.3.F.6.2[3396] circulated within a network of London goldsmiths and their associates. Henry Coldwell is probably the goldsmith of London who was active between 1548 and 1552.[28] Thomas Humfrey (or 'Humfray') may be the 'thomas humfrey goldsmyth of london' mentioned in 1509 in a statement of payments by Henry Hornby (*d.*1518), one of Lady Margaret Beaufort's executors.[29] Thomas Warley is probably the same Thomas Warley (fl. *c.*1520–57) who in 1530 annotated BodL, MS Rawl. B. 356: Warley, a member of Lord Lisle's household until 1540, signs and dates his name in this book ('T Warley 1530') and refers to himself in it as executor of the estate of a London goldsmith called John Whaberley.[30] John Warley, meanwhile, may be the Tower moneyer who was active in the 1590s and early 1600s.[31] Like Thomas Warley, John Warley would surely also have associated with contemporary goldsmiths. Indeed there were close connections between the Tower Mint and the London Goldsmiths' Company in this period, as are illustrated by the career of Ralph Robynson (1520–77): Robinson, the first English translator of More's *Utopia*, worked as a clerk at the Tower Mint before later becoming a member of the Goldsmiths' Company.[32]

These tentative identifications of annotators in this copy of Caxton's *History of Jason* span the full range of the sixteenth century, including after the date when the *Sammelband* must have been created. As such, it seems more likely than not that the entire *Sammelband*, and not just this one item in it, circulated among these goldsmiths and their associates. This hypothesis is supported by annotations in other items in the *Sammelband*. For example, the 'Henricus' who signed the third item may be the same Henry Coldwell who signed the second item.[33] The 'Thomas Humphrey'

ed. and trans. Lisa Jefferson, 3 vols. (Woodbridge, 2022), iii. 657–65; Gary G. Gibbs, *Five Parishes in Late Medieval and Tudor London: Communities and Reforms* (London, 2019), 158.

[27] CUL, Inc.3.F.6.2[3396], sig. l1r.

[28] C. E. Challis, 'Mint Officials and Moneyers of the Tudor Period', *British Numismatic Journal*, 45 (1975), 51–76 at 57.

[29] Cambridge, St John's College Archives, SJCM/1/3/6, f. 5v.

[30] BodL, MS Rawl. B. 356, ff. 52r, 95v. Cf. 'Warley, Thomas II', in John Baker, *The Men of Court 1440 to 1550: A Prosopography of the Inns of Court and Chancery and the Courts of Law*, 2 vols., Selden Society Supplementary Series, 18 (London, 2012), ii. 1627.

[31] Challis, 'Mint Officials', 76.

[32] *ODNB*, s.n. 'Robinson, Ralph (1520–1577)'.

[33] CUL, Inc.3.J.1.1[3491], f. 78v.

who is mentioned in a partially erased inscription in the first item may also be the same Thomas Humfrey who signed the second item.[34]

None of this information about provenance says much, however, about why the *Sammelband* was created in the first place. Perhaps it was put together simply to protect these four books. This suggestion is strengthened by the fact that the second item also shows signs of repair, like MS Nn.3.6. Indeed, this second item even has similar paper guards, seemingly from the same paper stock as the guards in the manuscript. But there are also thematic links between the texts in these four books. All three printed items are also translations into English, albeit from French rather than Latin. The second item's text even shares a classical theme with the Sallust translation. Similarly classicizing *Sammelbände* are more widely attested from this period. Consider the famous Rosenwald *Sammelband*, which Caxton put together shortly after 1480: this *Sammelband* includes Woodville's classicizing *Dictes or sayengis* translation and a 1481 Caxton edition that itself comprised three classical and/or classicizing translations—namely, of Cicero's *De senectute*, Cicero's *De amicitia*, and a humanist dialogue by Buonaccorso da Montemagno (1391×3–1429).[35] Like the MS Nn.3.6 *Sammelband*, then, both the Rosenwald *Sammelband* and Caxton's 1481 Cicero edition demonstrate how classicizing and humanist translations could be grouped together in premodern England. Also like our *Sammelband*, the Rosenwald *Sammelband* even contains the same combination of Caxton's *Mirror of the World*—albeit, this time, in Caxton's own first edition rather than Laurence Andrewe's sixteenth-century imprint—and Caxton's 1479 edition of Woodville's *Cordyale*.

As for our manuscript's provenance before it became part of this *Sammelband*, we know nothing. Admittedly, one might initially be tempted to hypothesize that it was copied from a now-lost printed book. The engrossed words, for instance, could imitate a printed book's use of larger, contrasting type fonts, as is the case in some contemporary manuscripts which we know were copied from print.[36] Similar display-script letters, imitating woodcut capitals, also appear in other contemporary manuscripts copied from print.[37] But MS Nn.3.6 also lacks features that would

[34] CUL, Sel.3.265, sig. y1^r.

[35] *Tullius de senectute* (Westminster, 1481), *ISTC* ic00627000, *STC* 5293; cf. Paul Needham, *The Printer and the Pardoner: An Unrecorded Indulgence Printed by William Caxton for the Hospital of St. Mary Rounceval, Charing Cross* (Washington, DC, 1986), 47–53.

[36] See e.g. CUL, MS Nn.3.10, a *c.*1500 manuscript copy of Woodville's 1479 *Cordyale*; cf. N. F. Blake, 'Manuscript to Print', in Jeremy Griffiths and Derek Pearsall (eds.), *Book Production and Publishing in Britain 1375–1475* (Cambridge, 1989), 403–32 at 420.

[37] See e.g. Cambridge, St John's College, MS G.19 (s. xv.ex/s. xvi.in), a copy of John

suggest a printed source: these features include a title page, running headers, folio or signature references, and a colophon. Nor are there errors that would especially suggest print transmission, such as the confusion of **d**, **b**, **p**, and **q**, all of which were easily inverted by a typesetter but less easily mistaken by a scribe copying from a manuscript. A further possibility is that MS Nn.3.6 was intended as copy for a printer. The manuscript, though, contains no evidence of casting-off. The uneven number of lines per page further rules out the possibility that the manuscript is a facsimile of a printed page. The evidence for print transmission or intended print transmission is therefore weak. Some aspects of the manuscript's presentation, however, nevertheless seem to have been influenced by features of contemporary printed books. Perhaps our scribe was one of several from the period who valued what Aditi Nafde calls a 'mechanical aesthetic'.[38]

SALLUST: TRANSMISSION AND TRANSLATION

The *Bellum Catilinae* was widely read in the Middle Ages. It usually circulated alongside Sallust's other, slightly longer 'historical monograph', the *Bellum Iugurthinum*; that monograph tells the story of Rome's conflict in the late second century BCE with the usurping Numidian ruler Jugurtha. (A 'historical monograph' concerns a single set of events, and differs from the annalistic style of history writing as practised, say, by Livy and Tacitus.) As Beryl Smalley showed, Sallust was celebrated in the Middle Ages for the moralizing bent of these monographs and their rhetorical value.[39] Their chief stylistic virtue was *brevitas*: both the *Bellum Catilinae* and *Bellum Iugurthinum* are concise in style and substance. Both monographs were also valued for their embedded letters and speeches. The speeches were largely invented by Sallust for rhetorical colour, as a means of increasing the verisimilitude of his histories: they held immense pedagogical value throughout the Middle Ages, not to mention early modernity, serving as rhetorical models for students of Latin to read and imitate. Sallust's monographs were top choices for the arts curriculum of medieval schools.

Sallust's monographs came to renewed prominence with the rise of

Mirk, *Liber festiualis* (Rouen, 1499), *ISTC* im00623500, *STC* 17966 (cf. Blake, 'Manuscript to Print', 428).

[38] Aditi Nafde, 'Replicating the Mechanical Print Aesthetic in Manuscripts before circa 1500', *Digital Philology*, 9 (2020), 120–44.

[39] B. Smalley, 'Sallust in the Middle Ages', in R. R. Bolgar (ed.), *Classical Influences on European Culture A.D. 500–1500: Proceedings of an International Conference Held at King's College, Cambridge, April 1969* (Cambridge, 1971), 165–75.

the *studia humanitatis*, or humanism, in Quattrocento Italy. Humanism instilled in its followers a belief in the value of returning *ad fontes* to original classical texts. Humanists also believed that reading ancient texts, which they called *bonae litterae* (literally, 'good letters'), was necessary for moral improvement and political renewal. Sallust's monographs came to be especially popular as sources for Quattrocento political thought—specifically, the growth of ideas surrounding civic humanism, republicanism, and political liberty. Many of these ideas were indebted to Sallust's concept of *virtus* as something that could only be achieved by individuals with *libertas* (i.e. rights and freedoms), and to his belief that *virtus* could lead to the winning of *gloria*.[40] No wonder, then, that Sallust's monographs came to function as handbooks for Quattrocento school students and other, often princely, readers who were keen to model this progression from *virtus* to *gloria*, winning excellence in political life and on the battlefield alike.[41] Indeed, the insights that both monographs offered into ancient battle tactics were selling points in and of themselves, especially among early Tudor readers.[42] Both monographs moreover offered attractive stylistic models for budding historiographers, including writers who were active at Henry VII's court such as Bernard André (*c.*1450–1522) and Polydore Vergil (*c.*1470–1555).[43]

Humanist readers were also voracious. The frequency with which Sallust appears in Paul Oskar Kristeller's *Iter Italicum* stands testament to the huge number of Sallust manuscripts that were produced in fifteenth-century Italy. Many were lavishly decorated and beautifully written in cursive humanist script.[44] Some travelled as far north as England, though

[40] See further Patricia J. Osmond, 'Princeps Historiae Romanae: Sallust in Renaissance Political Thought', in Batstone and Feldherr (eds.), *Sallust*, 400–44; James Hankins, *Virtue Politics: Soulcraft and Statecraft in Renaissance Italy* (Cambridge, MA, 2019); Quentin Skinner, *The Foundations of Modern Political Thought*, 2 vols. (Cambridge, 1978), i. 84–112. See also Patricia J. Osmond, 'Sallust in the Renaissance: From Exemplary and Analogical Reading to Scholarly Criticism', in C. B. Krebs (ed.), *The Cambridge Companion to Sallust* (Cambridge, forthcoming).

[41] On Sallust's popularity in Quattrocento schoolrooms, see Robert Black, *Humanism and Education in Medieval and Renaissance Italy: Tradition and Innovation in Latin Schools from the Twelfth to the Fifteenth Century* (Cambridge, 2001), 260–2.

[42] See Fred Schurink, 'War, What Is it Good for? Sixteenth-Century English Translations of Ancient Texts on Warfare', in Sara K. Barker and Brenda M. Hosington (eds.), *Renaissance Cultural Crossroads: Translation, Print and Culture in Britain, 1473–1640* (Leiden, 2013), 121–38.

[43] See C. W. T. Blackwell, 'Humanism and Politics in English Royal Biography: The Use of Cicero, Plutarch and Sallust in the *Vita Henrici Quinti* (1438) of Titus Livius de Frulovisi and the *Vita Henrici Septimi* (1500–1503) by Bernard André', in I. D. McFarlane (ed.), *Acta Conventus Neo-Latini Sanctandreani* (Binghamton, NY, 1986), 431–40.

[44] P. O. Kristeller, *Iter Italicum: A Finding List of Uncatalogued or Incompletely Catalogued*

others were made in England afresh: David Rundle refers to a fifteenth-century 'vogue' in England for copies of Sallust.[45] The most beautiful of the manuscripts made in England was copied by Richard Bole (*d.*1477), a Fellow of Balliol College in Oxford and sometime archdeacon of Ely.[46] Other Sallust manuscripts produced in fifteenth-century England include the work of one anonymous scribe and an otherwise little-known scribe called John Rybow.[47] In early Tudor England, these new manuscripts brushed shoulders with older ones: these included a twelfth-century copy of both monographs that John Leland (*c.*1503–52) recorded at Bury Abbey library and, for instance, a thirteenth-century copy of the *Bellum Catilinae* that passed through the library of Bishop Thomas Barlow (1608/9–91).[48] The older manuscripts also included a late fourteenth-century Italian copy of both monographs that was acquired in the fifteenth century by an English reader, probably Thomas Hill, who was a Fellow of New College, Oxford from 1449 to 1469.[49] Other Sallust manuscripts that were in circulation at the time but which have now been lost include the copy

Humanistic Manuscripts of the Renaissance in Italian and Other Libraries, 6 vols. (Leiden, 1963–92). For illuminated copies, see e.g. A. C. de la Mare and Laura Nuvoloni, *Bartolomeo Sanvito: The Life and Work of a Renaissance Scribe* (Paris, 2009), nos. 86, 90.

[45] David Rundle, 'Humanism before the Tudors: On Nobility and the Reception of the *Studia Humanitatis* in Fifteenth-Century England', in Jonathan Woolfson (ed.), *Reassessing Tudor Humanism* (Basingstoke, 2002), 22–42 at 41 n. 55.

[46] Oxford, Balliol College, MS 258. In 1461, Bole also copied two commentaries on Sallust's monographs, which Daniel Wakelin rightly suggests were probably assembled from other sources: see Oxford, Balliol College, MS 123; Daniel Wakelin, 'Early Humanism in England', in Rita Copeland (ed.), *The Oxford History of Classical Reception in English Literature*, i: *800–1558* (Oxford, 2016), 487–513 at 496. A clue that Bole compiled these from earlier sources is the fact that at least one gloss from his manuscript's first *BC* commentary also appears verbatim in 'Anonymous Amandensis', a commentary that survives in two 12th-c. MSS: see Balliol College, MS 123, f. 118ᵛ ('Municipia . castella a quibus Romani accipere munera vel tributa'); cf. Andrew J. Turner, 'Reading Sallust in Twelfth-Century Flanders', *International Journal of the Classical Tradition*, 21 (2014), 198–222 at 206. On Balliol MS 123, see further [A. C. de la Mare and Richard Hunt], *Duke Humfrey and English Humanism in the Fifteenth Century: Catalogue of an Exhibition Held in the Bodleian Library, Oxford* (Oxford, 1970), 30 (no. 50).

[47] Oxford, St John's College, MS 84; Oxford, Magdalen College, MS lat. 218. For a description of Rybow's manuscript, see David Rundle, 'Of Republics and Tyrants: Aspects of Quattrocento Humanist Writings and Their Reception in England, *c.*1400–*c.*1460' (D.Phil. thesis, University of Oxford, 1997), 448–51; cf. also Rundle, *The Renaissance Reform of the Book and Britain: The English Quattrocento* (Cambridge, 2019), 247–8.

[48] Cambridge, Pembroke College, MS 114; BodL, MS Barlow 45. On the 12th-c. copy, see N. R. Ker (ed.), *Medieval Libraries of Great Britain: A List of Surviving Books*, 2nd edn. (London, 1964), 19.

[49] BodL, MS Auct. F. 5. 8. For the Hill identification, see Otto Pächt and J. J. G. Alexander, *Illuminated Manuscripts in the Bodleian Library, Oxford*, ii: *Italian School* (Oxford, 1970), 18.

that Humfrey, duke of Gloucester presented to the University of Oxford in 1444. They also include the copy presented to Lincoln College, Oxford by Robert Flemyng (1416–83), a sometime dean of Lincoln.[50]

The *editio princeps* of both monographs was issued at Venice in 1470. Over a hundred books containing the *Bellum Catilinae* were then printed over the next fifty years: Peter Burke and Freyja Cox Jensen have shown that Sallust was the most popular ancient historian of the late fifteenth and early sixteenth centuries.[51] The text of these editions often varied because there was no established text of either the *Bellum Catilinae* or *Bellum Iugurthinum*.[52] The first editor to comprehensively tackle the textual problems was Pomponio Leto (1428–98), who used readings in 'old manuscripts'—or so at least he claimed—to prepare what can be considered the first critical edition of the monographs.[53] That edition first came out in 1490. In 1491 it was reprinted at Venice, this time with a 27,000-word commentary attributed to Leto's former mentor, Lorenzo Valla (1407–57). The Valla commentary—which was almost certainly not by Valla—takes a line-by-line and word-by-word approach to Sallust's Latin, glossing difficult vocabulary, figures of speech, and allusions to Roman history and culture.[54] As is standard for this period, the commentary is printed in smaller type and appears around Sallust's Latin (see e.g.

[50] *CBMLC* UO3.119, UO38.82.

[51] Freyja Cox Jensen, 'Ancient Histories of Rome in Sixteenth-Century England: A Reconsideration of Their Printing and Circulation', in Paulina Kewes (ed.), *Ancient Rome in English Political Culture, ca. 1570–1660*, special issue of *HLQ*, 83 (2020), 415–40; Cox Jensen, 'The Popularity of Ancient Historians, 1450–1600', *Historical Journal*, 61 (2018), 561–95; Peter Burke, 'A Survey of the Popularity of Ancient Historians', *History and Theory*, 5 (1966), 135–52. See also Patricia J. Osmond, '*Princeps historiae Romanae*: Sallust in Renaissance Political Thought', *Memoirs of the American Academy in Rome*, 40 (1995), 101–43 at 132–6.

[52] See further L. D. Reynolds (ed.), *Texts and Transmission: A Survey of the Latin Classics* (Oxford, 1983), 341–9.

[53] 'antiquis exemplaribus' (**1490**, sig. a3^{r}). The manuscripts Leto claimed to have used cannot be identified, and some of his emendations may lack the authority of an earlier witness. On other Renaissance editors who disingenuously advanced their own conjectural emendations under the cover of supposed earlier witnesses, see E. J. Kenney, *The Classical Text: Aspects of Editing in the Age of the Printed Book* (Berkeley, CA, 1974), 30–4. On Leto's edition in particular, see also Patricia J. Osmond and Robert W. Ulery, Jr., 'Pomponius Laetus, Editor of Sallust: *Corrector vel corruptor*?', in Giancarlo Abbamonte, Minna Skafte Jensen, and Marianne Pade (eds.), *Ipsissima verba: Essays in Honour of Johann Ramminger*, special issue of *Renæssanceforum: Nordic Journal of Renaissance Studies*, 19 (2022), 171–96. In the present edition, Renaissance names are given in the forms most commonly used in modern scholarship (hence e.g. 'Aldus Manutius', but 'Pomponio Leto').

[54] On the authenticity of the Valla commentary, see Patricia J. Osmond, 'The Valla Commentary on Sallust's *Bellum Catilinae*: Questions of Authenticity and Reception', in Marianne Pade (ed.), *On Renaissance Commentaries* (Hildesheim, 2005), 29–48.

Plate 1, *infra*). The Valla commentary appeared again in a 1495 version of Leto's edition that had been revised by Johannes Britannicus, a printer in Brescia. It also appeared in a 1500 edition of Sallust's *Opera* that additionally contained another, 16,000-word commentary on the *Bellum Catilinae*, attributed—again, spuriously—to Ognibene Bonisoli da Lonigo (*c*.1412–74).[55] After Britannicus's 1495 edition, Leto's edition was revised once more, in 1504, by the Parisian pedagogue and bookseller Jodocus Badius Ascensius. Ascensius printed his text of the *Bellum Catilinae* not with the Valla or ps.-Ognibene commentaries, but with a 41,000-word commentary of his own. This was one of Ascensius's 'familiar' commentaries, intended mainly for school students.[56] The final new edition of the monographs to appear in the first decade of the sixteenth century was edited by Aldus Manutius and came out in 1509.[57]

Many of the early printed editions of Sallust's monographs made it to England. For instance, out of the incunables containing the *Bellum Catilinae* that were consulted for this edition, eight have contemporary readers' marks that place them in England in the sixteenth century, if not earlier (the shelfmarks of these eight incunables are underlined in the Appendix). Most of these eight incunables were printed in Venice, which adds weight to Martin Lowry's suggestion that, by the 1480s, there was a direct link between Venetian publishing houses and English customers.[58] Besides the general reasons for Sallust's popularity as were outlined above, copies of Sallust's works were also popular specifically in England because they were studied at newly founded grammar schools, such as Magdalen College School in Oxford (founded 1480).[59] Sallust was

[55] The ps.-Ognibene commentary really dates from the 12th or 13th c.: see Robert W. Ulery, Jr., 'Sallust's *Bellum Catilinae* in the Edition of Venice, 1500: The Medieval Commentary and the Renaissance Reader', in Pade (ed.), *On Renaissance Commentaries*, 7–28.

[56] See further Paul White, *Jodocus Badius Ascensius: Commentary, Commerce and Print in the Renaissance* (Oxford, 2013), 73–6.

[57] On later editions and commentaries, and on earlier and contemporary commentaries that were never printed, see Patricia J. Osmond and Robert W. Ulery, Jr., 'Sallustius Crispus, Gaius', in †P. O. Kristeller, †F. E. Cranz, †V. Brown, and Greti Dinkova-Bruun (gen. eds.), *Catalogus translationum et commentariorum*, 13 vols. to date (Washington, DC, 1960–), viii. 183–326 and x. 375–91; Osmond, '*Princeps historiae Romanae*' (1995), 136–7.

[58] Martin Lowry, 'The Arrival and Use of Continental Printed Books in Yorkist England', in Pierre Aquilon and Henri-Jean Martin with François Dupuigrenet Desrousilles (eds.), *Le Livre dans l'Europe de la Renaissance: Actes du xxviiie colloque international d'études humanistes de Tours* (Paris, 1988), 449–59 at 453. See also Margaret Lane Ford, 'Importation of Printed Books into England and Scotland', in Lotte Hellinga and J. B. Trapp (eds.), *The Cambridge History of the Book in Britain*, iii: *1400–1557* (Cambridge, 1999), 179–201 at 188–9.

[59] See further Nicholas Orme, *English School Exercises: 1420–1530* (Toronto, 2013), 378–414, esp. 396–7.

sometimes studied at grammar schools alongside other historians such as Caesar. At other times, his works were read for their embedded orations. These orations could be used as a historical introduction to a study of Cicero's orations, especially his four *Catilinarians*, which similarly focused on Catiline's conspiracy (and alongside which the *Bellum Catilinae* was often copied or bound together in both manuscript and print).[60] The difficulty of Sallust's deliberately archaic Latin, however, meant that his works were typically studied only in the last years of a grammar school education. Sir John Cheke, a sixteenth-century Fellow of St John's College in Cambridge, alluded to Sallust's linguistic difficulty when he said that '*Salust* was not verie fitte for yong men, to learne out of him, the puritie of the Latin tong'.[61] Consequently, there was still plenty of scope to study Sallust at university. Hence, for instance, his works were stocked in fifteenth-century College libraries in Cambridge. He was also specified as an author to be read in the 1517 founding statutes of Corpus Christi College in Oxford. Several Sallust editions were moreover sold in Oxford in 1520 by the bookseller John Dorne, which further suggests Sallust's continuing appeal to a university market.[62]

SOURCES AND DATE

The Text

The Coniuracion closely translates Sallust's Latin, and it chiefly follows textual variants that first appeared in Pomponio Leto's 1490 edition. Crucially, some of these variants were not subsequently adopted in the revised versions of Leto's edition by Britannicus (1495) and Ascensius (1504), nor in Aldus's new edition of 1509. Consider, for example, when our translator writes that Catiline, despite extra safeguards that had been set up in Rome, went about the 'same thinges as he dyd afore'.[63] '[A]s he dyd afore' trans-

[60] For relevant syllabi, see T. W. Baldwin, *William Shakspere's 'Small Latine and Lesse Greeke'*, 2 vols. (Urbana, IL, 1944), i. 129, 132 and ii. 564–8.

[61] As quoted by Roger Ascham in *The Scholemaster* (London, 1570), *STC* 832, sig. S4^{v}.

[62] *Statutes of the Colleges of Oxford*, ii (London, 1853), part 10, 48; John Dorne, *Day-Book*, ed. C. R. L. Fletcher and Montagu Burrows, in *Collectanea* (Royal Historical Society), 4 vols. (Oxford, 1885–1905), i. 78–139 and ii. 457–62. For Sallust in Cambridge libraries, see Damian Riehl Leader, *A History of the University of Cambridge*, i: *The University to 1546* (Cambridge, 1988), 236, where Leader alludes to *CBMLC* UC29.152, UC48.*236b (Cambridge, Peterhouse, MS 258). The Sallust portion of this manuscript was lost by the end of the 16th c.: see Montague Rhodes James, *A Descriptive Catalogue of the Manuscripts in the Library of Peterhouse* (Cambridge, 1899), 323–4.

[63] 734. Here as elsewhere, see the Explanatory Notes for further discussion and citations.

lates 'quæ antea', a phrase that only appears in Leto's edition: these two words are omitted in all other incunables containing the *Bellum Catilinae*, as also in Ascensius's and Aldus's editions. As a second example, note that 'nature' at line 343 translates 'ingenii', which is the variant in all Leto editions. All other incunables instead print 'studium', as do Ascensius's and Aldus's editions.

Translations of Roman names offer further evidence for the translator's use of Leto's edition, and also for which imprint of Leto's edition he probably consulted. Of course, classical names were especially prone to variation more generally in late medieval scribal and print transmission.[64] If, however, the same unusual spelling appears in both MS Nn.3.6 and an early edition of the *Bellum Catilinae*, we can reasonably assume two things. First, that the unusual spelling in our manuscript is either the same as or very close to the translator's original spelling—and, indeed, MS Nn.3.6 was probably copied in close connection with the translator (see Revision). Second, we can assume that our translator carefully copied that unusual spelling from his source.

The two most revealingly spelled names are 'Puplius Siccio Nucerius' and 'Servius Yla' (i.e. the financier Publius Sittius of Nuceria and the conspirator Servius Sulla).[65] Early editions of the *Bellum Catilinae* provide a range of variants for both names (both of which always appear in the Latin in the accusative case). For the former, Britannicus editions (1495–) give 'Sicenium' or 'Siccinum', Ascensius editions (1504–) give 'Siccinum Nucerinum', and earlier incunables give either 'scithium nucerinum', 'scitium nucerinum', 'sicium nucerinum', or 'sicium micerinum' (or close variants thereof). The most plausible source for *The Coniuracion*'s spelling ('Puplius Siccio Nucerius') is the variant 'Siccium Nucerium', which only appears in a handful of imprints of Leto's edition: as listed in the Appendix, these are **1490**, **1491**, **1493.1**, and **1493.3**. For 'Servius Yla', most incunables print Servius 'Syllam' or 'Sillam', as do Britannicus's (1495–), Ascensius's (1504–), and Aldus's editions (1509–). The only exceptions are in imprints of Leto's edition. Among Leto editions that were printed with the Valla commentary, the variants are 'ylā' (**1491**, **1492**, **1493.3**), 'Syllam' (**1493.1**), 'ylam' (**1493.2**), 'yllā' (**1494**, **1497.5**), 'sillā' (**1495.2**), and 'yllam' (**1497.4**). *The Coniuracion*'s 'Yla' is closest to the variants in **1491**, **1492**, **1493.2**, and **1493.3**.

Considered together, the examples of 'Siccio Nucerius' and 'Servius Yla' suggest that *The Coniuracion*'s main source was one of two Venetian

[64] Cf. Daniel Wakelin, 'Not Diane: The Risk of Error in Chaucerian Classicism', *Exemplaria*, 29 (2017), 331–48.

[65] 532, 1083.

imprints of Leto's edition, either **1491** or **1493.3**. This conclusion is confirmed by other variants which are identified throughout the Explanatory Notes. One further example also deserves singling out, however, because it provides some evidence that our translator used **1491** instead of **1493.3**. This is where the translator writes 'for now it is nott', which more closely translates 'Nam nunc non agitur' (the variant in **1491**) rather than 'Nunc uero non id agitur' (the variant in **1493.3**).[66]

The translator's use of either **1493.3** or (more likely) **1491** provides a *terminus a quo* for *The Coniuracion* of 11 May 1491, which is when **1491** was first published. The translation was probably made sooner rather than later after that date: as time elapsed, the chances increase that our translator would alternatively have based his translation on the 1495 Britannicus or 1504 Ascensius editions. An earlier date is also consistent with the manuscript's main paper stock, whose watermark is attested in 1493 (see Materials). Due to the economics of the late medieval paper trade, paper was typically used soon after it was produced rather than stored for long periods of time.[67]

There is one complication, though: neither **1491** nor **1493.3** explains every textual variant that our translator followed. Conveniently, admittedly, most of the otherwise unexplained variants can be explained by variants that appear in the *lemmata* of the Valla commentary, which our translator drew on extensively (see *infra*, Commentaries). Nevertheless, there are two substantial variants in MS Nn.3.6 which cannot be explained in this way. One of these is the phrase 'his reason is nothing worthe'. This translates a Latin phrase which is omitted in all but one imprint of Leto's edition (**1491–2**), even though it appears in all earlier incunables. We can call this the 'animus nihil ualet' passage.[68] The other variant ('howe, shortly after, . . . made a citee') translates a Latin phrase which was even rarer in early editions of the *Bellum Catilinae*. In editions printed before 1510, it only appears in a group of (mostly) Parisian incunables which are designated *ParisT* in the Appendix. This Latin phrase was rare because it was not transmitted as part of the direct tradition of the *Bellum Catilinae*, only being introduced via its appearance in one of St Augustine's letters.[69] We can call this the 'ita breui' passage.[70]

[66] 1382.

[67] See further Orietta Da Rold, *Paper in Medieval England: From Pulp to Fictions* (Cambridge, 2020), 58–93.

[68] 1205–6; *BC* 51.3. NB. **1491–2** does not contain the Valla commentary.

[69] Cf. St Augustine, *Epistulae CI–CXXXIX*, ed. Kl. D. Daur, Corpus Christianorum Series Latina, 31B (Turnhout, 2009), *epistula* 138, §10.

[70] 157–8; 'ita breui multitudo diuorsa atque uaga concordia ciuitas facta erat' (*BC* 6.2). A

There are three possible explanations for how our translator came to translate the 'animus nihil ualet' and 'ita breui' passages. First, he may have added these missing passages to his copy of Leto's edition by collating it with an earlier *ParisT* incunable. This seems unlikely, however, since our translator appears not to have made a detailed collation of his copy-text against any other version of the *Bellum Catilinae*: his translation almost always follows either **1491** (or **1493.3**), or readings that he found in the Valla commentary. The second and third possibilities, which are not mutually exclusive, are more likely. The first of these possibilities is that our translator added both missing passages from another, already-corrected copy of the *Bellum Catilinae*. The other is that he added both passages based on second-hand information, perhaps via word of mouth. We should take this second idea at least as seriously as the first. Indeed, the translator himself gestures towards his second-hand knowledge in his preface, when he says he was taught 'in very youthe' by 'lernyd men' whom he describes as 'reders'.[71] 'Reders' probably translates *lectores*, which was the standard term for university lecturers in fifteenth-century Oxford and Cambridge. Perhaps, then, the 'animus nihil ualet' and 'ita breui' passages represent some of the 'thinges' which the translator knew from these 'lernyd men' and which he endeavoured 'to gader and adioyne'. Maybe he was even working from an old copy of the *Bellum Catilinae* that he had marked up in his student days. Although these 'thinges' had been 'a greate tyme laid by' and now seem 'full straunge' to him, he says that they are 'gretly belongynge' to the translation and that he has added them 'for fere of reprove of eny necligent ascape'.[72] Perhaps, one speculates, he was imagining the 'reprove' of one of his former teachers.

Some of the copies of Leto's Sallust edition that have early Tudor provenance add weight to this theory of second-hand textual transmission, and indicate how it may have worked in practice. For instance, one Tudor copy of the Venice 1492 imprint of Leto's edition has the missing 'ita breui' passage added in its entirety in the margin (Plate 1). This copy is signed by an Augustinian monk of Winchcombe called John. This

quibble: based on corrections to some classical names that were mangled in a later passage of Leto's edition (see e.g. 'L. Vargenteius', 'M. Porcius Leca' [396–7]), it is conceivable that our translator also knew readings from a subgroup of *ParisT* incunables that preserve a version of the *BC* edited by Filippo Beroaldo. Our translator's familiarity with readings from Beroaldo's edition, however, cannot ultimately be confirmed by the surviving evidence. On Beroaldo's edition, see further Patricia J. Osmond, 'Princeps Historiae Romanae' (2020), 424; Osmond, 'Jacopo Corbinelli and the Reading of Sallust in Late Renaissance France', *Medievalia et Humanistica*, 21 (1994), 85–110 at 87.

[71] 23–4.

[72] Quotations from 23–8.

copy has not been consistently collated against another copy of the text. So, perhaps John already knew at second-hand that this 'ita breui' passage was often wanting in *Bellum Catilinae* editions and therefore made a point of adding it to his newly acquired Venetian copy of the text.[73] Similar annotations are found in another copy of the Venice 1492 imprint that was owned and annotated by John Claymond (1468–1537). Claymond was an alumnus of Magdalen College and the first President of Corpus Christi College in Oxford. In Claymond's copy, the same 'ita breui' passage is also added in its entirety in the margin.[74] Claymond went on to make further corrections in his copy that our translator probably also made.[75] He also made other corrections, however, that our translator was either unaware of or chose not to follow.[76] Claymond, then, was not our translator. Both Claymond and John of Winchcombe were, however, the kinds of people whom our translator may have known and spoken with about the *Bellum Catilinae*, as colleagues or former teachers. Indeed, a monastic context may seem especially likely, since John of Winchcombe was not the only monk reading Sallust around this time. For example, a copy of Britannicus's edition survives which was signed by the Benedictine monks John Crystall and Thomas Rowland (or 'Rolhande'): both were at Abingdon Abbey by 1504 and studied at Oxford in the 1510s.[77] Like several other copies from this period, Crystall's and Rowland's copy even contains a few interlinear English glosses to the *Bellum Catilinae*. These glosses do not consistently mirror the translation choices made in *The Coniuracion*. Nevertheless, they suggest one way—hypothetically—in which *The Coniuracion* may have started out, as a series of vernacular glosses that were later pieced together and embellished.

Two final considerations remain to be addressed with respect to *The Coniuracion*'s main source. One is the possibility that our translator used a manuscript in combination with Leto's edition. After all, contemporary translators still used manuscripts in the age of print. Consider John Skelton, who for his translation of the first five books of Diodorus Siculus's *Library of History* (1478×90) must have worked from at least one manuscript of his main source, perhaps in combination with an early printed

[73] Cambridge, St John's College, Ii.2.27(1) (**1492.2**), sig. a5^{r}.

[74] Oxford, Corpus Christi College, ϕ.C.4.6(2) (**1492.2**), sig. a5^{r}. = *CBMLC* UO24.27b. See also on this copy R. M. Thomson, *The Fox and the Bees: The Early Library of Corpus Christi College, Oxford* (Cambridge, 2018), 62.

[75] Cf. e.g. 72–3*n*, 395*n*, 396–7*n*.

[76] Cf. e.g. 343*n*, 395–6*n*, 397*n*, 398–9*n*, 758*n*, 1025–6*n*.

[77] Shrewsbury School, F.VI.5 (**1495–1500.1**). On Crystall and Rowland, see A. B. Emden, *A Biographical Register of the University of Oxford A.D. 1501 to 1540* (Oxford, 1974), 156, 493.

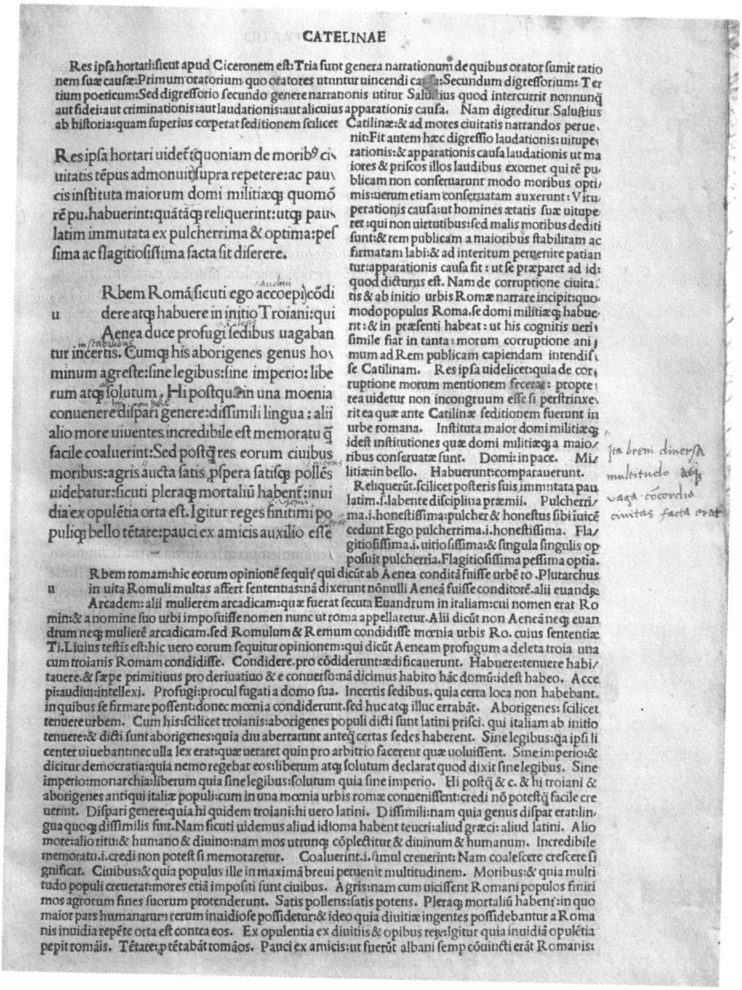

CATELINAE

Res ipsa hortari:sicut apud Ciceronem est:Tria sunt genera narrationum de quibus orator sumit ratio nem suæ causæ:Primum oratorium quo oratores utuntur uincendi causa:Secundum digressorium: Ter tium poeticum:Sed digressorio secundo genere narrationis utitur Salustius quod intercurrit nonnunq aut fidei:aut criminationis:aut laudationis:aut alicuius apparationis causa. Nam digreditur Salustius ab historia:quam superius cœperat seditionem scilicet Catilinæ:& ad mores ciuitatis narrandos peruenit:Fit autem hæc digressio laudationis:uituperationis:& apparationis causa laudationis ut maiores & priscos illos laudibus exornet qui rē publicam non conseruarunt modo moribus optimis:uerum etiam conseruatam auxerunt:Vituperationis causa:ut homines ætatis suæ uituperet:qui non uirtutibus:sed malis moribus dediti sunt:& rem publicam a maioribus stabilitam ac firmatam labi:& ad interitum peruenire patiantur:apparationis causa fit:ut se præparet ad id: quod dicturus est. Nam de corruptione ciuitatis & ab initio urbis Romæ narrare incipit:quomodo populus Roma.se domi militiæq; habuerit:& in præsenti habeat:ut his cognitis ueri simile fiat in tanta:morum corruptione animum ad Rem publicam capiendam intendisse Catilinam. Res ipsa uidelicet:quia de corruptione morum mentionem fecerat: propterea uidetur non incongruum esse si perstrinxerit ea quæ ante Catilinæ seditionem fuerunt in urbe romana. Instituta maior domi militiæq; idest institutiones quæ domi militiæq; a maioribus conseruatæ sunt. Domi:in pace. Militiæ:in bello. Habuerunt:comparauerunt. Reliquerūt.scilicet posteris suis immutata paulatim.s.labente disciplina præmii. Pulcherrima.i.honestissima:pulcher & honestus sibi inuicē cedunt Ergo pulcherrima.i.honestissima. Flagitiosissima.i.uitiosissima:& singula singulis opposuit pulcherria.Flagitiosissima pessima optia.

Res ipsa hortari uidet̄:quoniam de morib9 ciuitatis tēpus admonuit:supra repetere:ac paucis instituta maiorum domi militiæq; quomō rē pu.habuerint:quātaq; reliquerint:utq; paulatim immutata ex pulcherrima & optima:pessima ac flagitiosissima facta sit disserere.

Vrbem Romā:sicuti ego accoepi:cōdidere atq; habuere in initio Troiani:qui Aenea duce profugi sedibus uagabantur incertis. Cumq; his aborigenes genus hominum agreste:sine legibus:sine imperio: liberum atq; solutum. Hi postquā in una moenia conuenere dispari genere:dissimili lingua : alii alio more uiuentes incredibile est memoratu q̄ facile coaluerint:Sed postq̄ res eorum ciuibus moribus:agris aucta satis ꝓspera satisq; polles uidebatur:sicuti pleraq; mortaliū habent̄:inuidia ex opulētia orta est. Igitur reges finitimi populiq; bello tētare:pauci ex amicis auxilio esse

Vrbem romam:hic eorum opinionē sequit̄ qui dicūt ab Aenea conditā fuisse urbē ro .Plutarchus in uita Romuli multas affert sententias:nā dixerunt nōnulli Aeneā fuisse conditorē.alii euandrum Arcadem: alii mulierem arcadicam:quæ fuerat secuta Euandrum in italiam:cui nomen erat Romin:& a nomine suo urbi imposuisse nomen nunc ut roma appellaretur. Alii dicūt non Aeneā neq; euandrum neq; mulierē arcadicam.sed Romulum & Remum condidisse mœnia urbis Ro. cuius sententiæ Ti.Liuius testis est:hic uero eorum sequitur opinionem:qui dicūt Aeneam profugum a deleta troia una cum troianis Romam condidisse. Condidere.pro cōdiderunt:ædificauerunt. Habuere:tenuere habitauere.& sæpe primitiuus pro deriuatiuo & e conuerso:nā dicimus habito hāc domū:idest habeo. Accepi:audiui:intellexi. Profugi:procul fugati a domo sua. Incertis sedibus.quia certa loca non habebant. in quibus se firmare possent:donec mœnia condiderunt.sed huc atq; illuc errabāt. Aborigenes: scilicet tenuere urbem. Cum his:scilicet troianis:aborigenes populi dicti sunt latini prisci. qui italiam ab initio tenuere:& dicti sunt aborigenes:quia diu aberrarunt anteq̄ certas sedes haberent. Sine legibus:qa ipsi licenter uiuebant:nec ulla lex erat:quæ uetaret quin pro arbitrio facerent quæ uoluissent. Sine imperio:& dicitur democratia:quia nemo regebat eos:liberum atq; solutum declarat quod dixit sine legibus. Sine imperio:monarchia:liberum quia sine legibus:solutum quia sine imperio. Hi postq̄ & c. & hi troiani & aborigenes antiqui italiæ populi:cum in una mœnia urbis romæ conuenissent:credi nō potestq̄ facile creuerint. Dispari genere:quia hi quidem troiani:hi uero latini. Dissimili:nam quia genus dispar erat:lingua quoq; dissimilis fuit.Nam sicuti uidemus aliud idioma habent teucri:aliud græci: aliud latini. Alio more:alio ritu:& humano & diuino:nam mos utrunq; cōplectitur & diuinum & humanum. Incredibile memoratu.i.credi non potest si memoraretur. Coaluerint.i.simul creuerint: Nam coalescere crescere significat. Ciuibus:& quia populus ille in maximā breui peruenit multitudinem. Moribus:& quia multitudo populi creuerat:mores etiā impositi sunt ciuibus. Agris:nam cum uicissent Romani populos finitimos agrorum fines suorum protenderunt. Satis pollens:satis potens. Pleraq; mortaliū habent̄:in quo maior pars humanarum rerum inuidiose possidetur:& ideo quia diuitiæ ingentes possidebantur a Romanis inuidia repēte orta est contra eos. Ex opulentia ex diuitiis & opibus rerum:Igitur quia inuidiā opulētia pepit romāis. Tētare:ꝑtētabāt romāos. Pauci ex amicis:ut fuerūt albani semp cōiuncti erāt Romanis:

PLATE 1. Sallust, *Opera* (Venice: Theodorus de Ragazonibus, 9 July 1492), sig. a5r. *ISTC* is00077000, *USTC* 991410 (1492.2). Cambridge, St John's College, Ii.2.27

edition of the text.[78] Moreover, in 1517, a 'very old manuscript' supplied by Janus Lascaris (1445–1534) was used to correct readings in a heavily annotated copy of Leto's 1490 Sallust edition that passed through the hands of Aulo Giano Parrasio (1470–1522) and Antonio Seripando (1476–1531).[79] But there is nothing that especially commends the idea that our translator used a manuscript of Sallust's Latin. For the present edition, a survey was made of variants in five Sallust manuscripts that are known to have been in England in the fifteenth century.[80] None of these manuscripts contained readings that are unknown to the incunables and which might have influenced our translator's text of Sallust's Latin. In particular, none contained the rare 'ita breui' passage, either in the main text or as a marginal addition.

The second and last consideration is the issue of other vernacular translations of the *Bellum Catilinae*. By 1500, these included an Icelandic translation from the turn of the thirteenth century (which did not circulate widely), Italian translations by the Dominican friar Bartolomeo da San Concordia (early 14th century) and Ludovico Carbone (1430–85), and Spanish translations by Vasco de Guzmán (early 15th century) and Francisco Vidal de Noya (printed in 1493).[81] The first complete translations into German and French date from 1515 and 1528 respectively.[82] For the avoidance of doubt, there is no evidence that *The Coniuracion* was influenced by any of these translations.

Besides these translations, only one other potential vernacular intermediary needs to be considered: the *Fet des Romains*. This was an early

[78] That main source was a Latin intermediary by Poggio Bracciolini. On Skelton's sources, see further John Colley, 'Diodorus Siculus in the English Quattrocento: New Light on the Source of Skelton's *Bibliotheca historica*', *Medium Ævum*, 93 (2024), 389–407.

[79] This, at least, according to a note in this copy in Parrasio's hand: 'Anno Domini .M.D. xvij Ia. Parrhasius et Antonius Seripandus sequuti fidem uetustissimi codicis Iani Lascharis byzantii recensebant' (Cambridge, King's College, Bryant.XV.3.3 [**1490**], sig. q4^r^).

[80] Oxford, St John's College, MS 84; Oxford, Magdalen College, MS lat. 218; Oxford, Balliol College, MS 258; BodL, MSS Auct. F. 5. 8, Barlow 45.

[81] See *'Catilina' and 'Jugurtha' by Sallust and 'Pharsalia' by Lucan in Old Norse: Rómverjasaga, AM 595 a–b 4to*, ed. Jakob Benediktsson, introduction trans. Peter Foote (Copenhagen, 1980); Bartolomeo da San Concordio, *Il Catilinario e Giugurtino*, ed. Basilio Puoti (Naples, 1827); [Vasco Ramírez de Guzmán and Francisco Vidal de Noya], *The Texts and Concordances of Escorial ms. g.III.11 and Newberry Library inc. f-9511: Two Fifteenth-Century Translations of the 'Bellum Catilinarium sive de conjuratione Catilinae' and 'Jugurtha seu Bellum Jugurthinum' (Gaius Sallustius Crispus)*, ed. Jerry Rank (Madison, WI, 1989); Ludovico Carbone, *Le traduzioni da Sallustio di Ludovico Carbone*, ed. Alessandra Minisci (Pisa, 2017).

[82] Dietrich von Plieningen, *Zwo schon historien, nemlichen von des Catilinen und auch des Iugurthen kriegen* ([Landshut, 1515]), *USTC* 635245; Jean Parmentier, *L'hystoire catilinaire* (Paris, 1528), *USTC* 37936. On the vernacular translations, see also Osmond, '*Princeps historiae Romanae*' (1995), 137–9.

thirteenth-century compilation of classical history which combined French vernacular translations and paraphrases from Lucan, Suetonius, and Sallust.[83] Its translated excerpts from the *Bellum Catilinae* include key passages such as Catiline's speech to his co-conspirators (*BC* 20) and the syncrisis of Caesar and Cato (*BC* 54), a passage that especially attracted the interest of early readers (including, say, John Claymond).[84] Its excerpts also include Sallust's famous versions of Caesar's and Cato's speeches to the Senate on 5 December 63 BCE (*BC* 51–2), which advance arguments about the dangers and merits of putting some of Catiline's conspirators to death. The *Fet des Romains* was still read in the late fifteenth century, and beyond. The text was known to William Worcester (1415–*c*.1480×85), for instance, and an edition was issued by the Parisian publisher Antoine Vérard in 1490. Vérard's edition may even be the 'Salustius in lingua gallica' that ended up in the library of Henry VIII.[85] Our translator may well have known this work, and if he knew a contemporary vernacular (besides English) it would have been French. A close comparison of *The Coniuracion* with the *Fet des Romains*, however, yields nothing to suggest that it influenced *The Coniuracion* either directly or indirectly.

Commentaries

The Coniuracion draws extensively on the Valla commentary, which was first printed in the 1491 imprint of Leto's Sallust edition (and there is no evidence that this commentary circulated in England in manuscript at an earlier or indeed later date). Its use is apparent from the very start of our translator's preface, since it reworks some of the Valla commentary's preface.[86] Otherwise, there are three main ways in which *The Coniuracion* draws on the Valla commentary. First, for amplifications that clarify the meaning of Sallust's Latin. For example, the detail that the Romans had driven certain perils 'fer from themselffes' draws on a Valla gloss ('Propulerant: procul pepulerant') to amplify Sallust's 'propulerant'.[87] Second,

[83] On the text and its structure see Nigel Mortimer, *Medieval and Early Modern Portrayals of Julius Caesar: The Transmission of an Idea* (Oxford, 2020), 18–192.

[84] Almost the entire syncrisis (or 'collatio') is bracketed and highlighted with a marginal sidenote in Claymond's copy: see Oxford, Corpus Christi College, *ϕ*.C.4.6(2) (**1492.2**), sig. d5v.

[85] On Worcester's knowledge of the text, see *Boke of Noblesse*, ed. Nall and Wakelin, pp. lxxvii–lxxviii. A copy is also recorded in the library of Worcester's patron, Sir John Fastolf: see Richard Beadle, 'Sir John Fastolf's French Books', in Denis Renevey and Graham D. Caie (eds.), *Medieval Texts in Context* (London, 2008), 96–112 at 102. Vérard's edition is *ISTC* il00312000. For Henry VIII's French 'Salustius', see *CBMLC* H2.513.

[86] For a lightly edited transcription of the Valla commentary's preface, see Osmond, 'The Valla Commentary', 47–8.

[87] 170–1; *Val*, sig. a5v.

as stylistic inspiration for doublets and other lexical amplifications. Thus 'good science and faculte', amplifying 'artis bonae', follows another Valla gloss ('Bonæ artis: scientiæ et eruditionis').[88] Third, for amplifications that introduce new contextual details, as when *The Coniuracion* says Catiline 'sparid not to poyson his awne son'.[89] Sallust only says that Catiline killed his son, but the Valla commentary specifies the use of poison (by way of a detail in Valerius Maximus's *Facta et dicta memorabilia*). *The Coniuracion* also follows the Valla commentary when providing extra details about the dictator Sulla, the laws of Ambitus, the Plautian Law, the idiom *pedibus iturum*, the Portian Law, and what happened to the urban praetor Damasippus.[90] The Valla commentary is moreover used when Sallust's Latin is ambiguous.[91] Occasionally the translator even translates a version of Sallust's Latin that was transmitted via this commentary's *lemmata*, rather than from the main text as edited by Leto. So, most notably, the translator writes that Catiline called his company to his counsel 'aboute the begynnyng of Februarii', even though all editions of Sallust's Latin say 'circiter Kalendas Iunias' here. Our translator has simply translated word for word the gloss in the Valla commentary, in which the main text's 'Iunias' had been mangled as 'Ianuarias': viz., 'Kalend. Ianuarias: circa principium mensis februarii'.[92] Either our translator did not spot the discrepancy between the commentary and Sallust's main text here, or—at least in this one instance—he considered the commentary a more authoritative source.

At this stage we also need to dismiss the possibilities that the translator sometimes amplified from the ps.-Ognibene or Ascensius commentaries, which would have important implications for dating *The Coniuracion*. These possibilities are all the more important to tackle and dismiss because, at first glance, it may seem as though our translator used both. As for the former, the ps.-Ognibene commentary's gloss of 'municipia' as 'castella' may seem to inspire *The Coniuracion*'s translations of 'municipia' as 'strongeholdes' and 'holdes'.[93] As for the latter, there are a handful of moments where *The Coniuracion* may initially appear to rely on Ascensius's commentary. For example, 'invy of theire neighboures', which translates Sallust's 'inuidia', may seem to follow an Ascensius gloss ('inuidia .s. vicinorum et circum iacentium populorum est orta').[94]

Crucially, however, there are no smoking guns: nothing in *The Coniuracion* can only be explained by Ascensius's commentary or by the ps.-

[88] 83; *Val*, sig. a3r.

[89] 356–7.

[90] 135–6, 420, 736–7, 1194, 1279, 1308–13.

[91] 988, 1025–6, 1509–10.

[92] 386; *Val*, sig. b3r.

[93] Cf. 715*n*.

[94] 162; *Asc*, sig. a6r.

Ognibene commentary. In the 'castella' example here, our translator was probably aware of similar glosses of 'municipia' from other sources.[95] As for 'invy of theire neighboures', the translator could easily have devised his amplification ('of theire neighbours') on his own initiative, working from context in Sallust's Latin. It would also be surprising for our translator to have known Ascensius's longer and more detailed commentary and still to have amplified so extensively from the Valla commentary. Moreover, the Ascensius commentary is full of details that could have saved him from several mistakes.[96] Admittedly, there are also passages in the Valla commentary that could have prevented occasional misinterpretations or made for more accurate translations.[97] However, for reasons already explained (and as is shown throughout the Explanatory Notes), the translator's reliance on the Valla commentary is beyond doubt. All that needs to be qualified here is that he used the Valla commentary extensively, but never systematically.

The Coniuracion also has a handful of amplifications that lack obvious sources in any contemporary Sallust commentary. Sometimes these amplifications go awry, as when the translator suggests that Carthage, which was on the north coast of Africa, was a 'grete cite . . . in Grece'.[98] Conversely, however, the translator elsewhere gets something right that the Valla commentary gets wrong: this is when he translates 'tabulas nouas' as 'new grauntes in wryting of possescions', which correctly realizes that 'tabulas nouas' (i.e. 'the cancellation of debts') refers to the redistribution of wealth. The Valla commentary instead misguidedly suggests that 'tabulas' refers to paintings.[99] On this occasion we can tentatively suggest a source for the translator's amplification, since the correct financial sense of 'tabulas nouas' could have been gleaned from the appearance of this phrase in one of Cicero's *Catilinarians*. Its correct sense could also have been apparent from some of Cicero's letters to Atticus, which likewise were widely available in print at this time.[100] This is not the only occasion on which Cicero's works may directly or indirectly explain translation choices

[95] Cf. also 715*n*.

[96] Cf. e.g. 632*n*, 699–700*n*, 939–40*n*, 1563–4*n*, 1618*n*, 1654*n*. In a similar vein, one gloss in the ps.-Ognibene commentary could have prevented his misunderstanding of *exaequatus*: cf. 1649*n*.

[97] Cf. 466*n*, 502–3*n*, 687–8*n*, 853*n*, 1230–1*n*, 1489–90*n*.

[98] Cf. 241*n*.

[99] 528; 'Nouas tabulas: admirandas tabulas quæ possidebantur a diuitibus. sicut apud autores comprehendi potest preciosæ erant huiusmodi tabulæ in quibus artificiose pingebantur imagines ære uel argento et auro redimitæ' (*Val*, sig. b5^{r}). The English translation here is from Loeb.

[100] Cf. *In Catilinam* 2.18, in M. Tullius Cicero, *Orationes*, ed. Albert Curtis Clark, Oxford Classical Texts (Oxford, 1905); Cicero, *Ad Atticum*, 5.21.13, 10.8.2, 11.23.3, 14.21.4, in *Epi-*

in *The Coniuracion*.[101] Other amplifications, meanwhile, may derive from contemporary word lists such as Johannes Reuchlin's *Vocabularius breviloquus*, which had first been printed in 1478. Reuchlin's *Vocabularius* was available in England and had also been used by Skelton for his Diodorus translation.[102] Often the simplest explanation for some of our translator's amplifications, however, is that they were yet more 'thinges' that he knew from his 'reders' and which he endeavoured 'to gader and adioyne' to his translation.[103]

Besides the Valla commentary, there is also at least one other intermediary that our translator must have known either directly or indirectly. This is Vegetius' *Epitoma rei militaris* (also known as the *De re militari*), which probably dates from the late fourth century CE.[104] Vegetius manuscripts circulated widely in fifteenth-century England, in both Latin and French, and the text was available in print from the 1470s onward.[105] *The Coniuracion* draws on Vegetius at least twice. First, Vegetius underpins the comment that Catiline's army contained 'xij^{Ml}. ij^{C}. fotemen and M^{l}. iiij^{c}. and iij^{xx} horsemen' (i.e. 12,200 and 1,460). These numbers are not in the *Bellum Catilinae*, but they follow the numbers in Vegetius' description of the size of a Roman legion (6,100 infantry and 730 cavalry). 6,100 and 730 are multiplied by two because Catiline 'ordenyd two legiones'.[106] These numbers provide more detail than was available from the Valla commentary's glosses at §§32.1 and 59.1 of the *Bellum Catilinae*, which report that a Roman legion contained 6,666 men.[107] (This 6,666 figure was also

stulae, ed. W. S. Watt and D. R. Shackleton Bailey, 3 vols., Oxford Classical Texts (Oxford, 1958–82).

101 Cf. 938–9*n*, 951–2*n*.

102 Cf. e.g. 482–3*n*, 715*n*, 1618*n*. On Skelton's use of Reuchlin, see John Skelton, *Bibliotheca historica*, ed. F. M. Salter and H. L. R. Edwards, 2 vols., EETS OS 233, 239 (London, 1956–7), ii, pp. xxiv–xxvi.

103 22–4.

104 Others prefer a 5th-c. CE date; I follow the arguments and date in Vegetius, *Epitoma rei militaris*, ed. M. D. Reeve, Oxford Classical Texts (Oxford, 2004), pp. viii–x.

105 On Vegetius' reception in England, see Catherine Nall, *Reading and War in Fifteenth-Century England: From Lydgate to Malory* (Cambridge, 2012), 11–47; Daniel Wakelin, *Humanism, Reading, and English Literature 1430–1530* (Oxford, 2007), 80–92. See also Josette A. Wisman, 'Flavius Renatus Vegetius', in *Catalogus translationum et commentariorum*, vi. 175–84; Christopher Allmand, *The 'De Re Militari' of Vegetius: The Reception, Transmission and Legacy of a Roman Text in the Middle Ages* (Cambridge, 2011). One of the French translations was in Fastolf's library: see Beadle, 'Sir John Fastolf's French Books', 103–4. There were also two 15th-c. translations into English, one in prose and one in verse, though neither seems to have circulated widely: see *Knyghthode and Bataile: A XVth Century Verse Paraphrase of Flavius Vegetius Renatus' Treatise 'De re militari'*, ed. R. Dyboski and Z. M. Arend, EETS OS 201 (London, 1935); *The Earliest English Translation of Vegetius' 'De re militari'*, ed. G. A. Lester, Middle English Texts, 21 (Heidelberg, 1988).

106 1556, 1560; *Epitoma rei militaris*, 2.6.9.

107 *Val*, sigs. c2^{v}, e1^{r}.

interpolated in Bartolomeo's fourteenth-century Italian translation of the *Bellum Catilinae* and Barclay's 1522 translation of the *Bellum Iugurthinum*: premodern translators generally liked to add this kind of numerical detail.[108]) In *The Coniuracion*, the '6,100' and '730' numbers may come directly from Vegetius' text—whether in Latin or French—or from a later intermediary such as Vincent of Beauvais's *Speculum doctrinale* (*c.*1260); the *Speculum doctrinale* included these numbers about a legion's size in its chapter 'De legionibus'.[109]

The Coniuracion draws on Vegetius again when Catiline is said to have fielded '.vj. cohortes, abowte the nombre of oure accompting \`V´. M^{l}. i. C. and xxij men' (i.e. six cohorts, 5,122 men).[110] This passage stands out as the only time that a first-person pronoun is voiced in *The Coniuracion* by someone other than Sallust, as though the translator is proud to highlight this arithmetical interpolation as his own. Perhaps his pride was misplaced, however. Indeed, '5,122' can only be explained as the result of at least two separate mistakes. To start with, 5,122 is probably a scribal error for 4,122. The initial minim of 'iv' could easily have been dropped to become 'V'. 'V' also seems to have been written over an erasure, which increases the likelihood that some kind of error was made here. The number 4,122 can then be explained if Vegetius' number for soldiers in the majority of a legion's cohorts (555) has been mixed with his number for cavalry in a legion's first, larger cohort (132).[111] 555+132=687. 687×6=4,122. The calculator probably took these numbers directly from Book II of the *Epitoma rei militari*, since only in Vegetius' text—rather than later intermediaries, which often simplify the numerical details that Vegetius had provided—could the numbers of soldiers plausibly have been confused across different kinds of cohorts. Again, though, these numbers could also have been mediated to the translator at second hand, perhaps by his 'reders'.

There is another reason why 5,122 was surely not the number that the calculator intended: it is not divisible by six (i.e. the number of cohorts that Catiline is said to have fielded). Nor is 5,122 divisible by eight. Indeed, an added complication here is that Catiline, in all modern and contemporary texts of Sallust's Latin, is said to have fielded eight cohorts, not six. Only *The Coniuracion* says six ('.vj.'). Since 4,122 is not divisible by eight either, the calculator must have worked on the assumption that there

[108] Bartolomeo, *Il Catilinario*, 40 (cf. *BC* 32.1); Alexander Barclay, *The Famous Cronycle of the Warre which the Romayns had agaynst Iugurth, Usurper of the Kyngdome of Numidy*, ed. Greg Waite, EETS os 344 (Oxford, 2014), 69.

[109] Vincent of Beauvais (Vincentius Bellovacensis), *Speculum maius*, 4 vols. (Douai, 1624; repr. Graz, 1964–5), ii, col. 1021 (Book XI, chapter 46).

[110] 1653–4.

[111] *Epitoma rei militaris*, 2.6.3–4.

were indeed only six cohorts rather than eight. At some point, then, *vi* was probably written for *viii* in a draft version of *The Coniuracion*—an easy mistake for a scribe to make. That mistake can only have been introduced by our manuscript's scribe, however, if that same scribe was also responsible for making the '4,122' calculation in the first place. This would be an exceptional interpolation for a fifteenth-century scribe to make. A better explanation is that the muddling of *vi* for *viii* arose in the translator's own notes or foul papers, and that he inserted this calculation from Vegetius once he had already started translating Sallust's Latin. Working solely from his English translation or his notes, which now erroneously said *vi* rather than *viii*, the translator could have arrived at '4,122'.

OCCASION AND AUTHORSHIP

The translator says very little about himself. All that can be speculated about him (and as this Introduction has already noted: see Sources and Date) is (*a*) that he probably received a university education, and (*b*) that he may have discussed the *Bellum Catilinae* with colleagues or mentors in either a university or monastic context, or both. The translator also says little about why he translated the *Bellum Catilinae*, or for whom. Notably, for example, no patron is mentioned in his preface, though he hopes his translation will satisfy 'the desire of other men'.[112] This comment alludes fleetingly to a contemporary readership, though a readership is also implied by the preface's existence in the first place, not to mention the care which has been taken over the layout and presentation of MS Nn.3.6. Nor does the preface suggest any topical or political reason for translating this text. Some such reasons often guided other premodern authors who translated the *Bellum Catilinae* or more generally wrote about Catiline's conspiracy. For instance, when a neo-Latin rewriting of the *Bellum Catilinae* was translated into English by the sometime royal chaplain Thomas Paynell (*fl.*1528–67), Paynell in his preface drew parallels between Catiline's conspiracy and recent unrest in England; he was probably alluding to the Pilgrimage of Grace (1536) or Exeter Conspiracy (1538), if not both.[113] In the next century, parts of Heywood's

[112] 12.

[113] On the political contexts of Paynell's translation, see John-Mark Philo, *'An Ocean Untouched and Untried': The Tudor Translations of Livy* (Oxford, 2020), 43–5; David Womersley, 'Sir Henry Savile's Translation of Tacitus and the Political Interpretation of Elizabethan Texts', *Review of English Studies*, 42 (1991), 313–42 at 317–18. On Paynell's source, Costanzo Felici's *De coniuratione Catilinae* (printed 1518), see Patricia J. Osmond and Robert W.

translation of the *Bellum Catilinae* were inflected by the Gunpowder Plot (1605).[114]

Political resonance may still be heard indirectly in *The Coniuracion*, however, in its frequent references to 'treson' and 'comon wele'. '[T]reson' is the text's favourite translation of *coniuratio*, even though the more Latinate 'coniuracion' was adopted for the text's title (though 'coniuracion' is only then used twice in the translation itself). As scholars such as Paul Strohm and Megan Leitch have shown, the language of treason was widespread and highly charged in late fifteenth-century England: the country was only just emerging from decades of civil war, and ideas of treason remained a fault line for concepts of community and identity.[115] The language of commonweal, meanwhile, had recently risen to prominence in England with the reception of the *studia humanitatis*. 'Commonweal', indeed, is a calque of *res publica*, a term that fifteenth-century readers knew best from their avid reading of Cicero. Prominent among these readers were the likes of William Worcester, whose *Boke of Noblesse* (1475) even includes some translation from Cicero's *De senectute* (Worcester's complete English translation of the *De senectute*, made via a French translation of the Latin by Laurent de Premierfait, was the translation that Caxton printed in 1481).[116] Although *res publica* is translated three times as 'the cite' and once as 'impere' in *The Coniuracion*, commonweal language is employed almost fifty times. The frequency with which it appears echoes its frequent use in contemporary public life: John Watts shows that ideas of 'common wele' or 'common good' were deployed extensively at this time, both by those who rebelled against royal power and by those in positions of authority.[117]

Ulery, Jr., 'Constantius Felicius Durantinus and the Renaissance Origins of Anti-Sallustian Criticism', *International Journal of the Classical Tradition*, 1 (1995), 29–56; John Colley, '"Maniacal Ciceronianism"? Costanzo Felici's *De coniuratione Catilinae* and Historical Writing in the Early Cinquecento', *Erudition and the Republic of Letters*, 10 (2025), 115–43. Paynell translated from a 1535 edition of Felici's Latin (*USTC* 624975).

[114] See further B. N. De Luna, *Jonson's Romish Plot: A Study of 'Catiline' and Its Historical Context* (Oxford, 1967), 91–6.

[115] Megan Leitch, *Romancing Treason: The Literature of the Wars of Roses* (Oxford, 2015); Paul Strohm, *Politique: Languages of Statecraft between Chaucer and Shakespeare* (Notre Dame, IN, 2005), 187–8. '[T]reson' translates *coniuratio* 13 times (once via the Valla commentary rather than Sallust's Latin); it also once translates 'bella intestina' (127). *Coniuratio* is otherwise translated as 'rebellyon' (nine times), 'seducion' (once), 'insurreccion' (once), 'conspirise' (once), and 'coniuracion' (once).

[116] On Worcester and commonweal language, see further Catherine Nall, 'Moving to War: Rhetoric and Emotion in William Worcester's *Boke of Noblesse*', in Stephanie Downes, Andrew Lynch, and Katrina O'Laughlin (eds.), *Emotions and War: Medieval to Romantic Literature* (Basingstoke, 2015), 117–32; Wakelin, *Humanism*, 93–125.

[117] John Watts, 'Public or Plebs: The Changing Meaning of "The Commons", 1381–1549',

Commonweal language also asserted a degree of equivalence between the political systems of England and ancient Rome, which were increasingly likened to one another. So, the bishop and sometime Lord Chancellor John Russell (*c.*1430–94), himself a keen reader of Cicero, drew sustained comparisons between England's Parliament and the Roman Senate in a sermon he planned to deliver in 1483 at the first parliament of Edward V (who was dead, of course, before Russell could do so).[118]

Our translator may also have been influenced by the slowly rising tide of vernacular classical translation in fifteenth-century England. Some of these translations were only loosely related to their original ancient sources. The best-known example is Caxton's *Eneydos* (1490), which only contains fragments of translation from Virgil's *Aeneid*. Caxton's *Booke of Ovyde Named Metamorphose* is even less closely related to its Latin archetype, being a Middle English translation of a classicizing, prose version of the Middle French *Ovide moralisé*.[119] In contrast, *The Coniuracion* is striking for closely translating its Latin source. Only a handful of earlier classical translations into English had been similarly direct: they include the verse translation of Palladius' *De re rustica* produced in Duke Humfrey's circle (*c.*1439–43), translations of Vegetius' *Epitoma rei militaris* in 1408 (in prose) and 1460 (in verse), and the verse translation of Claudian's *De consulatu Stilichonis* by the Augustinian friar Osbern Bokenham (1392/3–in or after 1464).[120]

Whether our translator knew any of these earlier translations is an open question. There may be some evidence, though, that he knew Caxton's editions of vernacular translations. His comment about rendering Sallust 'in owre wolgare and Englisshe tonge', for instance, echoes the nationalistic

in Huw Pryce and Watts (eds.), *Power and Identity in the Middle Ages: Essays in Memory of Rees Davies* (Oxford, 2007), 242–60; Watts, '"Common Weal" and "Commonwealth": England's Monarchical Republic in the Making, c.1450–c.1530', in Andrea Gamberini, Jean-Philippe Genet, and Andrea Zorzi (eds.), *The Languages of Political Society: Western Europe, 14th–17th Centuries* (Rome, 2011), 147–63.

[118] See S. B. Chrimes, *English Constitutional Ideas in the Fifteenth Century* (Cambridge, 1936), 174. Russell purchased two printed collections of Cicero texts while in Bruges in 1467: these survive as London, Lambeth Palace Library, MS 765 and CUL, Inc.3.A.1.3a[12].

[119] On the sources of Caxton's *Eneydos*, see Matthew Day, *English Humanism and the Reception of Virgil c.1400–1550* (Oxford, 2022), 100–34. On Caxton's Ovid, see William Caxton, *The Booke of Ovyde Named Metamorphose*, ed. Richard J. Moll (Toronto, 2013); *The Middle English Text of 'Caxton's Ovid'*, Book I, ed. Diana Rumrich, Books II–III, ed. Wolfgang Mager, 2 vols. to date, Middle English Texts, 43, 53 (Heidelberg, 2011–).

[120] On which, see Wakelin, *Humanism, Reading, and English Literature*, 43–92. On Bokenham's Claudian, see also A. S. G. Edwards, 'The Middle English Translation of Claudian's *De consulatu Stilichonis*', in A. J. Minnis (ed.), *Middle English Poetry: Texts and Traditions* (York, 2001), 267–78.

rationale for vernacular translation which also surfaces in several of Caxton's prefaces.[121] A few conspicuous word choices also present the glimmer of a possibility that he knew John Skelton's classical translations. *The Coniuracion* uses the rare word 'haskerdes', for example, which was coined in Skelton's *Bibliotheca historica*, a translation that scholars usually date to the later 1480s.[122] *The Coniuracion* also uses the variant 'hastardes', which is only recorded elsewhere in Skelton's works: *OED*'s first citation is from Skelton's 1489 elegy on the death of the earl of Northumberland.[123] Significant too in *The Coniuracion* is 'pronosticates', which may echo the verb 'pronosticate' from Skelton's *Bibliotheca*. Our translator uses 'pronosticates' as a strikingly Latinate translation of either 'portenta' or 'prodigia', and the word antedates its first citation as a noun in *OED*.[124]

These lexical overlaps raise a tempting possibility: that our translator was none other than Skelton himself. Skelton had enjoyed a university education and had already translated Cicero's *Epistulae ad familiares* into English by 1490.[125] But there are good reasons to discount the idea of his authorship. For one, Skelton does not mention a Sallust translation in the comprehensive list of his works in his *Garlande of Laurell* (first printed in 1523). There are also reasons of style. The increasingly extreme style of amplification that Skelton works up to in his *Bibliotheca* is a world away from our translator's generally much closer translation style.[126] Skelton also filled his *Bibliotheca* with the anachronistic language of dames, dukes, and chivalry. Similar language is found in other classical translations from around the turn of the sixteenth century, such as Barclay's Sallust, Gavin Douglas's *Eneados* (1513), and a translation of the first five books of Livy's *Ab Urbe condita* by the Scots writer John Bellenden (1533).[127] *The*

[121] 13–14; cf. e.g. 'translate . . . in to our maternal tonge', 'reducynge . . . in to our engylssh tongue', in *The Prologues and Epilogues of William Caxton*, ed. W. J. B. Crotch, EETS OS 176 (London, 1928), 42, 43, 56, 87.

[122] 1570; *OED*, s.v. 'haskerd', n.; Skelton, *Bibliotheca historica*, i. 125. The *Bibliotheca*'s *terminus a quo* is 1478 and its *terminus ad quem* is 1490: see Colley, 'Diodorus Siculus', 389. For a slight preference, perhaps, for a post-1481 date, see also David R. Carlson, 'Skelton's English Diodorus and the 1481 Edition of Poggio's Latin Translation', *Notes and Queries*, 70 (2023), 61–4.

[123] 873; *OED*, s.v. 'hastard', n.; Skelton, *Upon the Dolorous Dethe*, line 24, in John Skelton, *The Complete English Poems*, ed. John Scattergood, rev. edn. (Liverpool, 2015).

[124] 695; Skelton, *Bibliotheca historica*, i. 176; *OED*, s.v. 'prognosticate', n. Cf. *OED*, s.v. 'prognosticate', v.

[125] Together with Skelton's *Bibliotheca*, Caxton mentions this translation in the prologue to his *Eneydos* (1490): cf. Caxton, *Prologues and Epilogues*, 109. Skelton also refers to his Cicero translation in his *Garlande or Chapelet of Laurell*, line 1185.

[126] On Skelton's amplifications, see Jane Griffiths, *John Skelton and Poetic Authority: Defining the Liberty to Speak* (Oxford, 2006), 47–55.

[127] For the latter two, see *The Eneados: Gavin Douglas' Translation of Virgil's 'Aeneid'*, ed.

Coniuracion, however, notably resists this kind of anachronism. Skelton's Latin was also more proficient than our translator's: our translator sometimes misinterprets Latin syntax, vocabulary, prepositions, and ablatives, including ablatives absolute.[128] Only one potential misinterpretation in *The Coniuracion* may have been deliberate, a coy euphemism when the Latin being translated refers to sodomy.[129] The weaknesses of our translator's Latin may even suggest that the Valla commentary, offering much-needed linguistic help, was the enabling factor for his making the translation in the first place. That explanation would also help to make sense of the 'greate tyme laid by' between his initial study of the *Bellum Catilinae* and when he came to make the translation.[130]

Our translator was aware of his limited Latinity too, it seems—at least, if we take his humble, self-effacing preface at face value. We should not do so automatically: 'dull', humble prefaces were conventional in the fifteenth century and were not always sincerely transparent.[131] But our translator seems in earnest. He begins his self-criticism by disclaiming 'the office of an interpreter'. This is a calque of *officium interpretis*, which played into a long-standing classical and medieval tradition of viewing translation as an act of interpretation rather than a slavish, word-for-word process of moving between one language and another.[132] He verges on self-criticism again when he claims to have 'overrunne' Sallust's Latin. This verb could neutrally mean 'survey' or 'consider'. In context, though, it seems to mean 'go through hastily' or 'superficially', as the word also means when it appears a few lines later.[133] The translator's preface more generally stresses that *The Coniuracion* was not intended as a definitive or fully polished translation. Instead, the translator positions his work as a personal exercise, helping him 'obteyne the knowleage and science' and to progress 'from the rude and derke stile to the good and commendable kynde of wryting'.[134] Perhaps these caveats about the purpose and success of the translation, suggesting

Priscilla Bawcutt with Ian C. Cunningham, 3 vols., Scottish Text Society, 5th ser., 17–19 (Woodbridge, 2020–2); John Bellenden, *Livy's History of Rome: The First Five Books*, ed. W. A. Craigie, 2 vols., Scottish Text Society, 1st ser., 47, 51 (Edinburgh, 1901–3).

128 See, respectively, 144*n*, 231–3*n*, 348–9*n*, 350*n*; 501–2*n*, 509–10*n*; 431–3*n*, 833–4*n*; 287–8*n*, 334–5*n*, 575*n*, 980–1*n*, 1195–6*n*.

129 Cf. 316–17*n*.

130 25.

131 Cf. David Lawton, 'Dullness and the Fifteenth Century', *English Literary History*, 54 (1987), 761–99. A conventionally 'dull' preface such as this is something else that we would not expect from Skelton, who often boasted about the high quality of his work: e.g. Skelton's *Garlande* claims that a reader of his *Bibliotheca* 'wolde rede it agayne' (line 1501).

132 14–15. On this tradition, see further Rita Copeland, *Rhetoric, Hermeneutics, and Translation in the Middle Ages: Academic Traditions and Vernacular Texts* (Cambridge, 1991), 9–62.

133 17, 38; cf. *MED*, s.v. 'overrennen', v.

134 30–1, 32–3.

the translator's lack of confidence, help to explain its limited circulation in its day. The idea of the translation as an exercise also resonates with a hypothesis that was advanced earlier in this Introduction (see Sources and Date), that *The Coniuracion* may have started out as a series of vernacular glosses to the *Bellum Catilinae* that were later drawn together and worked up into a full translation. Maybe the translator refers to exactly this kind of twofold translation process when he distinguishes the task of 'overrunning' Sallust's Latin ('to overrunne') from the task of writing ('to wryte').[135]

REVISION

Many of the manuscript's over 170 corrections are the humdrum kinds that might be expected of any manuscript from this period, such as corrections of eyeskip errors or of one letter to another. Many of the erasures and rewritings are also clearly corrections that the scribe made *currente calamo*, since they must have been made while the ink was still wet enough to be erased. Many interlinear, supralinear, sublinear, and marginal insertions could be explained as the scribe's additions of words which he initially missed when he first went through his exemplar. Some semantically unnecessary corrections of letters also suggest his fastidious attention to his exemplar's spellings (see *infra*, Manuscript: Language and Dialect).

Not all of the corrections, however, can be explained by the scribe's more careful reading of his exemplar. Two corrections are especially telling. One is where the scribe overwrites 'my' with 'oure'. The other is where he twice overwrites 'in' with 'by', giving '`by´ nature or `by´ maners' as a translation of 'natura' and 'moribus'.[136] These corrections were probably more retrospective, since they were completed by overwriting alone rather than erasure and overwriting. It also seems unlikely that the scribe in either case would have copied his exemplar incorrectly to start with: it would be odd for him to have written 'my' if his exemplar gave 'oure', and to have written 'in'—and not just once, but twice—if his exemplar gave 'by'. Two other explanations are preferable. The first is that the scribe initially followed his exemplar accurately, writing 'my' and 'in', and later corrected these words to 'oure' and 'by' on his own initiative. Indeed, the corrections in both of these instances could be considered revisions that improve on the quality of the translation. In the first example, the new pronoun ('oure') offers a more literal translation of the Latin being translated ('nostri'). In

[135] 17–18. [136] 46; 1601–2.

the second, 'by' better recognizes the function of Sallust's 'natura' and 'moribus' as instrumental ablatives.

This first explanation, however, assumes that the scribe could access Sallust's Latin. This explanation is also at odds with the fact that scribes of this period tended to copy 'with little variation', as Wakelin has shown.[137] The second possibility is therefore preferable: that is, that the scribe accurately followed his exemplar by writing 'my' and 'in', and that the revisions to 'oure' and 'by' were requested by someone else. The most likely candidate for requesting those changes is the translator himself. In the light of the translation's apparently minimal circulation, it would also make sense for this manuscript to have been produced in close proximity with the translator, in any case.

The translator's involvement may further help to explain some retrospective attempts to clarify the syntax (on which, see also Style). For instance, several minuscules are overwritten with majuscules to help emphasize the start of new units of sense.[138] Another semantically needless correction, where Tironian *et* is erased and 'And' is written over the erasure, employs majuscule a for the same clarifying effect.[139] Extra virgules are sometimes also added to better distinguish one *sententia* from the next. Other corrections in the manuscript, such as the addition of words between or above lines, could moreover be explained as revisions requested by the translator rather than things that the scribe initially overlooked in his exemplar and which he later added on his own initiative.

STYLE

The Coniuracion more closely translates its source than many other fifteenth- and early sixteenth-century English translations of ancient texts. One notable feature in this respect is that the balance of direct against indirect speech precisely follows Sallust's Latin. In contrast, Barclay in his *Bellum Iugurthinum* translation converts several passages of indirect speech into direct speech.[140]

Not all of *The Coniuracion*'s close translations are necessarily successful, however. Among the more successful features is the translator's use of the vivid present tense to translate Sallust's historic present. Less successful is the treatment of Sallust's syntax. A generous critic might still argue that

[137] Daniel Wakelin, *Scribal Correction and Literary Craft: English Manuscripts 1375–1510* (Cambridge, 2014), 43.

[138] 123, 383, 708.

[139] 1426.

[140] Barclay, *Famous Cronycle*, 106–7, 110–11, 194, 196, 199–200.

the translator shapes his syntax to imitate Sallust's prized *brevitas*. Hence he sometimes seems to imitate Sallust's asyndeton, successfully capturing some of the speed of Sallust's prose. Thus 'Youre stomake, your yeris, your manlynes dothe exhorte me' briskly and effectively translates 'Animus aetas uirtus uostra me hortantur'.[141] The translator may also seem to imitate Sallust's parataxis. A case in point is during Cato's speech before the Senate on 5 December, when Cato contrasts Rome's former glory with what he sees as the city's current moral turpitude. Here, the translator closely follows Sallust's paratactic Latin and thereby reproduces some of the rhetorical force of Cato's speech:

For these [i.e. past Roman virtues], we haue superfluouse lustis and covetousenes; in the causes of the comen wele, nedynes; in our howses, plentiousnes; we yeue the prayse to richesse and seeke ease; betwene the good and the badde no difference; all the gyftes that belonge to vertew f\`l′ateryng requestes now occupieth.

Pro his nos habemus luxuriam atque auaritiam, publice egestatem, priuatim opulentiam; laudamus diuitias, sequimur inertiam; inter bonos et malos discrimen nullum; omnia uirtutis praemia ambitio possidet.[142]

The translator's close translation of Latin syntax could also backfire, however. Sometimes the result was that sentences become overburdened with subordinate clauses, requiring recapitulatory pronouns to clarify the sense.[143] It is therefore probably less the case that our translator deliberately imitated Sallust's *brevitas* and more the case that he often adopted a 'stencil' approach to copying Sallust's syntax. A 'stencil' style was also employed by other fifteenth-century translators, most famously Caxton, and involved closely modelling a translation's syntax and lexis on its exemplar.[144] The results in *The Coniuracion* sometimes verge on the incomprehensible, as in the following sentence:

Therfore in the begynnyng, kynges \`(′for that name was had fyrste vpon the erthe of rewle and power\`)′, dyversly somme yave theim to the excersise of their body, somme to resonyng, for than the lyffe of man was ladde withoute covetousnes: every man was well satisfied with his awne.

Igitur initio reges—nam in terris nomen imperi id primum fuit—diuorsi pars ingenium, alii corpus exercebant. Etiam tum uita hominum sine cupiditate agitabatur; sua quoique satis placebant.[145]

[141] 1637–8.

[142] 1433–7; *BC* 52.22.

[143] Cf. e.g. 1554–7.

[144] See further *The Booke of Ovyde Named Metamorphose*, ed. Moll, 27–36; Samuel K. Workman, *Fifteenth Century Translation as an Influence on English Prose* (Princeton, NJ, 1940), 8–10. For some criticism of the idea of 'stencil' translation in relation to Caxton, see also Day, *English Humanism*, 100–34.

[145] 55–9; *BC* 2.1.

The translator renders Sallust's Latin virtually word by word here, and the round brackets have been added retrospectively to try to make sense of the resulting syntactical mess in English. There are similar instances where *The Coniuracion* tries to copy precisely the syntactical placement of Latin subordinate clauses, with awkward results.[146] Several odd turns of phrase also have their origins in a 'stencil' approach to copying Latin syntax.[147] Of course, the discussion of Revision in this Introduction has already showed that attempts were sometimes made to clarify the syntax, either by the scribe or translator. For the most part, however, the translator at least—if not, necessarily, the scribe—seems to have valued conspicuously knotty Latinate syntax as a model for what he calls 'the good and commendable kynde of wryting'.[148] Thus his preface imitates a crabbed style replete with subordinate clauses, as though it has been translated stencil-like from Latin (most of it was not). The translator also likes to match Sallust's impersonal constructions with Latin-sounding impersonal constructions in English. Hence 'Operae pretium est' becomes 'It is behovefull to beholde'. So too does 'incredibile memoratu est' become 'it is incredeble to be rehersyd' and, elsewhere, 'it is to mervelouse to tell'.[149] Similar impersonal phrases include 'It is requisite', 'It is foughten', and 'It is expedyent'.[150] This last example is especially notable, since it comes just after the translator's preface and at the beginning of the translation proper.

Although the translator keeps close to Sallust's syntax, however, he does not take a blandly *verbum pro verbo* approach to the translation as a whole. He introduces some metaphors, for instance, and there are some scattered instances of alliteration (e.g. 'fyrst stroke \`in´ fere the favorers', 'trewly trustyng').[151] There may even be attempts to make certain speeches more dramatic, as when he strews the interjection 'ye' throughout Cato's speech on 5 December. The added interjections make this speech sound more impassioned than Caesar's immediately preceding speech to the Senate. Three other areas of style also merit attention: amplification, anachronism, and lexis.

Amplification

Fifteenth- and early sixteenth-century English translations often amplified or reduced their sources. As for reduction, *The Coniuracion* only occasionally omits translations of words or short adverbial phrases.

[146] Cf. e.g. 1401, 1666.

[147] e.g. 1273–4.

[148] 32–3.

[149] 298; 156–7, 187. Cf. *BC* 12.3, 6.2, 7.3.

[150] 1199, for 'esse decet'; 1687, for 'certatur'; 37, for 'decet'.

[151] Cf. 208*n*, 575*n*; 585, 1453.

Except for the few omissions that may have been intentional (e.g. with respect to Roman dates), these omissions could all be explained as careless mistakes—the kind of mistake caused by having 'overrunne' Sallust's Latin, perhaps.[152] It would have been especially easy for the translator to miss stray words and phrases when he read back and forth so frequently between Sallust's main text and the Valla commentary in the margins of each page of his copy-text. Other omissions may have crept in during scribal transmission.

Meanwhile, the translator amplifies extensively. He almost doubles the 10,700 words of Sallust's Latin into 20,900 words of English. There are three main kinds of amplification. First, adjectives are often inserted in translations of nouns, and adverbs (especially 'sore') in translations of adjectives. Second, many amplifications are suggested by the Valla commentary. Amplification via commentary was a standard translation strategy for the period more generally: it is also a central feature of Barclay's Sallust and Douglas's *Eneados*, not to mention contemporary translations of the *Bellum Catilinae* into other European vernaculars.[153] Third, the translator uses doublets to render individual Latin lexemes. Doublets are two synonyms usually joined by 'and', and again are more widely a feature of later fifteenth- and early sixteenth-century translations: they appear frequently in Barclay's Sallust (which amplifies even more extensively than *The Coniuracion*), the *De amicitia* translation printed by Caxton in 1481 (and attributed to John Tiptoft), and an anonymous mid-fifteenth-century verse translation of Petrarch's *Secretum*.[154] *The Coniuracion* contains almost 150 doublets. Many are simply pleonastic, such as 'prosperity and welth' and 'hynderans and lett'.[155] The most common function of doublets seems to be stylistic, reflecting a preference for amplified language. But doublets could also have more specific functions, as in the famous syncrisis of Caesar and Cato: the sheer number of doublets here puts additional emphasis on the two Romans' respective virtues.[156]

[152] 17. On 'overrunne', cf. *supra*, pp. xliv–xlv.

[153] On Douglas's amplifications via commentaries, see Priscilla Bawcutt, *Gavin Douglas: A Critical Study* (Edinburgh, 1976), 110–27; Day, *Humanism and the Reception of Virgil*, 142–59. On Barclay's, see *Famous Cronycle*, ed. Waite, pp. xlvi–l; see also Greg Waite, 'Alexander Barclay's Translation of Sallust's *Jugurtha*: A Note on Sources', *Notes and Queries*, 58 (2011), 196–202. As for other vernacular *BC* translations, either the Valla or Ascensius commentaries (or possibly both) were used, for example, in the translations by Agostino Ortica (1518, *USTC* 854243–4), Parmentier (1528, *USTC* 37936), and Schrayer (1534, *USTC* 622276).

[154] Cf. Barclay, *Famous Cronycle*, ed. Waite, pp. liii–liv; Wakelin, 'Early Humanism', 502–3; *A Middle English Translation from Petrarch's 'Secretum'*, ed. Edward Wilson and Daniel Wakelin, EETS os 351 (Oxford, 2018), p. lvi.

[155] 286, inverted as 'welth and prosperite' at 1457; 657.

[156] 1515–36.

There are also instances where a doublet combines a better-known word with a more Latinate one, perhaps with the intention of glossing one with the other: thus 'fatigant' becomes 'oppressith and werith' and 'operam' becomes 'helpe and diligence'.[157]

Anachronism

The Coniuracion is less anachronistic than many contemporary translations of ancient texts. Its resistance to the language of chivalry has already been noted (see Occasion and Authorship). *The Coniuracion* also lacks the Christianizing domestication and moralization that characterize translations such as Barclay's Sallust (beyond the fact that Sallust's Latin was already moralizing to start with).[158] Nor does *The Coniuracion* adopt domesticating translations of more technical words such as *curia* (i.e. Rome's Senate House): our translator plumps for 'counseill house', whereas Barclay in his Englished *Bellum Iugurthinum* chooses 'court'.[159]

Some anachronism nevertheless creeps in, though. There is one obvious anachronism: Roman *sesterces* become *libri*.[160] Otherwise, there are several moments which may or may not be anachronistic depending on how much historical knowledge the translator is assumed to have had, and depending on the senses in which we suppose particular English words are used. Particularly difficult to judge is the language of slavery, when words such as 'bondage' and 'bondemen'—which had specific meanings in medieval England—translate references to *servi* or *servitia*. More general terms such as 'vile men' are also employed to translate Sallust's language of slavery. Writing of early modern English texts, Urvashi Chakravarty has argued that the language of Roman slavery was often translated with these kinds of domesticated terms as part of a strategy of deliberate anachronism.[161] Our translator may represent an important counter-example to this later trend. Indeed, the frequent appearance of potentially anachronistic terms such as 'bondage' and 'bondemen' as only one half of a doublet—for example, 'bondage and thraldome' and 'bondemen and haskerdes'—may suggest that he was sympathetic to the problems of translating such vocabulary. In other words, the doublets may reflect his awareness that these words do not quite approximate the Latin words being translated. Doublets in such

[157] 286, 959.

[158] Barclay, *Famous Cronycle*, ed. Waite, p. lvi. For some of Barclay's moralizing additions, see e.g. *Famous Cronycle*, 165 ('Than often be . . . and lesse circumspect'), 183 ('But certenly it . . . sadnes and sorowe'), 185 ('For shame it . . . maister sore laboreth').

[159] 440–1, 1009–10; Barclay, *Famous Cronycle*, 50; cf. *BJ* 15.2.

[160] 712–13.

[161] Urvashi Chakravarty, *Fictions of Consent: Slavery, Servitude, and Free Service in Early Modern England* (Philadelphia, PA, 2022), 54.

instances may therefore not have been intended as stylistic devices, but as opportunities to have two bites at the cherry when translating tricky terms.

There are also a few other moments when *The Coniuracion*'s language may suggest contemporary England rather than ancient Rome. These include the translations of 'imperium' as 'royall poour' and 'soueraigne'.[162] Both of these translations misrepresent the kinds of power that were actually wielded in Republican Rome. Some references to capital punishment are also muddled, as when the translator twice suggests that Roman senators were exempt from capital punishment and other penalties such as being beaten by rods. More correctly, all Roman citizens in Republican Rome were exempt from these punishments. On the first of these two occasions, the translator's narrowing of the exemption to senators—all of which is already part of an amplification of Sallust's Latin—contradicts a gloss in the Valla commentary which (correctly) specifies that every Roman citizen was exempt.[163] On the second occasion, the translator's contortion of the Latin is more drastic: this time, in order to narrow the exemption to senators rather than all Roman citizens, he has to translate *ciues* as 'senatour'.[164] These inaccuracies may still just be clumsy, of course. Alternatively, they may reflect the translator's assumptions about social class: he seems to think that ancient Rome was even less egalitarian than it really was.

Lexis

The translation is striking for its Latinate lexis. Many of its Latin-derived words had only entered English earlier in the fifteenth century, which was a time when several English writers—most famously Lydgate—had started to develop particular interest in aureate, classicizing diction.[165] Some of the text's recently coined Latinate words include 'admytte', 'ambassatour', 'amytie', 'creditours', 'displesure', 'exorte', 'oracion', 'pompowsnes', 'quarelouse', 'requisite', and 'surmyse'. Some of these closely reflect the Latin words that they translate: the translator often adopts a stencil approach to translating lexis just as he often adopts a stencil approach to syntax. Thus 'oracion' consistently translates *oratio* and forms of 'exhorte' consistently translate *hortari*. Other examples include the translations of 'continentia' as 'continense', 'conscientia'

[162] 687–8, 1463.

[163] Cf. 1230–1*n*.

[164] 1281.

[165] See further Jenni Nuttall, 'Literary Language', in Julia Boffey and A. S. G. Edwards (eds.), *The Oxford History of Poetry in English*, iii: *Medieval Poetry, 1400–1500* (Oxford, 2023), 61–75.

as 'consciency', and 'condicio' as 'condicion'.[166] Similar interest in Latin lexemes may explain the idiosyncratic spellings 'improwrys' for *imperatores* and 'impere' for *imperium*, where the English words closely approximate the Latin being translated.[167] Many other, less novel Latinate words also follow either Sallust's Latin or the Valla commentary. Hence 'vnexcersi[s]id', translating Sallust's *incultus*, probably follows the Valla commentary's gloss of *incultus* as 'sine exercitio'.[168]

Deploying pointedly Latinate vocabulary in these ways may sometimes have functioned as a defence mechanism, when the translator did not fully grasp the meaning of the Latin being translated.[169] At other times, though, he was being more ambitiously experimental. These include moments when he introduces Latinate words which are both suitable in sense and based neither on Sallust's Latin nor on the Valla commentary. Thus *haruspices* becomes 'augures', a term that our translator may have known from Gower or Lydgate.[170] A less surprising translation of *haruspices* might have been 'divinouris', a word used in English since the early fourteenth century; *divinouris* also translates both *haruspices* and *augures* in Bellenden's Livy.[171] Another arrestingly Latinate word is 'expedyent', which is also a word that had only entered English earlier in the fifteenth century and which appears throughout *The Coniuracion*.[172] Some of our translator's more innovative Latinate terms even antedate their first citations in the *OED* and may be coinages. These include 'prodygally', which variously translates *liberaliter*, *profusius*, and *largius*.[173] Another example is 'manymysid', which appears as part of a translation of *liberti* and which refers to the practice of manumission.[174]

The extensive use of Latinate vocabulary works in tandem with the translator's decision to leave some Latin words untranslated. Untranslated words—which typically appear in engrossed script—sometimes also seem to function as a defence mechanism, when the translator could not fully puzzle out the Latin. Hence 'nonas' and 'kalendas' are left untranslated, for example, perhaps because the Valla commentary had not explained either term—to our translator's despair, no doubt, since he more gener-

[166] 70–1, 361, 479.
[167] 62, 64.
[168] 76.
[169] Cf. e.g. 1618*n*.
[170] 1090; cf. *OED*, s.v. 'augur', n.[1].
[171] Bellenden, *Livy's History of Rome*, i. 72, 251; cf. Titus Livius, *Ab Urbe condita*, ed. John Briscoe, Robert Seymour Conway, Stephen Keymer Johnson, A. H. MacDonald, R. M. Ogilvie, and Charles Flamstead Walters, 6 vols., Oxford Classical Texts (Oxford, 1919–2016), 1.31.4, 3.7.6.
[172] 22, 37, 464, 1058; cf. *OED*, s.v. 'expedient', adj.
[173] 277, 323–4, 378.
[174] 1175; cf. *OED*, s.vv. 'prodigally', adv., 'manumise', v.

ally seems to have struggled with Roman dates.[175] But the translator's ignorance cannot always explain untranslated Latin in *The Coniuracion*. For instance, the word *legatus* (a Roman military rank) is once left untranslated as '*lygatus*', once translated periphrastically as someone who 'had þe commyssion and auctoryte', and once translated more simplistically as 'grete capytayn'.[176] The second and third of these translations show that our translator knew what the Latin meant. He therefore made a deliberate choice on one occasion—indeed, the third and last occasion—to leave the word untranslated as '*lygatus*'. Untranslated Latin is sometimes also combined with an English gloss, thereby rendering the Latin superfluous to the sense of the translation. One such case is when the translator refers to 'the light-harnessed men called *ferentarii*'.[177] Contemporary translators often domesticated this kind of technical vocabulary with more familiar, updated terms. Thus 'tribunus plebis', which *The Coniuracion* renders as '*tribunus* of the people', becomes 'Zunfftmeister' (i.e. 'guildmaster') in an early sixteenth-century German translation.[178] Our translator never domesticates Sallust's Latin so radically. There are nevertheless several instances where *The Coniuracion* omits technical terms and offers simplified explanations in English. For example, *pontifex maximus* becomes 'the grete dignitie of their religion', *triumuires* becomes 'doers of execucion', and 'centuriones' becomes 'cheffe capytayns'.[179] The translator also simplifies *sacerdos Vestae* (i.e. a Vestal virgin) as 'a mayde professid to perfeccion'.[180] Contrast Paynell and Heywood, who in their respective Catiline translations domesticate *sacerdos Vestae* as 'nunne'.[181] Our translator, then, often worked harder to keep close to the exact meaning of more technical words, when he understood what they meant, while retaining as much clarity in his English as possible.

In contrast with these Latinisms, *The Coniuracion*'s occasional vernacularisms are all the more striking. Some of these vernacularisms have already been mentioned, such as 'haskerdes' (see Occasion and Authorship). Among other alliterative vernacular phrases and idioms are 'by lytill and lytill', 'watche and warde', 'rappe and rynde', and 'wex wode'.[182] Some of the text's idioms again antedate first citations in the *OED*, including

[175] 433, 437; cf. also 430*n*, 694*n*.

[176] 985–6, 1664, 1674.

[177] 1681.

[178] 990; Georg Schrayer, *Chronica C. Crispi Salustii von dem Romischen Bundtschüch* (Strasbourg, 1534), *USTC* 622276, sig. C3^{v}.

[179] 1154–5, 1540, 1655.

[180] 351–2.

[181] Thomas Paynell, *The conspiracie of Lucius Catiline* (London, 1541), *STC* 10751, sig. B2^{r}; Thomas Heywood, *The two most worthy and notable histories* (London, 1609), *STC* 21625, sig. C3^{r}.

[182] 147, 256–7, 573, 1304; 717, 1184; 330–1; 243–4.

'in the dede of the nyght' and 'putt to a plunge'.[183] The translator also shows ingenuity by introducing Germanic, non-Latinate words such as 'dryffte'.[184] The sense of 'dryffte' as 'design' or 'scheme' on two of the three occasions on which it appears antedates this sense of the noun in the *OED*, which further suggests the translator's self-conscious interest in deploying innovative language, whether Latinate or vernacular.[185] Indeed, as is the case with 'dryffte', the vernacularisms generally stand out at moments when the translator more confidently reaches beyond a close translation of the Latin.

Other set phrases, meanwhile, may indicate the translator's broader familiarity with contemporary literary culture. His description of Sempronia as 'by hirsilff oone of all the worlde' appropriates the English syntactical type 'one the best man', which was well known from works such as Chaucer's *Troilus and Criseyde*. Perhaps the lexically closest analogue is Chaucer's description of Atalanta as 'A mayde, oon of this world the beste ypreysed', though the sense of 'oon' in this instance is partitive (i.e. 'one of the best') rather than intensive (i.e. 'the best'), as it is in *The Coniuracion*.[186] The phrase 'comen hasarder', which offers an idiomatic and personifying translation of 'alea', may also have been known from works such as the *Canterbury Tales*.[187] In addition, the doublet 'subiecte and obeysant' echoes the French-derived set phrase 'subgettis obeisauntes', as is also found, say, in Worcester's *Boke of Noblesse*.[188]

EDITORIAL CONVENTIONS

As per EETS guidelines, original orthography is preserved but word division is normalized to follow modern practice, where 'modern practice' usually follows entries in *OED*. A notable exception is 'comon wele', which is left as two words to underscore that it is a calque of *res publica*.

The scribe uses **u** and **v** interchangeably, though vocalic **v** is more frequent in engrossed words. In all cases, **u** and **v** are transcribed as found in the manuscript. The scribe also uses **i** and **j** forms interchangeably: this edition transcribes as **i** except when the scribe uses **j** as the last character

[183] 650–1, 764; 756, 1164.

[184] 628, 1046, 1139.

[185] *OED*, s.v. 'drift', n., sense I.5.

[186] 603–4; *Troilus*, V.1473, in *The Riverside Chaucer*, gen. ed. Larry D. Benson, 3rd edn. (Boston, 1987). On this type, cf. Tauno F. Mustanoja, *A Middle English Syntax: Parts of Speech*, introd. Elly van Gelderen (1960; Amsterdam, 2016), 297–9. Cf. similar, intensive usages in *Troilus*, I.1081, II.746–7, III.781, 1310, V.1056–7.

[187] 329; cf. e.g. *Canterbury Tales*, VI.596.

[188] 74; Worcester, *Boke of Noblesse*, lines 58, 541, 895, 1235.

in a roman numeral. Yogh is not used but thorn appears throughout and is transcribed as **þ**. Capitalization is normalized to follow modern practice. Word-initial **ff** is expanded as **f** or **F** as appropriate.

This edition follows the manuscript in its use of round brackets and introduces no other brackets, since these are distinctive and consistently used features of punctuation. Otherwise, following EETS guidelines, punctuation is modern and aimed at ease of comprehension. In particular, em-rules (—) are occasionally introduced to make sense of especially knotty sentences, and quotation marks ('. . .') are introduced for direct speech and embedded letters. Letters and speeches that are distinguished from surrounding passages in the manuscript are indented at the left. Although paragraph and section breaks are ultimately editorial, they aim to reflect as closely as possible the textual divisions in the MS.

All corrections, including retouched letters, are placed in superscript primes. Words or parts of words presumed lost to trimming are in ⟨angle brackets⟩. The method of revision and the original word or passage deleted are recorded in the textual notes at the bottom of each page.

Words that were clearly intended as untranslated Latin are presented in italic type; these words are often also engrossed in the manuscript. Admittedly, there are some ambiguous instances where a common noun in *The Coniuracion* could have been intended as either English or untranslated Latin (e.g. 'pretor', 'cohortes', 'censores'): these instances are interpreted on a case-by-case basis as either English (not italicized) or untranslated Latin (italicized). Thus 'cohortes' is taken as an English noun at line 1653 but as untranslated Latin at lines 1665 and 1679, since the word is introduced on both latter occasions as part of a lexical gloss ('the garde of the olde sowgers of Rome called *cohortes veterane*', 'wardes of the hoste callid *coh`o´rtes*'). *Pretor* likewise is usually interpreted as an English word, except when the noun is modified by a Latin adjective ('*pretor vrbanus*', 1073) and when it is explicitly introduced as a word 'in the Laten tonge' (1673). Potentially untranslated Latin words that are also proper nouns, such as 'Athenienses' (60, 209, 212) and 'Tullyanum' (1543), are generally not italicized because it is less obvious how such nouns should otherwise have been translated into English; it is therefore unclear that they were ever intended as untranslated Latin. But there are two exceptions to this rule of not italicizing Latinate proper nouns: first, where the noun is clearly part of a gloss that the translator has introduced to Sallust's text (e.g. 'the convocacion howse callid *Capitolium*', 'the hye contrey of Fraunce callid

Transalpina'); second, where the œ ligature in '*Pœnos*' indicates that this word must have been intended as untranslated Latin.[189]

To enable easy comparison with Sallust's *BC*, numbers between 1 and 60 are added in square brackets as anchor points to Sallust's Latin, corresponding with the numbering of sections in Reynolds's Oxford Classical Texts edition.

Editorial emendations appear in square brackets. Errors in the spelling of proper nouns are not emended because the variants may offer insight into which words were and were not familiar to the translator and/or scribe. Such errors were also a source of debate among contemporaries. Mistakes with proper nouns, for instance, number among Gavin Douglas's most frequent criticisms of Caxton's *Eneydos* (e.g. 'Thus ay for Tibir Tonyr puttis he, | Quhilk mony hundreth mylis syndry be').[190] A list of historically correct names is given in the Index of Proper Nouns, together with the variant spellings found in this MS.

Different policies apply to transcription from early printed books and manuscripts other than MS Nn.3.6 in the Explanatory Notes: there, original word division, punctuation, and spelling are maintained, all contractions and abbreviations are silently expanded, superscript letters are silently lowered, and hooked **e** (ę) becomes **ae**. Unless otherwise stated, Sallust (*Sal*) is always quoted from L. D. Reynolds's 1991 Oxford Classical Text.

Abbreviations in the text of *The Coniuracion* are silently expanded in line with the following procedures:

Curled Terminations

-es, **-ys**, or **-is** forms are used with roughly the same frequency in written-out plurals, but **-es** is narrowly the most common. The default expansion for the curled termination is therefore **-es**, but **-ys** or **-is** is used if either is more common for a particular word's written-out forms: thus, 'appetitis', 'dedys', 'frendys', 'goddys', 'mischevis', 'offensis', 'senatouris', 'tentys' (and by extension, 'ententys'), 'vicis', 'werkys'. The plural of *lust* appears once as 'lustis' and once as 'lustys'; this edition arbitrarily prefers 'lustis' as its expansion. There are just over fifty occasions on which the scribe also forms another kind of curled termination with long Anglicana **r**, most frequently for the plural of 'ambassatour'. This edition's default expansion is again **-es** (as for the other kind of curled termination), but **-ys** or **-is**

[189] 431–2, 1582; 1220. [190] Douglas, *Eneados*, I.prol.231–2.

if either is more common for a particular word's written-out forms (thus, 'yeris', 'senatouris').

Horizontal Strokes

Horizontal strokes are frequently used to signal abbreviated **m** or **n** and are expanded accordingly: they typically appear as a thick straight line or a line with a curl (e.g. for 'commaundyd', 1461), and occasionally with a dot appearing below the horizontal (e.g. for 'Picenum', 1584).

There are also almost three hundred instances where a (usually hairline) horizontal stroke either crosses or appears above the ascender of **h** in combinations of **-th**, **-ch**, **-gh**, or **-sh**, when these clusters appear near the ends of words (e.g. 'strengitħ', 'whicħ', 'rygħt', 'fressħ'). In the majority of such instances a vowel could hypothetically be added: almost always this is word-final **-e**. In roughly a tenth of instances, however, it is unclear how any vowel could be added (as e.g. for 'trowtħe', 'inasmocħe', 'thougħte', 'norissħe').[191] There are also instances throughout of similar **-th**, **-ch**, **-gh**, and **-sh** words that have no horizontal stroke above them, even though they could hypothetically take another vowel. Since the scribe's practice is therefore inconsistent at best, this edition treats all such strokes as otiose and ignores them. In doing so, this edition follows how editors have treated similar marks in other fifteenth-century manuscripts.[192]

On the other hand, any horizontal strokes which could signal an **m** or **n** expansion are expanded as such, since thicker horizontal strokes cannot consistently be distinguished from more hairline strokes (which, otherwise, might always have been treated as purely decorative). This policy often applies to 'sōme', where a horizontal crosses the ascender of long **s** or the top of majuscule **s**. Horizontal strokes above **-ship** (and, relatedly, twice over 'vp' and once over 'vpp') are also expanded, as **-(p)e**, in line with the scribe's preference in written-out forms for **-ppe** endings.[193] Horizontal strokes over **-con** and flourishes that extend from word-final **n** over **-con** are both expanded as **-cion** (**-cyon** is not attested in the MS).

Crossbars

Crossed **-br** is expanded as **-ber** or **-bre** in line with the scribe's preferred written-out forms (thus, 'nombre', 'chamber'). For the two **-br** words for which there are no corresponding written-out forms ('Nouemƀr',

[191] 8, 19, 10, 881.

[192] Cf. Worcester, *Boke of Noblesse*, ed. Nall and Wakelin, p. cv; *Paston Letters and Papers of the Fifteenth Century*, i, ed. Norman Davis, EETS ss 20 (Oxford, 2005), p. lxxxii.

[193] 752, 1498, 1646.

'rememƀr'), this edition expands as **-bre**, since the scribe uses this written-out form more frequently. Where the expansion is already written out, the crossbar on word-final **-bre** is treated as otiose. Barred (and usually word-final) double **ll**, which never needs to be expanded with **-e**, is treated as a decorative flourish rather than as signalling abbreviation. Barred single **l**, however, is expanded as **ul** in 'multitude', where a **u** is needed.[194] Barred **p** is expanded as **par-** or **per-** in line with the most common spelling of each word's written-out form.

Superscript Letters and Symbols

Superior **a** is lowered to **-au-**, or to **-a-** where the **u** is already present. Superior **a** is treated as otiose when **-au-** is already present. Superscript **r** is lowered to **-ur**. Superscript **u** is lowered to **u** with the exception of **þ**$^{\mathbf{u}}$, which becomes **þou** (in line with the scribe's preference for 'thow'). **w**$^{\mathbf{t}}$ becomes **with** and **þ**$^{\mathbf{t}}$ becomes **þat**. The word-final '9' symbol is expanded as **-us**. Tironian *et* is expanded as 'and'.

Flourishes

Flourishes on word-final **m** and **n** need never be expanded with **-e** and are treated as otiose, with the exceptions of (*a*) flourishes on word-final **n** that clearly expand as **-er**, and (*b*) aforementioned instances where **-con** becomes **-cion**. Various marks that clearly signal **-er-**, **-r-**, **-re-**, **-ri-**, or **-ro-** expansions are also expanded as appropriate. The tongue that sometimes extends from word-final **g** is treated as otiose, except when the tongue is connected to a flourish that clearly signals **-er** (e.g. 'messanger', 811). Also treated as otiose are the tails and tongues that sometimes appear on word-final **d**, **f**, and **t** (especially **tt**).

A greater challenge is presented by the text's over five hundred instances of short **r**, which is always flourished when it appears at the end of a word. This graph is also flourished on one of the two occasions when it appears medially ('retourned', 890). There is one occasion where flourished short **r** must be expanded with **-e** for phonological reasons ('degre', 956); elsewhere it must also be expanded with **-er** for semantic reasons ('nerer', 1539). Otherwise, this edition generally treats the flourish as otiose, especially when the flourish is small, seemingly throwaway, or curly rather than angular. Short **r** is only expanded with **-e** when the flourish has a significant kinch or hook, angularity, or a thicker lobe, or a combination of these features. There are clear hooks or kinches, for example, in the one

194 157.

instance ('degre') where **-e** must be added, and especially in the above-noted instance where **-er** must be added ('nerer'). The result of this policy is that just over a quarter of instances of short **r** are expanded with **-e** in this edition. Many of these instances overlap with the nine words that sometimes end with short **r** and elsewhere appear in written-out forms with word-final **e** ('desire', 'impire', 'fayre', 'manere', 'matere', 'nature', 'oure', 'require', and 'where'). The manuscript's two instances of word-final flourished long **r** are also expanded with **-e**: in the first case the flourish has a clear kinch ('oure', 46); in the second, there is both a clear kinch and a relatively thick lobe ('demenure', 870).

This policy of expanding or ignoring flourished short **r** depending on the nature of the flourish is necessarily subjective, and another editor who implemented it would doubtless arrive at slightly different results. The policy is preferable, however, to the alternative of expanding every flourished short **r** with **-e**, since this clearly was not the scribe's intention. The policy adopted here also echoes the ad hoc approach to expanding flourished **r** that was adopted by Norman Davis for his edition of the Paston Letters. Davis commented of the manuscripts he edited that word-final **e** was 'in any case so irregularly written' that it had 'little importance'.[195] The same caveat applies to MS Nn.3.6, since word-final **e** also appears irregularly in this manuscript's written-out forms. The extent to which short **r** is flourished in this manuscript also seems often to be guided not by phonological or semantic concerns, but more simply by the scribe's whim and where he was in his stint of copying. Hence instances of short **r** with more elaborate flourishes are often found grouped together, in patches. The same is true of instances of short **r** that have more perfunctory flourishes.

195 *Paston Letters*, ed. Davis, p. lxxxii.

BIBLIOGRAPHY

MANUSCRIPTS

Cambridge, Pembroke College, MS 114 (p. xxv n. 48)
Cambridge, Peterhouse, MS 258 (p. xxviii n. 62)
Cambridge, St John's College, MS G.19 (p. xxii n. 37)
Cambridge, St John's College Archives, SJCM/1/3/6 (p. xxi n. 29)
Cambridge University Archives
  ULIB 7/3/28 (p. xix n. 23)
  ULIB 7/3/74/65 (p. xix n. 24)
Cambridge, University Library
  MS Nn.3.6
  MS Nn.3.10 (p. xxii n. 36)
  MS Oo.7.57 (p. xix n. 22)
Oxford, Balliol College
  MS 121 (pp. 71, 98)
  MS 123 (p. xxv n. 46, pp. 99, 105)
  MS 258 (p. xxv n. 46, p. xxxiv n. 80)
Oxford, Bodleian Library
  MS Auct. F. 5. 8 (p. xxv n. 49, p. xxxiv n. 80)
  MS Barlow 45 (p. xxv n. 48, p. xxxiv n. 80)
  MS Rawl. B. 356 (p. xxi)
Oxford, Magdalen College, MS lat. 218 (p. xxv n. 47, p. xxxiv n. 80)
Oxford, St John's College, MS 84 (p. xxv n. 47, p. xxxiv n. 80)

INCUNABLES CITED IN SPECIFIC COPIES

Cambridge, King's College, Bryant.XV.3.3 (p. xxxiv n. 79, pp. 69, 81, 91, 93, 99)
Cambridge, St John's College, Ii.2.27 (p. xxxii n. 73; Plate 1)
Cambridge, University Library
  Inc.3.A.1.3a[12] (p. xlii n. 118)
  Inc.3.F.6.2[3396] (pp. xx–xxiii)
  Inc.3.J.1.1[3491] (pp. xx–xxiii)
  Sel.3.265 (pp. xix–xxiii)
London, Lambeth Palace Library, MS 765 (p. xlii n. 118)
Oxford, Corpus Christi College, ϕ.C.4.6 (p. xxxii n. 74, p. xxxv n. 84, pp. 57, 67, 69–71, 84, 93)
Shrewsbury School, F.VI.5 (p. xxxii n. 77, p. 59)

NON-INCUNABLE EARLY PRINTED BOOKS CITED IN SPECIFIC COPIES

Cambridge, University Library, Tc.54.58 (p. 59)
Oxford, Bodleian Library
8° F 75 Linc. (pp. 82, 87)
8° H 183 Art. (p. 75)
Broxb. 79.3 (p. 59)
DD 20 Art. (pp. 59, 88, 107)

PRINTED PRIMARY SOURCES

Ascham, Roger, *The Scholemaster* (London, 1570), *STC* 832.

Augustine, *De ciuitate Dei libri XXII*, ed. Bernhard Dombart and Alfons Kalb, 2 vols., Corpus Christianorum Series Latina, 47–8 (Turnhout, 1955).

—— *Epistulae CI–CXXXIX*, ed. Kl. D. Daur, Corpus Christianorum Series Latina, 31B (Turnhout, 2009).

Barclay, Alexander, *The Famous Cronycle of the Warre which the Romayns had agaynst Iugurth, Usurper of the Kyngdome of Numidy*, ed. Greg Waite, EETS OS 344 (Oxford, 2014).

Bartolomeo da San Concordio, *Il Catilinario e Giugurtino*, ed. Basilio Puoti (Naples, 1827).

Bellenden, John, *Livy's History of Rome: The First Five Books*, ed. W. A. Craigie, 2 vols., Scottish Text Society, 1st ser., 47, 51 (Edinburgh, 1901–3).

Bernard, Edward, *Catalogi librorum manuscriptorum angliæ et hiberniæ*, 2 vols. (London, 1697–8).

Blount, John, 'An Edition with Introduction and Commentary of John Blount's English Translation of Nicholas Upton's *De studio militari*', ed. Craig G. Walker, 2 vols. (D.Phil. thesis, University of Oxford, 1998).

Bourchier, John, Lord Berners, *The thirde and fourthe boke of Sir Iohn Froissart* (London, 1525), *STC* 11397.

Carbone, Ludovico, *Le traduzioni da Sallustio*, ed. Alessandra Minisci (Pisa, 2017).

'Catilina' and 'Jugurtha' by Sallust and 'Pharsalia' by Lucan in Old Norse: Rómverjasaga, AM 595 a–b 4to, ed. Jakob Benediktsson, introduction trans. Peter Foote (Copenhagen, 1980).

Caxton, William, *The Booke of Ovyde Named Metamorphose*, ed. Richard J. Moll (Toronto, 2013).

—— *The Middle English Text of 'Caxton's Ovid'*, Book I, ed. Diana Rumrich, Books II–III, ed. Wolfgang Mager, 2 vols. to date, Middle English Texts, 43, 53 (Heidelberg, 2011–).

—— *Myrrour of the worlde* (London: Laurence Andrewe, 1527?), *STC* 24764.

—— *The Prologues and Epilogues of William Caxton*, ed. W. J. B. Crotch, EETS os 176 (London, 1928).

—— *The veray trew history of the valiaunt knight Iason* (Antwerp: Gerard Leeu, 2 June 1492), *ISTC* il00112100, *STC* 15384.

Chaucer, Geoffrey, *The Riverside Chaucer*, gen. ed. Larry D. Benson, 3rd edn. (Boston, 1987).

Cicero, M. Tullius, *Epistulae*, ed. W. S. Watt and D. R. Shackleton Bailey, 3 vols., Oxford Classical Texts (Oxford, 1958–82).

—— *Orationes*, ed. Albert Curtis Clark, Oxford Classical Texts (Oxford, 1905).

Cope, Anthony, *The historie of two the moste noble capitaines of the worlde* (London, 1544), *STC* 5718.

Dietrich von Plieningen, *Zwo schon historien, nemlichen von des Catilinen und auch des Iugurthen kriegen* ([Landshut, 1515]), *USTC* 635245.

Dorne, John, *Day-Book*, ed. C. R. L. Fletcher and Montagu Burrows, in *Collectanea* (Royal Historical Society), 4 vols. (Oxford, 1885–1905).

Douglas, Gavin, *The Eneados*, ed. Priscilla Bawcutt with Ian C. Cunningham, Scottish Text Society, 5th ser., 17–19 (Woodbridge, 2020–2).

The Earliest English Translation of Vegetius' 'De re militari', ed. G. A. Lester, Middle English Texts, 21 (Heidelberg, 1988).

Elyot, Thomas, *Bibliotheca Eliotae* (London, 1542), *STC* 7659.5.

—— *Dictionary* (London, 1538), *STC* 7659.

—— *'The Image of Governance' and Other Dialogues of Counsel (1533–1541)*, ed. David R. Carlson (Cambridge, 2018).

Felici, Costanzo, *De coniuratione L. Catilinae* (Leipzig, 1535), *USTC* 624975.

Heywood, Thomas, *The two most worthy and notable histories* (London, 1609), *STC* 21625.

Higden, Ranulf, *Polycronicon*, trans. John Trevisa (Westminster, 1482), *ISTC* ih00267000, *STC* 13438.

Kempe, Margery, *The Book of Margery Kempe*, ed. Barry Windeatt (Cambridge, 2000).

Knyghthode and Bataile: A XVth Century Verse Paraphrase of Flavius Vegetius Renatus' Treatise 'De re militari', ed. R. Dyboski and Z. M. Arend, EETS os 201 (London, 1935).

A Late-Medieval History of the Ancient and Biblical World, ed. Cosima Clara Gillhammer, 2 vols., Middle English Texts, 63–4 (Heidelberg, 2022).

Livius, Titus, *Ab Urbe condita*, ed. John Briscoe, Robert Seymour Conway, Stephen Keymer Johnson, A. H. MacDonald, R. M. Ogilvie, and Charles Flamstead Walters, 6 vols., Oxford Classical Texts (Oxford, 1919–2016).

Lucan, Suetone, et Salluste [i.e. *Li fet des Romains*] (Paris, 1490), *ISTC* il00312000, *USTC* 766079.

Lydgate, John, *Fall of Princes*, ed. Henry Bergen, 4 vols., EETS ES 121–4 (London, 1924–7).

—— *Siege of Thebes*, ed. Axel Erdmann, 2 vols., EETS ES 108, 125 (London, 1911–30).

Manutius, Aldus, *Humanism and the Latin Classics*, ed. and trans. John N. Grant, I Tatti Renaissance Library, 78 (Cambridge, MA, 2017).

Martialis, M. Val., *Epigrammata*, ed. W. M. Lindsay, 2nd edn., Oxford Classical Texts (Oxford, 2007).

A Middle English Translation from Petrarch's 'Secretum', ed. Edward Wilson and Daniel Wakelin, EETS OS 351 (Oxford, 2018).

Mirk, John, *Liber festiualis* (Rouen, 1499), *ISTC* im00623500, *STC* 17966.

Palsgrave, John, *Lesclarcissement de la langue francoyse* (London, 1530), *STC* 19166.

Parmentier, Jean, *L'hystoire catilinaire* (Paris, 1528), *USTC* 37936.

Paston Letters and Papers of the Fifteenth Century, i, ed. Norman Davis, EETS SS 20 (Oxford, 2005).

Paynell, Thomas, *The conspiracie of Lucius Catiline* (London, 1541), *STC* 10751.

Quintilianus, M. Fabius, *Institutionis oratoriae libri duodecim*, ed. M. Winterbottom, 2 vols., Oxford Classical Texts (Oxford, 1970).

[Ramírez de Guzmán, Vasco, and Francisco Vidal de Noya], *The Texts and Concordances of Escorial ms. g.III.11 and Newberry Library inc. f-9511: Two Fifteenth-Century Translations of the 'Bellum Catilinarium sive de conjuratione Catilinae' and 'Jugurtha seu Bellum Jugurthinum'* (*Gaius Sallustius Crispus*), ed. Jerry Rank (Madison, WI, 1989).

The Register of the Goldsmiths' Company: Deeds and Documents, c.1190 to c.1666, ed. and trans. Lisa Jefferson, 3 vols. (Woodbridge, 2022).

Reuchlin, Johannes, *Vocabularius breviloquus* (Basel, 1478), *ISTC* ir00155000, *USTC* 748529.

Sallust, *Catilina; Iugurtha; Historiarum fragmenta selecta; Appendix Sallustiana*, ed. L. D. Reynolds, Oxford Classical Texts (Oxford, 1991).

—— *Opera*, comm. attrib. Lorenzo Valla (Venice, 1491), *ISTC* is00076000, *USTC* 991411.

—— *Opera*, comm. Jodocus Badius Ascensius (Paris, 1504), *USTC* 182604.

—— *Sallust's 'Bellum Catilinae'*, ed. and comm. John T. Ramsey, 2nd edn. (Oxford, 2007).

—— *The War with Catiline; The War with Jugurtha*, trans. J. C. Rolfe, rev. John T. Ramsey, Loeb Classical Library, 116 (Cambridge, MA, 2013).

Schrayer, Georg, *Chronica C. Crispi Salustii von dem Romischen Bundtschüch* (Strasbourg, 1534), *USTC* 622276.

Skelton, John, *Bibliotheca historica*, ed. F. M. Salter and H. L. R. Edwards, 2 vols., EETS OS 233, 239 (London, 1956–7).

—— *The Complete English Poems*, ed. John Scattergood, rev. edn. (Liverpool, 2015).

Starkey, Thomas, *A Dialogue between Pole and Lupset*, ed. T. F. Mayer, Camden Society, 4th ser., 37 (London, 1989).

Statutes of the Colleges of Oxford, ii (London, 1853).

Tullius de senectute (Westminster, 1481), *ISTC* ic00627000, *STC* 5293.

Udall, Nicholas, *Apophthegmes* (London, 1542), *STC* 10443.

—— *Floures for Latine spekynge* (London, 1534), *STC* 23899.

Upton, Nicholas, *De studio militari libri quatuor*, ed. Edward Bysshe (London, 1654).

Valerius Maximus, *Factorum et dictorum memorabilium libri IX*, ed. John Briscoe, ii: *Libri VII–IX* (Stuttgart, 1998).

Vegetius, *Epitoma rei militaris*, ed. M. D. Reeve, Oxford Classical Texts (Oxford, 2004).

Vincent of Beauvais (Vincentius Bellovacensis), *Speculum maius*, 4 vols. (Douai, 1624; repr. Graz, 1964–5).

Woodville, Anthony, *Cordiale quattuor novissimorum* (Westminster, 1479), *ISTC* ic00907000, *STC* 5758.

—— *The dictes or sayengis of the philosophres* (Westminster, 1477), *ISTC* id00272000, *STC* 6826.

Worcester, William, *'The Boke of Noblesse' and the English Texts from Its Codicil*, ed. Catherine Nall and Daniel Wakelin, EETS OS 362 (Oxford, 2023).

SECONDARY SOURCES

Allmand, Christopher, *The 'De Re Militari' of Vegetius: The Reception, Transmission and Legacy of a Roman Text in the Middle Ages* (Cambridge, 2011).

Baker, John, *The Men of Court 1440 to 1550: A Prosopography of the Inns of Court and Chancery and the Courts of Law*, 2 vols., Selden Society Supplementary Series, 18 (London, 2012).

Baldwin, T. W., *William Shakspere's 'Small Latine and Lesse Greeke'*, 2 vols. (Urbana, IL, 1944).

Batstone, William W., and Andrew Feldherr (eds.), *Sallust*, Oxford Readings in Classical Studies (Oxford, 2020).

Bawcutt, Priscilla, *Gavin Douglas: A Critical Study* (Edinburgh, 1976).

Beadle, Richard, 'Sir John Fastolf's French Books', in Denis Renevey and Graham D. Caie (eds.), *Medieval Texts in Context* (London, 2008), 96–112.

Benskin, Michael, and M. L. Samuels (eds.), *So meny people longages and tonges: Philological Essays in Scots and Mediaeval English Presented to Angus McIntosh* (Edinburgh, 1981).

—— and Margaret Laing, 'Translations and *Mischsprachen* in Middle English Manuscripts', in Benskin and Samuels (eds.), *So meny people longages and tonges*, 55–106.

Berry, D. H., *Cicero's 'Catilinarians'* (Oxford, 2020).

Black, Robert, *Humanism and Education in Medieval and Renaissance Italy: Tradition and Innovation in Latin Schools from the Twelfth to the Fifteenth Century* (Cambridge, 2001).

Blackwell, C. W. T., 'Humanism and Politics in English Royal Biography: The Use of Cicero, Plutarch and Sallust in the *Vita Henrici Quinti* (1438) of Titus Livius de Frulovisi and the *Vita Henrici Septimi* (1500–1503) by Bernard André', in I. D. McFarlane (ed.), *Acta Conventus Neo-Latini Sanctandreani* (Binghamton, NY, 1986), 431–40.

Blake, N. F., 'Manuscript to Print', in Jeremy Griffiths and Derek Pearsall (eds.), *Book Production and Publishing in Britain 1375–1475* (Cambridge, 1989), 403–32.

Brennan, T. Corey, and Andrew Lintott, 'praetor', *Oxford Classical Dictionary*, https://doi.org/10.1093/acrefore/9780199381135.013.5305.

Briquet, C. M., *Les Filigranes: Dictionnaire historique des marques du papier dès leur apparition vers 1282 jusqu'en 1600*, 4 vols. (Paris, 1907).

Brockliss, L. W. B., *The University of Oxford: A History* (Oxford, 2016).

Burke, Peter, 'A Survey of the Popularity of Ancient Historians', *History and Theory*, 5 (1966), 135–52.

Carlson, David R., 'Skelton's English Diodorus and the 1481 Edition of Poggio's Latin Translation', *Notes and Queries*, 70 (2023), 61–4.

Chakravarty, Urvashi, *Fictions of Consent: Slavery, Servitude, and Free Service in Early Modern England* (Philadelphia, PA, 2022).

Challis, C. E., 'Mint Officials and Moneyers of the Tudor Period', *British Numismatic Journal*, 45 (1975), 51–76.

Chrimes, S. B., *English Constitutional Ideas in the Fifteenth Century* (Cambridge, 1936).

Colley, John, 'Diodorus Siculus in the English Quattrocento: New Light on the Source of Skelton's *Bibliotheca historica*', *Medium Ævum*, 93 (2024), 389–407.

—— '"Maniacal Ciceronianism"? Costanzo Felici's *De coniuratione Catilinae* and Historical Writing in the Early Cinquecento', *Erudition and the Republic of Letters*, 10 (2025), 115–43.

Connolly, Margaret, *Manuscripts in the University Library, Cambridge (Dd–Oo)*, Index of Middle English Prose, 19 (Cambridge, 2009).

Copeland, Rita, *Rhetoric, Hermeneutics, and Translation in the Middle Ages: Academic Traditions and Vernacular Texts* (Cambridge, 1991).

Cox Jensen, Freyja, 'The Popularity of Ancient Historians, 1450–1600', *Historical Journal*, 61 (2018), 561–95.

—— 'Ancient Histories of Rome in Sixteenth-Century England: A Reconsideration of Their Printing and Circulation', in Paulina Kewes (ed.), *Ancient Rome in English Political Culture, ca. 1570–1660*, special issue of *Huntington Library Quarterly*, 83 (2020), 415–40.

Da Rold, Orietta, *Paper in Medieval England: From Pulp to Fictions* (Cambridge, 2020).

Day, Matthew, *English Humanism and the Reception of Virgil c.1400–1550* (Oxford, 2022).

[De la Mare, A. C., and Richard Hunt], *Duke Humfrey and English Humanism in the Fifteenth Century: Catalogue of an Exhibition Held in the Bodleian Library, Oxford* (Oxford, 1970).

—— and Laura Nuvoloni, *Bartolomeo Sanvito: The Life and Work of a Renaissance Scribe* (Paris, 2009).

De Luna, B. N., *Jonson's Romish Plot: A Study of 'Catiline' and Its Historical Context* (Oxford, 1967).

Earl, D. C., *The Political Thought of Sallust* (Cambridge, 1961).

Edwards, A. S. G., 'The Middle English Translation of Claudian's *De consulatu Stilichonis*', in A. J. Minnis (ed.), *Middle English Poetry: Texts and Traditions* (York, 2001), 267–78.

Emden, A. B., *A Biographical Register of the University of Oxford A.D. 1501 to 1540* (Oxford, 1974).

Ford, Margaret Lane, 'Importation of Printed Books into England and Scotland', in Lotte Hellinga and J. B. Trapp (eds.), *The Cambridge History of the Book in Britain*, iii: *1400–1557* (Cambridge, 1999), 179–201.

Gibbs, Gary G., *Five Parishes in Late Medieval and Tudor London: Communities and Reforms* (London, 2019).

Griffiths, Jane, *John Skelton and Poetic Authority: Defining the Liberty to Speak* (Oxford, 2006).

Hankins, James, *Virtue Politics: Soulcraft and Statecraft in Renaissance Italy* (Cambridge, MA, 2019).

James, Montague Rhodes, *A Descriptive Catalogue of the Manuscripts in the Library of Peterhouse* (Cambridge, 1899).

Kennedy, Benjamin Hall, *The Revised Latin Primer*, ed. James Mountford (London, 1962).

Kenney, E. J., *The Classical Text: Aspects of Editing in the Age of the Printed Book* (Berkeley, CA, 1974).

Ker, N. R. (ed.), *Medieval Libraries of Great Britain: A List of Surviving Books*, 2nd edn. (London, 1964).

Knight, Jeffrey Todd, 'Fast Bind, Fast Find: The History of the Book and the Modern Collection', *Criticism*, 51 (2009), 79–104.

—— *Bound to Read: Compilations, Collections, and the Making of Renaissance Literature* (Philadelphia, PA, 2013).

Kristeller, P. O., *Iter Italicum: A Finding List of Uncatalogued or Incompletely Catalogued Humanistic Manuscripts of the Renaissance in Italian and Other Libraries*, 6 vols. (Leiden, 1963–92).

—— †F. E. Cranz, †V. Brown, and Greti Dinkova-Bruun (gen. eds.), *Catalogus translationum et commentariorum*, 13 vols. to date (Washington, DC, 1960–).

Laing, Margaret, 'Multidimensionality: Time, Space and Stratigraphy in Historical Dialectology', in Marina Dossena and Roger Lass (eds.), *Methods and Data in English Historical Dialectology* (Bern, 2004), 49–96.

—— and Roger Lass, 'Early Middle English Dialectology: Problems and Prospects', in Ans van Kemenade and Bettelou Los (eds.), *The Handbook of the History of English* (Chichester, 2006), 417–51.

Lass, Roger (ed.), *The Cambridge History of the English Language*, iii: *1476–1776* (Cambridge, 2000).

Latte, Kurt, 'Sallust: Diction and Sentence Structure, Narrative Style and Composition, Personality and Times', in Batstone and Feldherr (eds.), *Sallust*, 24–84.

Lawton, David, 'Dullness and the Fifteenth Century', *English Literary History*, 54 (1987), 761–99.

Leader, Damian Riehl, *A History of the University of Cambridge*, i: *The University to 1546* (Cambridge, 1988).

Lee, Brian North, *British Royal Bookplates and Ex-Libris of Related Families* (Aldershot, 1992).

Leitch, Megan, *Romancing Treason: The Literature of the Wars of Roses* (Oxford, 2015).

Levick, Barbara, *Catiline* (London, 2015).

Lowry, Martin, 'The Arrival and Use of Continental Printed Books in Yorkist England', in Pierre Aquilon and Henri-Jean Martin with François Dupuigrenet Desrousilles (eds.), *Le Livre dans l'Europe de la Renaissance: Actes du xxviiie colloque international d'études humanistes de Tours* (Paris, 1988), 449–59.

McGushin, P., *'Bellum Catilinae': A Commentary* (Leiden, 1977).

McIntosh, Angus et al., *An Electronic Version of A Linguistic Atlas of Late Mediaeval English* (Edinburgh, 2013), http://www.lel.ed.ac.uk/ihd/elalme/elalme.html.

McKitterick, David, *Cambridge University Library, A History: The Eighteenth and Nineteenth Centuries* (Cambridge, 1986).

Memory of Paper, The, https://www.memoryofpaper.eu/BernsteinPortal.

Momigliano, Arnaldo, and Andrew Lintott, 'senatus consultum ultimum', *Oxford Classical Dictionary*, https://doi.org/10.1093/acrefore/9780199381135.013.5821.

Mortimer, Nigel, *Medieval and Early Modern Portrayals of Julius Caesar: The Transmission of an Idea* (Oxford, 2020).

Mustanoja, Tauno F., *A Middle English Syntax: Parts of Speech*, introd. Elly van Gelderen (1960; Amsterdam, 2016).

Nafde, Aditi, 'Replicating the Mechanical Print Aesthetic in Manuscripts before circa 1500', *Digital Philology*, 9 (2020), 120–44.

Nall, Catherine, *Reading and War in Fifteenth-Century England: From Lydgate to Malory* (Cambridge, 2012).

—— 'Moving to War: Rhetoric and Emotion in William Worcester's *Boke of Noblesse*', in Stephanie Downes, Andrew Lynch, and Katrina O'Laughlin (eds.), *Emotions and War: Medieval to Romantic Literature* (Basingstoke, 2015), 117–32.

Needham, Paul, *The Printer and the Pardoner: An Unrecorded Indulgence Printed by*

William Caxton for the Hospital of St. Mary Rounceval, Charing Cross (Washington, DC, 1986).

Nuttall, Jenni, 'Literary Language', in Julia Boffey and A. S. G. Edwards (eds.), *The Oxford History of Poetry in English*, iii: *Medieval Poetry, 1400–1500* (Oxford, 2023), 61–75.

Orme, Nicholas, *English School Exercises: 1420–1530* (Toronto, 2013).

Osmond, Patricia J., 'Jacopo Corbinelli and the Reading of Sallust in Late Renaissance France', *Medievalia et Humanistica*, 21 (1994), 85–110.

—— '*Princeps historiae Romanae*: Sallust in Renaissance Political Thought', *Memoirs of the American Academy in Rome*, 40 (1995), 101–43.

—— 'Princeps Historiae Romanae: Sallust in Renaissance Political Thought', in Batstone and Feldherr (eds.), *Sallust*, 400–44.

—— 'Sallust in the Renaissance: From Exemplary and Analogical Reading to Scholarly Criticism', in C. B. Krebs (ed.), *The Cambridge Companion to Sallust* (Cambridge, forthcoming).

—— 'The Valla Commentary on Sallust's *Bellum Catilinae*: Questions of Authenticity and Reception', in Pade (ed.), *On Renaissance Commentaries*, 29–48.

—— and Robert W. Ulery, Jr., 'Constantius Felicius Durantinus and the Renaissance Origins of Anti-Sallustian Criticism', *International Journal of the Classical Tradition*, 1 (1995), 29–56.

—— —— 'Sallustius Crispus, Gaius', in †Kristeller, †Cranz, †Brown, and Dinkova-Bruun (gen. eds.), *Catalogus translationum et commentariorum*, viii. 183–326 and x. 375–91.

—— —— 'Pomponius Laetus, Editor of Sallust: *Corrector vel corruptor*?', in Giancarlo Abbamonte, Minna Skafte Jensen, and Marianne Pade (eds.), *Ipsissima verba: Essays in Honour of Johann Ramminger*, special issue of *Renæssanceforum: Nordic Journal of Renaissance Studies*, 19 (2022), 171–96.

Pächt, Otto, and J. J. G. Alexander, *Illuminated Manuscripts in the Bodleian Library, Oxford*, ii: *Italian School* (Oxford, 1970).

Pade, Marianne (ed.), *On Renaissance Commentaries* (Hildesheim, 2005).

Philo, John-Mark, *'An Ocean Untouched and Untried': The Tudor Translations of Livy* (Oxford, 2020).

Reynolds, L. D. (ed.), *Texts and Transmission: A Survey of the Latin Classics* (Oxford, 1983).

Rissanen, Matti, 'Syntax', in Lass (ed.), *The Cambridge History of the English Language*, 187–331.

Rundle, David, 'Humanism before the Tudors: On Nobility and the Reception of the *Studia Humanitatis* in Fifteenth-Century England', in Jonathan Woolfson (ed.), *Reassessing Tudor Humanism* (Basingstoke, 2002), 22–42.

—— 'Of Republics and Tyrants: Aspects of Quattrocento Humanist Writings and Their Reception in England, *c.*1400–*c.*1460' (D.Phil. thesis, University of Oxford, 1997).

—— *The Renaissance Reform of the Book and Britain: The English Quattrocento* (Cambridge, 2019).

Salmon, Vivian, 'Orthography and Punctuation', in Lass (ed.), *The Cambridge History of the English Language*, 13–55.

Samuels, M. L., 'Spelling and Dialect in the Late and Post-Middle English Periods', in Benskin and Samuels (eds.), *So meny people longages and tonges*, 43–54.

Schurink, Fred, 'War, What Is it Good for? Sixteenth-Century English Translations of Ancient Texts on Warfare', in Sara K. Barker and Brenda M. Hosington (eds.), *Renaissance Cultural Crossroads: Translation, Print and Culture in Britain, 1473–1640* (Leiden, 2013), 121–38.

Sharpe, Richard, and Teresa Webber (gen. eds.), *Corpus of British Medieval Library Catalogues*, 16 vols. to date (London, 1990–).

Singh, Devani, *Chaucer's Early Modern Readers: Reception in Print and Manuscript* (Cambridge, 2023).

Skinner, Quentin, *The Foundations of Modern Political Thought*, 2 vols. (Cambridge, 1978).

Smalley, B., 'Sallust in the Middle Ages', in R. R. Bolgar (ed.), *Classical Influences on European Culture A.D. 500–1500: Proceedings of an International Conference Held at King's College, Cambridge, April 1969* (Cambridge, 1971), 165–75.

Smith, Jeremy J., 'Tradition and Innovation in South-West-Midland Middle English', in Felicity Riddy (ed.), *Regionalism in Late Medieval Manuscripts and Texts: Essays Celebrating the Publication of 'A Linguistic Atlas of Late Mediaeval English'* (Cambridge, 1991), 53–65.

Strohm, Paul, *Politique: Languages of Statecraft between Chaucer and Shakespeare* (Notre Dame, IN, 2005).

Thomson, R. M., *The Fox and the Bees: The Early Library of Corpus Christi College, Oxford* (Cambridge, 2018).

Turner, Andrew J., 'Reading Sallust in Twelfth-Century Flanders', *International Journal of the Classical Tradition*, 21 (2014), 198–222.

Ulery, Robert W., Jr., 'Sallust's *Bellum Catilinae* in the Edition of Venice, 1500: The Medieval Commentary and the Renaissance Reader', in Pade (ed.), *On Renaissance Commentaries*, 7–28.

Waite, Greg, 'Alexander Barclay's Translation of Sallust's *Jugurtha*: A Note on Sources', *Notes and Queries*, 58 (2011), 196–202.

Wakelin, Daniel, *Humanism, Reading, and English Literature 1430–1530* (Oxford, 2007).

—— 'Classical and Humanist Translations', in Julia Boffey and A. S. G. Edwards (eds.), *A Companion to Fifteenth-Century English Poetry* (Cambridge, 2013), 171–85.

—— *Scribal Correction and Literary Craft: English Manuscripts 1375–1510* (Cambridge, 2014).

—— 'Early Humanism in England', in Rita Copeland (ed.), *The Oxford History of Classical Reception in English Literature*, i: *800–1558* (Oxford, 2016), 487–513.

—— 'Not Diane: The Risk of Error in Chaucerian Classicism', *Exemplaria*, 29 (2017), 331–48.

Wasserzeichen-Informationssystem, https://www.wasserzeichen-online.de.

Watts, John, '"Common Weal" and "Commonwealth": England's Monarchical Republic in the Making, c.1450–c.1530', in Andrea Gamberini, Jean-Philippe Genet, and Andrea Zorzi (eds.), *The Languages of Political Society: Western Europe, 14th–17th Centuries* (Rome, 2011), 147–63.

—— 'Public or Plebs: The Changing Meaning of "The Commons", 1381–1549', in Huw Pryce and John Watts (eds.), *Power and Identity in the Middle Ages: Essays in Memory of Rees Davies* (Oxford, 2007), 242–60.

White, Paul, *Jodocus Badius Ascensius: Commentary, Commerce and Print in the Renaissance* (Oxford, 2013).

Wisman, Josette A., 'Flavius Renatus Vegetius', in †Kristeller, †Cranz, †Brown, and Dinkova-Bruun (gen. eds.), *Catalogus translationum et commentariorum*, vi. 175–84.

Womersley, David, 'Sir Henry Savile's Translation of Tacitus and the Political Interpretation of Elizabethan Texts', *Review of English Studies*, 42 (1991), 313–42.

Workman, Samuel K., *Fifteenth Century Translation as an Influence on English Prose* (Princeton, NJ, 1940).

THE CONIURACION OF LUCIUS SERGIUS CATELINA

How moche Salvstius is to be praysed afore oder wryters of histories in the Laten tonge Qvintilianus declarith, in that he gevith hym the laude above Thucidides, which by the iugement of hym and many oder famose clerkys excellid ferre Herodotvs or Livius. Marcialis also, that noble poete, approvinge the same, d`ow′ted not above all oder Saluste in glorie to avaunce. But Saynt Augustine (to whose auctorite of ryght all good men gevith faithfull credens) in his booke *De civitate Dei* not alonly callith hym right eloquent, `b′ut also the notable wryter of trowthe of the historye—the which, howe may be gretter prayses geven to eny suche wryter? f. 1r

Therfore I thoughte it a right convenyent besynes for me to bestowe summe labour and studye in his werkys, and after my lytill power to attempte in satisfying the desire of other men to haue his tr`e′atise of the coniuracion of Catelyne owte of Latyn in owre wolgare and Englisshe tonge declared. I dar not sey wher I am not aboute to take vpon me the office of an interpreter, for the greate lakke of knowleage of bothe those langages, ner yet intende so greate a charge and diligens, but it shal be sufficient for me the same to overrunne and after, as it shall for the tyme comme to mynde, so to wryte.

Forthermore, inasmoche as the maners of the old Romaynes be had so notable and excellent, and by the shewynge of Saluste seme to be so gretly accordynge to the nature and | dew lyvynge of men, I thoughte it also expedyent to endevour me to gader and adioyne to the same somme suche thinges concernyng those behalffes the which in very youthe, herynge the famouse lernyd men my reders, summewhat I savored, and beryng therof aparte in mynde nowe a greate tyme laid by and I from them a longe space withdrawen. Albeit they seme vnto me full straunge, yet for that they are to this mater so gretly belongynge, for fere of reprove of eny necligent ascape it is not to be done in silence to leve them onspoken of, where the tendre aige is also excusable and moost of all the intent of my purpose by excersise of wryting, at the laste, trustyng to obteyne the knowleage and science, the which is also the allonly waye, as many excellent clerkys wryte and recorde, that reducith men from the rude and derke stile to the good and commendable kynde of wryting. Thus therfore the more boldly I entre into the mater. | f. 1v

5 d`ow′ted] o *retouched,* w *over eras. letter* 8 `b′ut] b *over vertical stroke, perhaps the start of* T 12 tr`e′atise] e *over* a

f. 2r

Caius Cryspus Salustius In his boke of hystoryes of the coniuracion of Lvcius Sergius Catelina

[1] It is expedyent to all men that myndes themselfes to be above other bestys to endevour them with all laboure and diligens that they overrynne not their lyffe nothing doyng lyke shepe, the which nature hathe ordenyd to be inclynyd and obeysant to the bellye. But all oure possibylite is putt in the doyng of the sowle and of the body, the sowle to haue the rewle, the body to be subiectt. The oon we haue comyn with the goddys, the othire with w`y′lde bestys. Wherfore it semy`th′ me more ryght to serche to wynne glorye by the warkys of the reason than by the actes of the body, and bycause this maner lyffe that we occupy is but shorte, to make `oure′ memoryall mooste longeste to endure. For the glorye of welthe and goodlynesse is vnstable and not abydyng; the actes of vertew be noble and euerlastyng.

[1.5] But a longe tyme ther was a `greate′ striffe and contencion | f. 2v amonges men whethir the obtenyng of victorye stode more by manlynes of the body or by wisdome of the soule, for afore that thow shalt begynne to do anything, it requyrith the to cowncell with thy reason, and necessaryly to all resonyng belongith also incontynent to folowe the actuall dede of þe body. So ethir of them beying inperfite withoute the other hathe nede to the helpe of the other. Therfore in the begynnyng, kynges `(′for that name was had fyrste vpon the erthe of rewle and power`)′, dyversly somme yave theim to the excersise of their body, somme to resonyng, for than the lyffe of man was ladde withoute covetousnes: every man was well satisfied with his awne. But after whan Cirus in Asia, the Lacedemones and the Athenienses in Grece, began vpon an appetite `of′ rewle to make quarell of bataill, to subdew citees and contrees vnto theim, and to iuge mooste glorye in hym that had the mooste large impere, than sone after in perelles and greate actes it was well percevyd þat in bataill wisdome myght do moche. For `and′ yf kynges and improwrys had ben of as wyse and vertuouse disposicion in tyme of peas as in theire warrys, the state of men shuld haue ben ferre more stable and longer enduryng. Thow | f. 3r shuldyste not than haue seen oon overturne another and so many chaunges and confusyons, for the hye dignyte is easely kept by the same wayes with the which in the begynnyng it is wonne.

43 w`y′lde] *minim changed to* y  semy`th′] th *over eras.* d 46 oure] *initially* my*; first minim turned into* o *and hooked* r *written over* y 49 greate] *interlineated, marked with caret* 53 resonyng] *follows crossed-out long* s 55–6 `(′ . . .`)′] *round brackets added retrospectively* 60 of] *over eras. letter or letters* 64 and] *interlineated, marked with caret*

[2.5] But whereas in the place of laboure slothe is entred, and for continense and iustice lustis and wilfulnesse be vsed, fortune chaungeth togader with their maners, wherby imperys be translatyd from the badde to better men. For vertew alweis will rewle: to hir all thinges vpon land and see be subiecte and obeysant. Howbeit many men, dyspysing vertu, folowed sensualitie and bestowed theimselffes in mete, drynke, and slepe. Theire witt vnlernyd, their body vnexcersi[s]id, they ouerpassed their lyffe lyke straungers, vnknowen men and vnspokyn of. To thees men sewrly, ayenst nature, the body was their pleasure, the sowle right a grete burden. The lyffe and dethe of theim I accompte all alyke worthe bycause ther is nought spoken of ethir.

But of trothe he allonly aftir my iugement lyvith and occupieth reason that ethir is sette vpon the renowme of a valeant acte or ellys sekyth the prayse of a good science and faculte. And in the greate multytude of so many thinges to wynne honour by, to every man nature dyversly hathe yeven another wey. It is a goodly thing to doo noble enterprysis for the comen wele, and | to be well lernyd is not amysse. A man mey wynne f. 3v
honour in warrys, ye and lyvyng also in peas, for many men that haue done the actes and many þat hathe but wryten other mennys dedys be praysid.

[3.2] But to me of trouthe, though there folowe not lyke glorye to the wryter and to the d`ooe'r, yet of all thinges it semyth an harde bysenes a man to declare in wryting the noble and valeant actes. Fyrst, because his sayinges muste be egall and accordyng to the dedys. The seconde, that many men will thinke his reprovis of other mennys offensis to be spoken of malice and invye. Also, whan he shall speke of t`h'e grete vertew and glorye of good men, as for those that euery man thinkith that he mey lightly do, he takith well aworthe. Yf they be above his estymacion, those he iugeth fayned and false matere.

Bvt in tendre age and in my begynnyng, as many other yonge men dyd, I lefte lernyng and was putte forthe to the comen wele, in the which reynid many vicis, for for drede of shame, for abstinence and doyng no violence, for vertewis and noblenes, ther reygned boldnes to all myscheffe, pompowsnes, and inordynate coveting of dignite and richesse, the which though the reson shunnyd, that was not accustomyd to those evill craftes, yet amonges so grete vycis the feble age was taken with the corrupcion of desyre of honour. For whereas I cowde not agree me to the other evill maners, neuerthelesse | yet coveting of honour vexed me, lykewise as other f. 4r

76 vnexcersisid] vnexcersidid *over eras. and* e *over another letter* 82 is] *follows crossed-out long* s 91 d`ooe'r] oo 95 t`h'e] h *over* e

men, as well in deffence of my fame ayenst myn aduersaries as in the labour and bysenes to wynne the honour of it.

[4] Bvt after many perelles and myserys therof, `w′ha`n′ the mynde was restyd and that I had determyned to bestow the remnaunt of my yeres ferre from medelyng in the causis of the comen wele, to consume the good tyme in slouthe and idelnes it was no wisdome, nor yet convenyent to spend my lyffe in the vile offices of plowing or huntyng. But from that study that evill covetyng of honour pullyd me fyrst fro, now ayen retornyd and dryven to the same I haue taken vpon me to wryte the hystoryes of Romaynys, `not′ of all theire actes at lengith, but suche thinges as semyd me mooste worthy to be had in memorye. And I do this the rather because my mynde is free from hope or drede in the partetakynges within the comen wele.

Therfore of the seducion of Catelyne as trewly as I may brevely I shall declare, for that dede methynkith is to be had chefely in remembraunce for the gretnes of the matere and of the parell also, `o′f the which mannys condicions fyrst is somwhat to be shewed afore I begynne my `t′rayties. |

f. 4v [5] Lvcius Catelina was comyn of a right noble `ly′n`age′ of the citee of Rome, a stronge man bothe of stomake and of body but of an evill and a shrewed disposicion, for of very youthe in treson, mordre, thefte, ravissh-ment of women, debates and stryves was his delyte, and therin excersysid hymselffe. Of his body he myght abyde and suffre hunger, colde, watche aboue any mannys thynkyng; a bolde and hardy stomake, crafty, vary-able, and in euerything he vsed coloure and dyssymylacion; of his awne prodygall, verey desirous of other mennys; fervent in his wilfull `appetitis, metely′ well spoken, but lytill wisdome; a wastefull mynde, coveting hye thinges without reason or mesure.

[5.6] Thys man, after he had sene how Lvcius Sylla by force aforetyme had taken in rewle the hole comen welle, was sett on fyre mooste fervently to subdew the cite to hym, and that he caryd not by what meanes he myght wynne it so he myght haue it. Dayly more and more his ferse mynde was styrred theronto by his fallyng into pouertie and lakkyng of his awne to meynteine his pleasures. The remembraunce also of his horrible offencis mevid hym not a lytill, the which thinges encresid dayly by his maners

110 `w′ha`n′] w *and* n *over eras. letters* 117 not] *interlineated, marked with caret* 123 `o′f] *majuscule over minuscule* o 124 `t′rayties] t *over another letter* 125 `ly′n`age′] ly *over eras. letters, two minims retouched as* a, g *over* e, *and terminal* e *added* 132–3 appetitis, metely] d *retouched as* a, *with some of* a *and* ppetitis *over eras., and* metely *over eras. word with medial* y *and word-final* tt *or* ll

afore rehersid and in esspeciall `by´ the corrupte maners of the cite, the which with the fowle vicis, lustis, and covetyse were sore vexed. |

The very thing and the tyme also requyrith, bycause I haue spoken of f. 5r
the maners of the cite, to call to mynde and to describe brevely here the instruccions of our eldres in the comen wele bothe in tyme of peas and in their warrys, and how large they leffte it, and how by lytill and lytill it chaunged from the mooste noble and the beste and bycam the worste and mooste vicious.

[**6**] The cite of Rome, as I haue lernyd, was byeldid and inhabite in the bygynnyng by the Troianys, the which vnder Eneas their capytayn were fled from ferre contres and had no bydyng place. With these men were also a people of antiquytie ther callid *latini*, a rewde kynde of men withoute lawes and withowte hed, fre and withoute any correccion. These men, after they were gadred into oon place, beyng of dyuers kyn`d´es and of onlyke langages and levyng after dyverse and sundry maners, it is incredeble to be rehersyd how lightly they encresid and howe, shortly after, that multitude, that was dyuerse and wandryng, by peas was made a citee.

[**6.3**] But after whan their power was incresyd and `semyd´ myghty, of citezins, of good maners, of possescions ryght welthy and ryght stronge, incontinent, | as the custome is allweys amonges mortall men, ayenst their f. 5v
plenteousnes rose `the´ invy of theire neighboures. Wheruppon the kynges and people þat ioynyd to theim began to attempte bataill ayenst theim, and ryght a few were there of their frendys that wolde eyde theim. All other, stryken with fere, ab`s´entid theim from theire perelles. But the Romaynys were ryght dyligent bothe in theire warrys and in the tyme of peas and hastely they made them redy, oon exhortyng another, and sett forward to mete theire enmyes to deffend with armour their fredome, theire contrey, their faders and their moders.

And after whan they had by theire valyantnes dryven fer from themselffes all perelles, than they toke in hand to deffend their frendys causis. They purchasid theim favour by their gyftes and desertes to other men more than by recevyng of other mennys benefytes. They ordenyd theim by lawis a rewler whome they `nami´d a kyng and they chase owte also a certeyn nombre of theim þat for age had weke bodyes, but stronge brayns in wisdome, to be councelers for the comen wele, the which ethir bycause of theire age or for theire auctoryte were namyd Faders. But after whan the

142 by] *interlineated, marked with caret* 154 withoute] *follows crossed-out* at 155 kyn`d´es] d *retouched from one- to two-compartment* d 159 semyd] *added in right-hand margin* 162 the] *over* to 165 ab`s´entid] s *over eras. letter* 174 `nami´d] nami *over eras. letters*

rewle of kynges, which was ordenyd in the begynnyng to conserue their fredome and for the incresyng of their comen wele, was turnyd into pryde f. 6r and wilfulnesse, they chaunged than their | customes and made yerely two governours, the`yre′ auctoryte enduryng allonly by the space of oon yere, for by that manere they thoughte the mynde of man cowde not fall into pryde vpon suche libertie. Than in that tyme every man began to putte hymselff more forwarde to be sett by and covetid to haue their manlynes and wisdo`me′ more opyn and knowen, for vnto kynges the good men be had more susspect than the vile, and allweys to theim anoder mannys vertew and `polecy′ is right dredefull. But it is to mervelouse to tell, havyng that fredome, how bigge the cite grew right shortly, they were taken with so grete desyres of glorye.

[7.4] Than þe youth in their begynnyng, as sone as they were able for bataill, streight were putte into places assigned for their tentys and for `þe′ excersyse of armour, where they lernyd by the vse of labour to be men of warre. They had more delyte in goodly armour and in warly horses then in hoorys and bankettes. Therfore to suche men was no labour vnknowyn, no place paynefull or daungerous. There came non enmye with strengith of armour that was feryd: their valiantnes subdewed all thinges. But to wynne glorye was their grete stryffe and besynes, so that every man that fyrst sett vpon his enmy or scaled fyrst þe wallis at a sege, and he ware beholden whan he did those dedys, that he callid his richesse, the good fame, and grete noblenes. Of lawde and prayse they were moste desirous, of their f. 6v goodes liberall, honour they covetid exceding, | richesse competent.

I myght here reherse the places in the which the Romaynys with a small power ouerthrew grete multitudes of their enmyes, and how grete citees mooste strongly warded and fensyd by theire warrys they toke and subdewed, were it not that þat matere shuld to longe withdrawe me fro my purpose.

[8] But sewrly fortune rewlith all thinges. She of hir will more than of the right settyth all thinges vppon hight `a′nd downe full lowe. The actes of the Athenienses, as I thinke, were ryght large and ryght notable, but yet sumwhat lesse than the fame spekith of theim. But bycause there were bredde of wryte`r′s the[r] excelent brayns, therfore over all the worlde the dedys of the Athenienses be lawded for the best, wherby the valeantnes of those persones that dyd the actes there is taken for as grete as their noble

181 the`yre′] *initially* ther; y *written over* r *and word-final hooked short* r *added* 185 wisdo`me′] me *over two earlier letters* (*?*) 187 polecy] *over eras.* valiantnes 191 þe] *initially* to; *y-shaped* þ *written over* to, *where* o *is partially erased; superscript* e *added* 208 `a′nd] a *retouched from one- to two-compartment* a 211 wryte`r′s] r *over another letter* (*?*) ther] the

wisdomes by wordes cowde sett theim vpon hyght. But the Romaynys had neuer suche company of wryters for the wisist of theim: every man yaue hymsilff mooste pryncipally to the noble actes. To study allonly no man yaue hym withoute he excersisid his body in the warris also. Every of the best of theim had rather do the dedys than to teche and speke of them, and rather they wolde haue their noble dedys to be praysid of oþer men than they to talke of oþer mennys dedys. [**9**] Therfore as well at home as in theire warris good maners were kepte and observid; amonges theimselffes best acorde, leste covetousnes; þe right and good wayes | they `vsed and´ kepte f. 7r more by lawe of nature than by the forse of lawis. All brallynges, malices, and hates they excersisid ayenst their enmyes. The citezens emonxte themselffes had but oon stryffe: who shulde excelle other in vertew and noblenes. In thaire sacrifices to the goddys verrey plentiouse, at home they vsed mesure, and righte faithfull were they to their frendys. By thise two wayes, Manlynesse in bataill and Iustice in the tyme of peas, they deffendid theimselffes and the comen wele also, of the which two thinges thise mooste cheffe examples I haue knoleage of, that in theire warrys they dyd oftetymes execucion vpon theim that faughte with their enmyes contrary to þe commaundment of their soueraigne and on them that taryed longer after in the felde than they that callid them thense by the signes, and on them also that yf they were overturnyd from their place durste be so hardy to yelde themselffes. But in the tyme of peas the impire was gouerned more by theire good desertes than by coarcion of fere, and in all wronges done to þem they were better wyllinge to foryeue than to be revengid.

[**10**] But whan by excersise and iustice their comen wele was growyn so myghty that their rewle spred ouer all the worlde, the grete kynges conquerid by thaim in batelles, the wilde nacions and grete multitude of peoples subdewed by force, þat grete cite Cartago in Grece that was invious to the impire of Rome overturnyd by the rootes, and whan all sees and landes to theim were open and obesaunt, than | fortune began `to wex f. 7v wode and´ to chaunge all thinges. They that dyd easely and paciently suffre the laboures, the perellz, the hard and doutfull thinges iuged alweys ease and riches the burdeyns of all wretchednes, the which vnto other men be moste coveted and desyred, and vpon the same, coveting of goodes fyrste entred emonxte theim after the desire of rewle, and those two thinges were the verrey matere of all evilles and mischeffis. For covetousnes overturnyd fidelite, `g´entill disposicion, and all other vertewis maners and brought in

222 vsed and] *over eras. word* 241 grete] *follows crossed-out* there 243 than] *precedes crossed-out* they 243–4 to wex wode and] *supralinear addition, marked with caret* 250 `g´entill] g *over the start of another letter*

for theim pryde, crewelnes, to sett lytill by the goddys, and for mony to bye and sell all maner thinges. The fervent desire of dignite drove many men to moche falsehed, to beyre oon thing closed in the breste and anoder redy on the tonge, to iuge theire frendys and their enmyes not ac[c]ording to right but after as they were for theire profytte. They occupied more a good countenaunce than a goode disposicion. These two thinges fyrst grew on by lytill and lytill, yet amonge they were punished. But aftyr the contagiouse therof lyke a pestilence had infected theim, the cite was clene altred and from the mooste ryghtwes and best impere it become the moste crewell and to wikked. But in þe begynnyng þerof þe desir of honour occupied mennys myndes moche more than covetousnes, the which vice neuertheles yet was \`nerrer´ vnto vertew, for glory, honour, and rewle þe good man sekith and f. 8r the badde man in lyke wise, howbeit he endevorith | hym by trew and right weyse, the oþer, that hathe no good maners, laborith by crafty wayis and deseytes. Covetousnes hathe the fervent desire of richesse, the which the wise man neuer covetyd, for she lyke a full venemouse \`evyll´ thing makyth bothe the body of the man and the reason also right vyle. She is withoute mesure and onsaciable foreuer, for nethir with habundaunce ne scastye she lessyth.

[11.4] Bvt after that the victorye of Lvcius Sulla turnyd from their good begynnynges to evill chaunces and mischevous maners, all they fyll to oppression. Oone toke from \`hym´ his howse, anoþer his landes, and he that myght wynne the victorye nethir had he mesure nor gentilnes, but right horrible and crewell dedys dyd they ayenst the citezens. And to this moreouer the hooste of Sylla, that he had the rewle of in Asia, to gete hym their fauour was suffred by hym to do what they lysted and were kepte to prodygally with lycens and fredomys contrary to þe manere of oure forfaders. The swete and plesaunt howsis with ease anon made the bolde stomakes of sowgers to be right softe. There fyrst byganne the hoste of Rome to fall to love, to haue their greate bankettes, to sett moche by theire goodly pictures and ymages sett with golde and precious stones, to haue the fressh facions of plate, the which thinges they dred not to stele, bothe f. 8v pryvely and openly, and spoylid the temples also, ye and spared not | to polute and to do morder in theim \`all´. Therfore thees saugers, whan they had gotten the victory, they lefte no maner thing to theim that were ouercomen. Sewrly prosperity and welth oppressith and werith the reasons of

254 according] acoording 262 nerrer] *interlineated, marked with caret* 266 evyll] *interlineated, marked with caret* 272 hym] *interlineated, marked with caret* 276 they lysted] theylysted*; two vertical strokes have been added to mark word division* 280 to sett] *one or more letters eras. before* to, t *partly rewritten* 284 all] *supralinear addition, marked with caret*

wyse men also, that scant they can refrayne from the vicious maners of the wilfulnes of victorye.

[12] After onys that richesse began to make honour, and that glory, iurysdiccion, and poour folowid therunto, vertu`y′s anon were `noght′ sett by, pouerty was taken for reproffe and shame, innocency and pleyn levyng was had in hate and dispyte. Therfore vpon this ease and welth oure youthe ware taken with lustys, covetousnes, and oppression also. They robbyd and consumyd all thinges, sett lytill store by their owne, other mennys goodes fervently covetyd, toke no regarde ether to shame or honestye. Whether hit belongid to the goddys or to men they rekkyd not: all was lyke to them. They had nethir consideracion nor mesure.

It is behovefull to beholde the noblenes of oure elders, and whan ye haue seen their howsis and their places bylded in the maner of citees to loke also vpon the temples that they made as moste devoute and religious men. Certenly they anournyd the temples with holynesse and sacrifice, their howsis with honour and glory. And in their victoryes, they neuer dyd more to man but allonly toke from hym his liberty and power to wronge theim. | But these folkes contrary, moste vyle men, by grete wykkydnes f. 9r
toke vyolently from their awne felowis those thinges that the moste valeant men our eldres in their warrys dyd leve to their enmyes. So it cam to at the laste that allonly he that by power dyd oppression and wronge had the rewle and dignite. [13] And what to tell you of their lustis and plesures the which no man wil beleve but they allonly that haue seen them? Many meane men made playn`s′ of the `hye′ mountayns and drye groundes [with] ferre compas within the sees to bylde them royall castelles in of the fresshest maner, t`he w′hich men methinkyth dyd make a scorne of theire richesse, for why those thinges that they myght honestly haue had and occupied they went abowte to abvse theim in foly and vylenes. But of the fowle viciousnes they sparid non advoutre, comyn women, bawdre, and all other moste vylonowse offensys. The women were redyer and that openly to offer it than the men to desyre it, and for their bankettes ther was nethir land nor see shuld be vnsought. To slepe they wolde yeue theim afore they had luste therto. Hunger, thryst, coolde, or laboure they wolde abyde non but prevent all them after their appetytis and lustis. All these thinges dyd sette the youthe vpon mischeffe `after′ whan they had clerely wasted their substaunce. The mynde infectid with evill maners myght not lyghtly be

290 vertu`y′s] y *over* o  noght] *interlineated, marked with caret*  310 playn`s′] *initially* playnenes*;* nes *erased and* s *written over* e hye] *interlineated, marked with caret* 311 with] *om.* 312 t`he w′hich] he w *over eras. letters, with the* w *retouched* 315 non] *follows crossed-out* not 321 after] *interlineated, marked with caret*

f. 9v withowte `h′is | pleasures, but after the more excedyngly and more prodygally yeven to charges and pompowsnes by what wey somever they myght comme by it.

[14] In so grete and so corrupte a citee, Catelyne, thinkyng to wynne the rewle that þat was full lyght to do, gadred the multytude of all the vicious and mischevous men as a company of a garde abowte hym. For whosoeuer were paste shame, adwoutrer, or levyd by bawdre, or comen hasarder, or vpon his belly and prodygalite had wasted all that he myght rappe and rynde, and he that had caste hymselfe ferre in dett for the redemyng and dischargyng of his wykkyd dedys, all they also that had kyld thair fadres or commytted sacrylege, and they that ethir were condempnyd by the lawys or feryd iugement vpon their dedys, and they lykewise that their hand had doone thefte or m`u′rder, their tonge commytted false wytnes or periurye, and brevely whosomeuer in his con`s′iens was prykkyd of his opyn mischevis or vexid with necessite after he had wasted all, into the famyliaryte and affyans with Catelyne he shulde be recevid. And yf it happid any man that was not gylty in suche maners to fall into his favour, by theire dayly f. 10r company and with his flatery and pleasures anon he was made egall | and lyke to the other. But moste of all he covetid the famyliaryte of the yonge men (their myndes beyng softe, and theire age freyll, they were takyn with deceytes withoute difficultie), for, as he asspied theire nature and accordyng to the desyre of the yerys of eche of theim, to somme he offred women, with other he bargenyd for horsys and doggys, and at the laste nethir sparid he for charges nor for mesure so he myght wynne theim to be obesaunt and faithfull vnto hym. I know certeyn men that iuged that the yonge men that hawnted Catelyns howse vsed right vilonowse maners ther, the which was of trouthe more than euer was puplished or spoken of.

[15] In the begynnyng of his yeris Catelyne commytted many wikkyd and fowle ravishmentes and adwowtrees with an noble virgyn, with a mayde professid to perfeccion, and suche other horrible dedys ayenst the lawys of god and of man. And after that, taken with the love of Avrelia Orestella, of whome never good man praysid thing but oonly hir beauty, bycause she dowted to be maryed to hym, dredyng leste his sone comen to age shuld do hir displesure, it is had for trowthe that he sparid not to poyson his awne son to make mete his howse for thair wykkyd maryage. The which thinges mesemyth was the fyrst cause of the rypyng of his

323 `h′is] h *added retrospectively* 328 and] *follows crossed-out* people 335 m`u′rder] *second minim of* u *initially written as* r, *then retouched* 336 con`s′iens] s *over* c 352 other] *follows crossed-out* h

mischeffe, for sewrly his mynde, | beyng vnclene ayenst the goddys and f. 10v malicious to men, kowde nethir with watche ner with reste be peasid: the consciency troubled so sore the wilde mynde. Therfore the coloure of his face salowe, the eyn bl`odye′, his pace `now′ swifte now slowe, and in the visage and the countenaunce apperid alweys fersenes and mischeffe.

[16] Bvt the yonge men, the which as I said before he drew to hym by many maner weys, he lernyd theim false craftes to beyre vntrew witnesse, to countrefete mennys signes, fydelite, prosperous fortune, and perelles to haue no consideracion vnto, and after he had distroyde theire good name and the fere of shame, than he sett theim vpon greter maters, and yf he had not at that tyme th'occasion redy to worke apon his horrible dedys, he wolde fall than vppon theim that were innocentes to disceve theim, ye and also sley theim as and they had bene his aduersaries. For bycause he wold not that the hand ner the stomake of the yonge men shuld for lakke of excersise forgete theire maners, therfore rather than to fayle, withoute any cause yeven he wolde be myschevous and crewell.

In thees frendys and felyshippe Catelyne havyng his hope, and therto seyng that all the contreys abow`te′ the citee were sore pillaged in þe warrys | and oppressid with dett, also that many of the sawgeorus of Silla f. 11r that had prodygally wasted theire substaunce bare in mynde their prayers and olde victorye and covetid moche to haue bataill among the citezens, determyned anon to attempte to subdew the comyn wele. In all Italye was no senator of strengith of armes. Gneius Pompeius was in ferre contreys occupied in warrys. He hymselfe stode in the eleccion to be chosen consul, wher`of′ he had right a grete hope—`t′he Senate withoute mystruste, all thinges peasable and quyete. But thees thinges were mete and accordyng to þe appetyte of Catelyne.

[17] Therfore aboute the begynnyng of Februarii, Lvcius Cesar and `C′aius Figulus than beyng consulles, fyrst Catelyne callid his company to his counseill by oon and oon, and somme he temptyd in the matere, some he exhortid thervnto, and shewd theim what assistaunce he dowted not to haue and how vnredy the comen wele was, and how grete rewardes they shuld haue that wolde take his parte in the rebellion. So whan he had compassid his matters after his mynde, than he callid all theim that stode in daunger and greate necessite within the citee, and were of moste boldnes, tog`a′der into oon place. Thether come of the noble degre of senatouris

362 bl`odye′] o *over* e *and* dye *over eras. letters* now] *over eras. letters, perhaps* pac 376 abow`te′] t *over eras. letter* (*perhaps* e) *and word-final* e *added* 383 wher`of′] of *over eras. letters* `t′he] *majuscule* T *over another letter* 387 `C′aius] *engrossed* C *over smaller* c 394 tog`a′der] o *partially erased then retouched as* a

f. 11v Puplius Lentulus Sura, P. Antronius, Lvcius Cassius Longinus, | Marcus Cethegus, P. Servius Sila, L. Vargenteius, Qvintus Annius, M. Porcius Leca, Lvcius Calphurnius, L. Bestia, Q. Curius; also, of the degre of meane gentilmen, Marcus Fulvius, Lucius Statilius, P. Gabinivs, Caius Cornelius, P. Capito; and many moo besyde these ware gadred to that place that were but of low and symple degre yet in their porte right noble and wors`h′ipfull. Moreouer many other right greate men were assent to this same counseill after a more secrete manere, the which hope of rewle mevyd more therunto than pouerty or othir necessitie. But the more parte of the youth, and mooste of all the yonge men of the noble degre, favored the weys of Catelyne, the which covetid to be lordes that they myght leve in ease plesauntly and pompously. Their will was to aventure vpon the vnc[er]teyn and to leve the certayn, and desyrid rathir to haue warre then pease. There were men that tyme that thoughte Marcus Lucius Crassus was not all ignorant of their counseill, and bycause that Gneius Pompeius, that invyed and bare hym malice, was of so greate strengith and powere of `a′rmys, they demyd he wold haue bene wylling that any man shulde haue growen myghty ayenst his power, and also for that he shuld haue trusted f. 12r that yf the rebellyon had obtenyd, lightly | he myght haue ben made prynce amonges theim.

[18] Bvt afore this besynes there were also certeyn men that conspired the destruccion of the comen wele, amonge the which Catelyne was oon, the which matere as playnly as I can I shall shew you. Whan—Lvcius Tullo and Marcus Lepido beyng consulles—Puplius Antronius and P. Silla were electid to succede theim into the dignite of consulles, they were thervpon accusid in the lawis of *ambitus* that they had wonne the favour of the people by corrupcion of money, for the which they suffred opyn punyshment. Within a shorte space after, Catelyne, standyng to be made consull, was put by it because he was accusid at that tyme of extorcion and pillage that he had done in the contreys lately afore which he had þe iurisdiccion of, and had not sufficient leyser after the cowrse of the lawis to make his tryall therin before the dey of eleccion of the consulles.

There was also the same tyme Gneius Piso, a yonge man of noble kynred, of an haute and bolde mynde, nedy and quarelous, whome necessite and evill maners styrred to make trouble in the comen wele. With hym Catelyne and Antronius made apoyntment and preparyd them to

401 wors`h′ipfull] h *over eras. letter* 407 vncerteyn] vncreteyn 411 `a′rmys] a *retouched from one- to two-compartment* a 425 sufficient leyser] sufficientleyser*; two vertical strokes have been added to mark word division*

haue slayne Lvcius Cota | and Lvcius Torquatus, than consulles, in the convocacion howse callid *Capitolium* vpon the dey of their congregacion thether in the *kalendas* of Ianuary, þat they by suche forse myght haue occupied their auctoryte of ˋcˊonsulles and than to haue sent Pyso forthe with strengith of armour to subdew the contreys of Speyne. And whan this mater was asspied and knowen, than they dyfferryd their purpose of this morder vnto the *nonas* of February next folowing, at which tyme they had ymagenyd the distruccion not allonly of the consulles but of many other also of the senatoris, insomoche that and Catelyne had not preventid and to hastely made the signe appoynted amonges theim afore the counseill house to his felowis, that day had bene commytted the greatyst mischeffe that euer come to Rome synnes the cite was fyrst made. But the greate company of the men of armes were not than gadred nor all thing redy at his calling, the which thing brake all theire purpose and intent. f. 12v

[**19**] Sone after, Pyso had the commyssion graunted hym to be pretor into the nerer contrey of Spayne thorow the laboure of Marcus Crassus, bycause he knew well he was the greate enmy of Pompey, and the Senate yet dyd not admytte hym to the auctoryte of that contrey ayenst theire will, but sewrly they were ryght willing to haue suche a mischevouse man to be ferre of from the comen wele. Also there were many good men thoˋghtˊ | they shulde haue a syngler deffence of hym bycause that the mighty powere of Pompei was to be gretly drad ˋaˊt that tyme. But the same Piso in his iourney toward that province was slayne of the gentilmen horsemen of Spayne, the which he ledde with hym in his hoste. Many men said that his commaundmentes were so wrongefull, so cruell, and so wilfull that straungers myght not abyde ne suffer theim. Other men said that the same Spaynyardes were olde frendys and faithfull to Pompey and that by his ˋadvisesˊ they sette vpon Piso, for it was neuer herd of the Spaynyardes aforetyme that euer they commytted any suche offense, for all that they had sufferd aforetyme many grevouse oppressyons, but that matere I leve. f. 13r

Thus of the fyrst rebellyon this is sufficient.

[**20**] Catelyne whan he had gadred them togader that I spake of here a lytill afore, ˋalbeitˊ he had had many talkynges with eche of theim by theimselffes, yet he thoughte hit expedient for his matere to call theim all vnto hym to exorte theim, and into a secrete place of the howse he getyth hym ferre from the heryng of straungers and there he spake to them aftyr this maner folowing: |

434 ˋcˊonsulles] c *over* s 450 the] theim, *with* im *crossed out* thoˋghtˊ] ght *over eras. letters* 452 ˋaˊt] i *retouched as* a 458 advises] *over eras.* 463 albeit] *over eras. word*

f. 13v And yf youre manlynes and faithfulnes were not well assured vnto me, this mater were fallyn nothing mete to oure desyres: the grete hope of rewle that now is offerd vnto our handes shuld be but voyde. Ner I wold not by foly and vpon truste of light braynes leve the thing certayne and take in hand thinges vncerteyn, but bycause I haue in many and grete dawngers founden you stronge and faithfull vnto me, therfore my stomake is bolded to sett vpon the moste noble and gretest acte, consydering also that all that shall be good or evill to me shal be in lyke maner vnto you, for amonges faithfull frendys is all oon will and all oon consente. And what my purpose is ye haue knowen it eche of you afore, but dayly more and more it settith my mynde on fyre whan I considre what condicion of lyffe is to comme withoute we ourselffes wyne ayen our fredome. For sythen the comen wele is fallen into rewle and iurisdiccion of a few men of myght and power, to them kynges and prynces beyrith tribute. The people, the nacions, mennys wages and their rewardes hangith vpon them. All other valeaunt, good, noble, and vile men, we be all comons of lyke reputacion, withoute favour, withoute auctoryte, and subiectes to theim, that and the comen wele were anything worthe they shuld haue vs in drede. So, all power,
f. 14r honour, richesse is emonxte | theim or where the[y] wyll haue theim. To vs they leve rebukys, dyshonoures, perelles, condempnaciones, and necessities, the weche how longe will ye s`u´ffer, ye mooste manly men? Were it not yet better with noblenes to dye than this wretched and vile lyfe, in the which ye serue to thair pryde and scornys, to lose it with shame? [**20.10**] But sewrly by the faith of the goddys and of men, the victorye for vs is at hand. We haue youthe and lusty yeris, we haue stomake and hardynes, and they contrary, for what for yeris and richesse all in thaim is aged. Here lakkith nothing but to sett vpon this matere. The residew the thing of the self will spede. And who is leving here that hathe a mannys stomake that can be contentid to suffre theim to haue these excedyng habundaunces of goodes, to bylde pompouse howsis in the sees, to make for their pleasures playnys of the hye mountaynes, and we to lakke that that is necessarie to mannys lyving? And they also haue contynually kepte two how`sh´oldes or moo, and we to haue neuer a chamber of our awne? They by theim goodly pictures, fressh and shynyng ymages. The olde maners they disspise. Those that were latly byeldyd they pull downe and othir new they sett vp. But all

487 they] the 489 s`u´ffer] *over eras. letter* 491 lyfe] *precedes crossed-out* lyve 501 how`sh´oldes] how soldes; s *added and* h *written over eras.* s, *thereby also removing MS word division*

maner wayes they draw home richesse, they laboure and hale abowte it mooste bysely: they cannot ouercome their richesse. And to vs at home is pouerty and owteward grete dett | f. 14v to oder men: an evill thing, the hope moche harder. So, in the extreme of it, what haue we lefte vs besyde the wretched lyffe? [**20.14**] Wherfore now aryse and bestyrre you. Beholde well, here is the fredome that ye haue oftentymes gretly desyred. Also richesse, worshippe, glorye be sett afore oure eyn. Fortune hathe ordenyd all those in rewardes to theim that haue the victorye. The thing, the tyme, oure perelles, our necessitie, the greate rewardes of the bataill shuld more styrre you than my speche chose you. As a capytayn or a sawiour vse me. Nether the stomake nor the body shall goo bakke from you. Thees maters as I truste I shall do them beyng consull with your helpe togader, withoute peradventure youre mynde deceyue me and that ye `be´ better willing to be in bondage and thraldome than in auctoryte and rewle.

[**21**] After whan these men had hard these wordes, the which were full of all evilles, for their substaunce was nothing, ne nought they had to truste vnto or yet to haue any good hope in, thowe they sawe grete prayes to trouble the comen wele that was in quyete, neuertheles yet many of them desyred that he shuld shew theim what condicion they shuld be in by reason of that bataill and what rewardes they shuld truste to haue for that they | f. 15r enterprysid to make suche warre, and what assistaunce or lyklyhode of victory ther was.

Than Catelyne promysid theim new grauntes in wryting of possescions, the riche mennys goodes to be attaynted, the hye dignyties, the greate and welthy offices, the prayes, and also all othir thinges that bataill and wilfulnes of the victorye covetith. Moreouer he shewed that Piso was in the nerrer contrey of Spayne, Puplius Siccio Nucerius in Mauritania in Affrica with greate hostes, the which were of assent to his counseill, also that Caius Antonius stode for the eleccion to be made consull, whome he trusted to haue his felowe in that dignyte, a man verrey famyliar and frendly to hym and sore trobled with all displeasures and necessities. With hym, he beyng consull, he wolde begynne than to sett vpon bataill, and with this he dispraysid all the good men with many dispytefull wordes and called to euery oon of his affyans by name. Summe he greatly lawded, other he instructed and yaue theim monycions, oon for to recouer his necessitie, another to obteyne his farvent desyres, many to loke vpon þe daungers

518 be] *interlineated, marked with caret* 520 the which] *follows* the which (*dittography*)

and shame that they stode in, many to remembre their rewardes in the victory of Sylla the which they wanne at that tyme. And whan he sawe all their myndes sett vpon a good hope and ioyfull, than he besought theim to haue in consideracion his sewte for þe dignyte of consull and so departed. |

f. 15v [22] There were men that made reporte that at the same tyme whan Catelyne had thise sayinges to theim, and whan he dyd requyre the greate othe of theim that favored his mischevous entent, that he shuld than haue gon abowte and yeven theim in cuppis the blode of mannys body myxed with wyne, and whan they all had recevid therof after they had made the greate vowe and promys of confeddresye, accordyng to the maner that is accustomed in the solempne sacrifices, that then he shuld haue openyd his entent. And rehersyng their vowes he shuld haue done this, they said, to th'entent that they shulde be more faithfull oone to another bycause they had assented to so wykked and horrible dede.

Summe men thought that thise sayinges and many other were fayned of those men that trusted to appease the malice that was borne afterward ayenst Cicero, thorow theire aggreving of the mischevous dedys of theim that suffred shamefull deth. Bvt to me that matere is right lytill knowen of the gretnes that they do speke of.

[23] Bvt in this rebellion was Quintus Curius, borne of no lowe howse, oppressid with vicious maners and wykked dedys, whom censores deprivid as vnworthy from the degre of senatours for greate vylony and shame. In this man was no | (f. 16r) lasse falsehed than folehardynes, nether cowde he kepe that he hard ner yet hyde his awne mischevous dedys, for nether what he said ne what he dyd had he consideracion vnto. Ther was an olde customed famyliarite of vice betwixt hym and Fulvia, that had a comen name in vice, to whome whan he waxed lesse welcom, bycause for poverty he had lasse to yeue hir, anon with an haute mynde he beganne to promys hir londes, sees, and all thinges, and sometyme he thretenyd to sley hir without she applied and obeyd to his desyres. Moreouer he fared fowler and more dredfully with hyr than he was wonte to doo. But Fvlvia, seyng this straunge and prowde dealyng of Cvrivs, be lytill and lytill she vnderstode of hym all the matere, the which kepte no secretnes of the perell of the comyn wele, but whan his bakke was turnyd that had vttred hit vnto hir, of the coniuracion of Catelyne, what she had herd and howe, she sparyd not to shew to many men.

[23.5] This thing moste cheffely styrred mennys myndes to putt the dignite of consull to Marcus Tullius Cicero, for aforetyme the more parte

566 an] *initially* and*; start of a* d *crossed out* 568 for] *follows crossed-out* of

of the noble men bare hym fervent hate and they thoughte þe dignyte of consull shuld be poluted yf he dyd obteyne that dygnyte: thowe he ware an excellent man, yet he was newly callid vp to worshippe. But whan this daunger was happenyd, malice | and pryde were laied by. Wherfore, in the f. 16v day of the commyssyon, Marcus Tullius and Caius Antonius were electid consulles, the which dede fyrst stroke \`in´ fere the favorers of the rebellyon. But for all that the fersenes of Catelyne lessid not, but dayly he devisid many thinges and prepared strengith of armour abowte Italye in the mete places for his bataill. And suche money as he cowde gete vpon his owne credens or borow by meanes of his frendys he conveid into Fesulanum, to oon Manlius, the which afterward was the cheffe doer of makyng of bataill.

At that season it is said that Catelyne drew many vnto hym, bothe men and women of all sortes, and somme had he of suche maner women that in theire begynnyng had wonne greate money by the viciousnes of their body, and after where their yeris was paste of lucre, and yet withoute mesure in the desyris of lecherye and covetousnes, had caste theimselffes in greate daunger of dett by theim. Catelyn belevid he myght purchase hym the favour of the vile men of the cite, and he thought also that they were mete to sett the towne on fyre and to cause their husbondes to assent to hym or ellys to sley theim.

[**25**] Bvt amonges these was Sempronia, oon the which oftetymes had commytted many bolde and horrible dedys lyke as she had ben a \`man´. | This woman of hir byrth and of hir bewty was by hirsilff oone of all the f. 17r worlde and right fortunate to an honourable husbond and to children and goodly lernyd bothe in the Greke and in the Latyne tunge. Syng and daunce she cowde, mych more fresshly than nedyd to a good woman, and many othir suche thinges that be the instrumentes and delytes of lustis and pleasaunce. But she regarded more and loved better all maner thinges than hir honour or fere of shame. It were herd \`f´or the to iuge whether she sparid more hir goodes or hir good name, they were so comyn. She wolde be so desyrous in lechery that oftner she called men to it than she was desyred of theim. But oftetymes afore she cared not to breke hir fydelyte and to forswere hir creditoures of hir dettes, and other men of those thinges that she was putt in truste of, ye and to helpe forwarde to the mordre of dyvers men also. But with thise craftes she fyll anon into greate mesery and nede. Yet she had a propur witt to make ryme, to make solace and myrth to men whansoeuer they lustyd. She had maner redy allweys of

585 in] *over eras. letter or letters* 602 man] *over eras.* woman 609 \`f´or] f *over* t

euery behavour bothe goodly and of swete wordes, ye and of wantones also. Sewrly ther was in hyr moche myrth, deyntynes, and fressh disporte.

[26] These thinges done, Catelyne neuertheles yet was in good hope to f. 17v stand the next yere | folowing for the eleccion of consulles, trustyng that yf he myght gete the graunte to succede theronto that he shulde easely vse Antonius at his will. Ner yet in the meanetyme was his mynde quyete, but all manere wayes he devysed and soughte the destruccion of Cicero. But he was not to seke of crafte and polycye to ouercom all that, for from the begynnyng of his auctoryte, by hys greate gyftes and promyses to Fvlvia, he brought to passe that Qvintus Curius, of whome I spake a lytill afore, shuld make hym prevy to all the counseill and dryfte of Catelyne. Besyde this he drove his felawe Antonius, in their covenaunt for devyding of their iurisdiccion to the auctoryte of the provinces, for the savegarde of the citee, that he shuld not varye ne intermedell in þe parties ayenst the comen wele. And grete diffensis of his frendys and seruauntes he kepte secretly abowte hym.

After whan the day of the commyssion camme and nethir Catelynes seute for the dygnyte ne yet his besynes that he was aboute to dystroy Cicero camme to effecte, than he determyned to make warre and to aventure in the extremyte of all thinges, because that thoose maters that he had attempted vnder subtell and prevy meanes provyd ryght froward and vyle. |

f. 18r **[27]** Therfore he sent forthe Caius Manlius to Fesula`s´, also into the same party of Tvscan, oon callid Lucius Septimius towarde the marchesses of Italye, Caius Iulius into Appulia, and moreouer every man his waye aboute to suche places as he thoughte they shuld be convenyent for his purpose.

In that tyme in Rome he went abowte many thinges. He ordenyd prevy sawtes to haue distroyed the consull, prepared crewell fyres, besette the mete places of the cite with men of armes. He hymsilffe ware prevy weypon, also other men he commaunded, exorted that they shulde be dylygent and redy. All dey and nyght he watched and hastenyd to those maters. Nethir with labour ner watche was he weryed. At the laste, whan nothing wolde prospere of so many thinges as he had ymagenyd, yet ayen in the dede of the nyght he callid togader þe cheffe capitayns of the rebellyon, by Marcus Porcius than his messangere, and att their metyng he complayned gretly of thair foly and shewed them that he had sent Manlius afore to that multytude the which he had prepared for his bataill, also diuers other into oder convenyent places, the which shuld fyrste begynne to make warre,

620 yet] *follows eras. letter* 639 Fesula`s´] s *over* n

and that he wolde hymsilffe go forthe to the hoste after that he myght fynde the wayes to overturne Cicero, that was þe greate hynderans and lett of his purpose.

[28] And whereas many of them sore drad and dowted that matere, Caius Cornelius, of the degre of meane gentilmen, promysed his besynes therin, and | (f. 18v) with hym Lvcius Varguteius, a senator, covenaunted at the same tyme to haue gon vnto Cicero right shortly after with a company harnessed as to haue visite hym and so, he beyng vnpurveid, they to haue sodenly murdred hym. Cvrius, where he vnderstode what greate perell hynge vpon the consull, incontinent he sendith knoleage by Fvlvia to Cicero of the deceyte that they prepared, so that \`att' theire commyng his gates were kept shett, and they dysapoynted of their mische\`v'ouse entent.

[28.4] In this meanetyme Manlius in Tushan reysid the people that was desirous of a chaunge, bothe for their nedynes and also for the paynfulnes of thair wronges, for in the tyme of the victorye of Sylla they were putt fro as well their possessions as their goodes. Moreouer many thevis and vagaboundes of all soortes fyll to hym of which was a grete multitude in that \`re'gion, somme also of the olde frendys of Silla that then were laborers, the which their pleasures and viciousnes had nothing leffte theim of their prayes and spoylinges.

[29] Whan thise thinges were shewed to Cicero, | (f. 19r) his mynde was sore troubled with dowtfull evilles of bothe handes, that nethir he cowde lenger diffend the citee of his awne police and wisdome ner yet knewe he the certentye howe greate the hoste of Manlius was or of what purpose. This matere he sheweth to the Senate, the which was strekyn afore with the rumour of the people therof, whervppon the Senate, as they are accustomed oftetymes in grevous maters, decreed that the consulles shuld do their dyligence and provyde that the comen wele toke no harme. This power is assigned of mooste myght and gretest auctoryte by the Senate, accordyng to the custome of Rome, to oon of the dignyties to prepare an hoste, to make bataill, to constrayne \`by' all maner weys his felowis and citezens, and as well within the citee as in their warris to occupy the royall poour and extreme iugementes. Otherwise, withoute their decre and assente also of the people, non of those thinges be lefull for the consull to doo.

[30] After a few dayes Lvcius Servius, a senatour, rehersid lettres afore

666 att] *interlineated above crossed-out* after 667 mische\`v'ouse] v *over eras. letter* 673 \`re'gion] *majuscule* r *and backwards* e *over minuscule* re 678 awne] *follows crossed-out* oo 682 the] *initially* they, *with* y *eras.* 686 by] *interlineated, marked with caret*

the Senate the which he said were sent to hym from Fesulas, in the which was wryten that Caius Manlius had resyd an hoste with a grete multitude vj. dayes afore the begynnyng of Novembre. Also, as it is wonte to be f. 19v in suche a thing, somme tolde signes and pronosticates | therof, somme shewed how the people made insurreccions and mustred in harnes at the cite of Capva, and the vile persones of Appulia made them redy for warre in lyke wise.

Wheruppon by the ordynaunce of the Senate, Qvintus Marcius was sent with greate auctoryte to Fesulas, Qvintus Metellus Creticus to Appulia and into all the parties aboute those contreys. They bothe at their commyng vp to Rome from their contreys were putte by of the grete honour and tr`y′humphe that they had well deseruyd in their conqueste thorow the false accusacion of somme men, the which were accustomed for lucre to bye and sell all maner thinges bothe vile and worshipfull. And the pretores were sent forthe also, Qvintus Pompeius Rufus to Capva, Qvintus Metellus Celer into the marchesse of Italye to the citee callid Picenum. `T′o thise men aforesaid was assigned that, for that tyme, because of the perell, they shulde reyse an hoste of people to make warre. Also the Senate decreed that whosomeuer cam in and pupplisshed the treson that was conspyred ayenst the comen wele shuld haue large rewardes: to a bond or vile man, his fredome and in money CC.l. *libri*; to a free man, his pardone therof and .v^{c}.M^{l}. *libri* in rewarde. Also they made statute that the quarelouse people and suche howseholders as dyd teche the excersise of wepyns shuld be sent owte of Rome to Capva and to other suche holdes, having delyuerd to them in goodes after the rate of their substaunce and f. 20r possescions, also that in Rome thorow all the cite watche and | warde shulde be kept, the which t`h′e secondare dignitees shulde ordre and oversee.

[31] With which thinges the cite was gretly troubled and the sight `of′ the towne gretly altred from excedyng myrth and pleasures, the which continuall rest had bred in it. Sodenly entred into theim all maner sorowes: accombred were they with many contrary myndes and trembled vpon the grounde they stode on, nethir in place ner man had they assured truste in, to make bataill they knew not howe ne yet to haue the contynewaunce of pease. Every man iuged their perelles after their fere. Moreouer the women, the which because of the grete myght of the comen wele were not wonte aforetyme to drede any maner warre, now taken therwith, turmentyd theirselffis, held vp their handes devoutly to the heveins, bewaylid

703 tr`y′humphe] y *over eras. letter* 708 `T′o] *majuscule* t *over eras. letter*
718 t`h′e] h *over* e 720 of] *over* in

their litill children, prayde lowly to the goddys, feryd all thinges, and layde awey their pryde and playsures and despaired theirsellffes and their contrey.

[31.4] Bvt the cruell mynde of Catelyne neuertheless went abowte the \`s´elff same thinges as he dyd afore, \`f´or all the defensys an\`d´ sauega\`r´des that were ordenyd. | Than Lvcius Pavllo, the which was *tribunus*, accused f. 20v hym afore the people of his treson and required by the lawe ordenyd by Plavcius that he shuld be compellid to make aunswer to all suche thinges as shuld be laid to his charge. So att the laste, to coloure his matere and to purge hymselff, into the Senate he commyth lyke as he had ben forsed therunto by false accusacion. \`T´han Marcus Tullius, the consull, either dowting his presence the\`i´r or ellz stirred with wrathe, had a notable oracion and right profitable for the comen wele, the which afterward he wrote and puplisshed.

But whan he had fynysshed his saying and was sett downe, Catelyne, as he was full redy to dissemule all thinges, with a lowly countenaunce and a demure speche began to requyre of the Fadres that they shuld not vndiscretly beleve any suche thinges in hym that was comen of that howse, and so had led his lyffe from tendre age that he iuged euer all good thinges to hange allonly in his good fame, and that they shuld not thinke that it cowde be profitable to hym, a man borne of noble senatours, the which he hymsilffe and his auncetoures had done so grete actes for the Romayns, to haue the comen wele perisshed where Marcus Tullius, a man new comen vppe, shuld kepe it. To thise malicious wordes where he laid on mo and mo, all the Senate cryed alowde and callid hym their enmye and rebell. Than he full of fure lyke a mad man, 'Sithen', quod he, 'that I am | thus bysett f. 21r abowte, and of m\`y´n enmyes sodenly putt to a plunge, I shall quynch this flame with all mischeffe', and so wounde hym home to his awne howse, owte of the temple, where he bethoght hym of many thinges, that nether his sawtes to sley the consull went forward, and percevid that the cite by their watches was deffendid from brennyng, thoghte that it shuld be best for hym to encrese his hoste, and fyrste, afore that the Senate shulde take vp þe sowgers, he to prevente theim and to take aforehand many suche thinges as belongeth to bataill.

In the ded tyme of the nyght he toke his iourney with a few persones

734 \`s´elff] s *over another letter* \`f´or] f *over eras. letter* the] *follows crossed-out* d an\`d´] d *retouched from one- to two-compartment* d sauega\`r´des] *long* r *over eras. z-shaped* r 737 make] *follows crossed-out* a 740 \`T´han] *majuscule* T *over* w 741 the\`i´r] i *over eras. letter* 756 m\`y´n] y *over two minims*

to Manlius tentys. [**32.2**] But to Cethegus and Lentulus and other of the which he had knowen redy boldnes and hardynes, he yeueth in charge that they do strengith the favour of his partye, that they s`e´tt in hand with sawtes ayenst the consull and prepare for the mordre, fyres, and other the mischeffis of bataill. Moreouer he sheweth to theim that shortly he hymselff with a greate hoste wolde draw nere to þe cite.

While these thinges be doyng in Rome, Caius Manlius of his company sendes messangeres to Qvintus Marcius, that had the greate commission, | f. 21v with messagis aftir this maner:

> [**33**] We take recorde of the goddis and of all men that we intende no warre ayenst our contrey by our resyng of people, ne yet to putt oþer men to any daunger or perell, but that our bodyes may be kepte saffe from wronge, the which be in thraldome and necessite, and thorow the malice and cruelnes of the inordinate covetise men many banasshed from our contrey, but all spoyled of our fame and goodes. Ner we cowde not any of vs haue the lawe after the custome of our eldres, ner whan our goodes were taken from vs yet myght we haue fredome ner liberte, the vengeaunce of the covetouse men and of the pretor was so grete. Oure elders many tymes of their pyte to the comens of Rome, by þe graunte of the hole counseill, hathe yeven greate aydes of their tresoure to redeme the necessite of them, and now right lately in our tyme for the exceding grete dett that they were in, by the consent of all good men, the Senate of their comen hutche quyteth them oute of their daun`g´ere. Offtetymes the people mevid with desire of rule, or bycause they myght not suffre the wilfulnes of the gouernours, hathe fallen clerely from the Senate. But we nethir aske auctoryte ner richesse, the which be the f. 22r causis of all stryves and batailles emonxte men, | but allonly our fredome, the which no good man wil be putt from withoute he departe from his lyffe also. We therfore instance you and the Senate that ye considre vs that be citezens, and in mesery, that we mey haue restored the socour of our lawis, the which the wikkednes of the pretor hathe taken vyolently from vs, leste ye putt that necessite vnto vs that we seke all maner weys to be moste revenged vpon our distruccion.

[**34**] To this Qvintus Marius made aunswer that yf they wolde require anything of þe Senate, they shulde lay awey their armour and come lowly to

767 favour] *follows crossed-out* forwarde s`e´tt] e *over* o 787 daun`g´ere] g *over two minims* 796 we] *follows crossed-out* all

Rome with humble supplicacion, where they myght be sewre the Senate and þe hole cite of Rome was allweis of that mercy and gentilnes that no maner man shulde in vayne desire socour or helpe of theim.

Bvt Catelyne vpon his iourney sent letters to many of the senatouris, and specially to the cheffe noble men, that he was oppressed with wrongefull accusacions, and bycause he was not able to withstond the myghty power of his aduersaries he was fayne to yeld to fortune and to departe the towne into exile to Manlius, not to be assistaunte to his grevous | offensis, f. 22v
but that the comen wele shuld be in quyete and that the`r′ shuld `ry′se no trouble to the cite vpon his quarell.

Bvt Qvintus Catullus rehersid afore the Senate that Catelyne shuld haue sent a messanger with lettres to hym all after a contrary wey, of þe which th'exsample here folowith:

[35] Lvcius Catelina yeveth salutacion to Qvintus Catullus.

Youre greate faithfulnes, the which the dede hathe provid ryght thankfull in my grete daungers, yeveth truste and assuraunce of my commendacion vnto you, wheruppon I haue determyned not to question and to defend to you these new wayes that I do take. Ner I thinke not to make excuse of any trespas that I know mysilff culpable of, the which by the hye goddys thowe it be well knowen vnto you of trothe, bycause I was so sore oppressid with sclaundres and grete wronges that I myght not accordyng to my diligence and desertes maynteine the rowme of my honour, I haue after myn olde custome take in hande the cause and comyn deffence of them that be in mesery, n`ot′t for that my possescions were not able to content all my credetoures, where the substaunce of Aurelia and hir doughter is plentyouse enowe to pay to euery man their dewty, but that I saw theim þat were ferre vnworthy honoured with þe grete dignyties, | and I vppon their falsse susspeccion sore hyndered f. 23r
and imparid. In this opynyon I haue entertayned sufficient hope of worshippe for my falle to contynew the remnaunt of my honour that was leffte vnto me. Other many thinges, whan I wolde haue wryten vnto you, it was yeven me in knolege that they resyd power ayenst me. Now I commytte my wiffe Orestella onto you and I bequeith hir to your faithfullnes that ye se hir diffendid from wronge. Wryten at the requeste of youre sonnys, and thus fare ye well.

[36] Bvt he after a few dayes tarying in the felde of Arretyn while he

808 the`r′] r *over eras.* y `ry′se] ry *over eras.* ra 823 n`ot′t] ot *over two earlier letters*

appoynted his company redy for the warre, the whiche afore were very desirous of bataill, with his signes borne afore hym and other astate that belongith to an emperour hastely he commyth downe to Manlius.

These thinges whan they were knowen in Rome, the Senate proclamed Catelyne and Manlius rebelles. To other their company the Senate assigned certen days to leve their harnes and to come into their pardone withoute punysshment, excepte allonly those persones that stode condempned by the lawis for other offensis. Moreouer they decreed that the consulles shuld be putt to the choyse of the devyding of their gouernaunce, f. 23v wheruppon Caius Antonius | was commaunded to haste hym forward with the strengith of Rome to pursew Catelyne, Cicero to provide for the saffegarde of the cite.

[**36.4**] And at that tyme methoughte the empire of Rome was in the gretyst thraldome and mooste mesery that euer it was in, whan dayly from the sonne rysing to his goyng downe all thinges ther obeyd to armour. At home was richesse and ease plentiously, the which of all thinges men desire mooste, notwithstandyng there were citezens that with obstynate myndes iuged themselffes but loste and the comen wele also, for for all the cryes that were made by the Senate, of all that grete multitude ther came no man vpon mynde of their rewarde to yeue theim knoleage of the treson, ne yet any maner man of Catelyns hooste that wolde departe thens. The gretnes of the sore was so moche that the contagiousnes therof infected many myndes of the citezens, for not allonly they were evill sett that were assent to the treson, but all the hole people also favored the weys of Catelyne the wheche were gretly mynded to haue a chaunge. But that was done evyn after their f. 24r olde manere, for euer | in a cite, they that be of no substaunce hathe envy at the good men and yevith the mooste prayse to the vicious men: they hate the olde customes, they covet new thinges, for hate to their awne they wolde haue all thinges to chaunge, they be norisshed with trouble and stryves withoute any care, for poverty goothe forthe at all adventures withoute losse. [**37.4**] But the commyns of the cite were ryght perelouse and mooste daungerous of all other people for many causis. Fyrst, for they that in the contreys were in mooste shame and of mooste viciouse maners, also they that by thair vnthrifftynes had loste their patrymonye and were vagaboundes, moreouer they that for wikkid or myschevouse demenure were drevyn owte of their cuntre, all they resortid to Rome as the water in the shippe rennyth to the pumppe. Than were ther many also that bare in mynde the victorye of Sylla, that they sawe than of hastardes summe made senatouris, somme so ryche that euer after they ledde their lyffe in

welthe lyke kynges. Every of theim trusted that and they had warre, by the victory they myght comme to the same. Moreouer the yonge men laborers that by their handwarke yernyd their lyving in the feldes remembred the grete gyfftes that they had knowen in suche tymes bothe owte of the comyn wele and also of pryuate persones, and gladly they wold haue lefte their paynfull labour to wynne the ease of the citee. Theim and all the other the viciousnes of the cite dyd norisshe. Wherfore it his | the lesse to mer- f. 24v
vayle that nedy men corrupted with ill maners, havyng so grete hope laid afore theim, dyd thinke that beste wey which they myght haue mooste pro-fett by. And also they that their faders were atteynted after the victorye of Sylla, their goodes taken from them, their fredome lessid, they had non other mynde but abode the chaunce of bataill. Besydes these, whosoeuer toke vpon hym a party of rewle otherwise than accordyd to the maner of þe Senate, they covetid rather the decaye of the comen wele than their myght to be mynysshed in any condicion. This grevouse evill thing after many yeris retourned ayen into the citee, [38] for after that—Gneius Pompeius, Marcus Crassus beyng consulles—the auctoryte of *tribunus* was restored, the yonge men whan they had obtenyd that hye power—their yeris, their stomake fers—begane in accusing the Senate to styrre the people, after with their liberalyte in gyfftes and large promyses to sette theim more on fyre, so by those meanes they to be myghty and notable. Ayenst theim many of the noble men toke entreprise with all possibilitie, as for the cause of the Senate and of their grete honoure. And that I shuld brevely declare the trothe vnto you after that tyme, whosomeuer made bysenes ayenst the comyn wele vnder honest colour, somme as they shuld deffende the lawes and right of the comens, other for the meyntenyng of the | auctoryte of the f. 25r
Senate, dissimulyng thus þeir dede for the behoffe of the comen well, every of them made warre for their awne strengith and power, ner in their stryffe was mesure or ende. Bothe parties crewelly excersised their victorye.

[39] Bvt after that Pompeius was sent forthe in the warres to the see, and afterwardes ayenst Metridates the kynge of Pontus, than the might of the people sore lessid and the power of the Senate, a fewe company, incressyd. They kepte the greate offices and the auctorytes into the contreys and all suche rewles, they dyd no wronges, they levid in quyete and passed ouer their lyffe withoute drede, and other of their company they putt in fere and ponysshed by ryghtfull iugementes, that the people vnder their gouernaunce by that exsample shulde be more peasably rewlid. Bvt after onys that in the renewing of doutefull thinges an hope was offred to theim, the olde stryffe bytwixte the Senate and the people was resyd. Wherfore,

876 Moreouer] *follows eras. stroke*

and it had fortuned Catelyne in his bataill to haue goten the victorye or to haue departed from the felde in strengith, sewrly the comen wele had had a grete fall and shuld haue ben oppressid with moche mischeffe. Ner and they had obtenyd at that tyme, they cowde non otherwise haue kept it, f. 25v beyng so weyke and so feble of their hurtes in the felde, but who þat | had ben myghtiest shuld haue taken by force the gouernaunce of all thinges.

There were also many that were not prevey to the treson that ranne in the bygynnyng to Catelyne, in the which was Fvlvius, that was comen of senatouris, the which was taken on his wey and by his awne faders commaundment was slayne.

[**39.6**] In this tyme within the cite Lentulus, as Catelyne bad hym, brought in by hymselff and by other men to their opynyon all suche as for their vnthryfty maners or hard fortune he thoughte shulde be mete to covite a chaunge, and that not allonly the citezens but all maner havour of men that he trowed were able to comme forthe to `a′ felde. Therfore to oon Pupplius Vmbrenus he commytted the besynes to seke owte the ambassatoures of Fraunce and to dryve them yf he cowde to assiste theim in their bataill, thynkyng in his mynde that bycause they were so sore oppressed with dett as well in their comen wele as the pryvate persones of theim also, and for that the Frenchmen of natur be so war`l′y people that easely they f. 26r myght be ledde to suche | an entent.

[**40.2**] Vmbrenus, by reson of many herrandes that he had had into Fraunce, was well acquaynted with many of the cheffe capitayns of their citees and knew their condicions right well, wherfore withoute tarying, as sone as he had fyrste aspied the ambassatoures in the place of comen resorte, he questioned sumwhat with theim of the state of the cite and disposicion of the Senate, and as bevayling the rvyne therof asked what ende they trusted to haue that were in so grete thraldome and sorowe. After whan he saw theim compleyn of the covetousnes of theim tha`t′ had the dignities of Rome and accused the Senate that there was no grace to gete of theim, and said they loked for no remedy but to dye in mysery and wretchednes, 'But I', quod he, 'shall shew you the wayes and ye will do lyke men that ye shall escape those grete evilles.' Whan he had said that, the ambassatoures were full of ioye and of a grete hope and besought Vmbrenus to haue pite vpon theim, and said vnto hym that there was not that thing so hard nor paynfull but mooste gladly they wolde do it yf their contre myght therby be deliuerd of their thraldome and dett. Than he

928 a] *interlineated, marked with caret* 933 war`l′y] l *over* r 942 tha`t′] t *over* d

brought theim to Decius Brutus howse, because it was nere to the comen place and of his affynyte by reson of the hauntyng thedyr of Sempronia, but Brutus at this tyme | was owte from Rome. Than Vmbrenus, that there f. 26v shuld be more credens and auctoryte takyn in his saying, callid Gabinius thedir before whome he shewed theim of all their treson and the namys of his company, and moreouer of many other bothe of noble and low degre that were right innocent in the mater, to make the stomake of the Frenchmen more bolde and more gladly to [a]pplie vnto it. To thise maters whan they had promysed their helpe and diligence he suffred theim to departe to their logeinges.

[41] But the ambassatoures hynge longe in doute what wey were best for theim to take: ˋon þeˊ one syde was dette and nedynes, the desir of bataill grete, and large offers vppon hope of vyctory, but on the oder syde ferre myghtier power, wise and stronge counseill, for vncerten hope sewre truste and grete rewardes of theim that shulde puplisshe the treson. And in these theire doutefull thoughtes at the laste the fortune of the comyn wele ouercamme and they lyked beste to truste to our comen wele, wherfore they counselid herein with Quintus Fabius Zanga, the which had ben a singler frende and helper to their contrey in all their sewites, and openyd to hym all the mater as theˋyˊ had vnderstond. And he incontinent gothe to Cicero and yaue hym knoleage of all thinges, wheruppon Cicero commaunded the ambassatoures by Zanga that they vtterly shuld dissimule and colour the besynes | of thair treson, and willed theim to goo forder f. 27r to þe oder company and to make theim fayre promyses and to endevour theim to haue mooste opyn and evident proffe of theim all.

[42] Abowte the same tyme bothe in the nerre contrey and in the farder contrey of Fraunce, also in the cite of Picenum and lykewise in Appulia, was rysing of people, for those that Catelyne a lytill afore had sent abowte vndiscretly and lyke madde men dyd all thinges at all adventures, made metynges in the nyght tyme, carryed their armour abowte hyder and thyder, made excedyng haste and grete besynes. They did all thinges vpon mynde of moche fere more than ther was perell. Off that nombre Qvintus Metellus Celer, the pretor, caste many into pryson of Catelynes felˋyˊshippe whan he had knoleage of their matere. Also in the nerre contrey of Fraunce Caius Murena dyd lykewise, the which had þe commyssion and auctoryte vpon those parties.

958 applie] pplie 962 on þe] *in right-hand margin* 970 theˋyˊ] y *added retrospectively* 984 felˋyˊshippe] y *over another letter*

[43] Bvt at Rome Lentulus, with other that were the cheffe doers of the f. 27v rebellyon, whanne Catelyne they thoughte had made redy a grete | hooste, appoynted that at suche tyme as Catelyne with his company shuld comme downe to Fesulas in Tuschan, Lvcius Bestia, the *tribunus* of the people, at a convocacion of theim shuld grevously complayne of the dedys of Cicero and to lay vnto hym the grevous defaulte of all the trouble, which was so noble and so faithfull a consull. And by that signe, the next nyght folowing, all þe other that were assente to the treson shuld execute their purposes, the which were appoynted after this manere, as it was said, that Statilius and Gabinius with a grete strengith shuld do sett on fyre .xij. sondry and mooste mete places of the cite, for their entent that thorow that soden trouble ther myght be the esear commyng to the consull and to the oder that they prepared sawtes vnto; Cethegus to besett C`icer′os howse and by force to sett vpon hym; and lykewise every of theim to oder that they bare malice vnto, but mennys sonnys of the which the mooste parte were of the noble men shuld at the same tyme slee their faders. And so they all what with fyryng and what with mordre stryken in myscheffe shuld rynne forthe to Catelyne. In the ordenyng and makyng redy of these thinges Cethegus allweys compleyned hym of the foly of his company and said that they had overpassed many mete seasons with castyng dowtes and makynge `d′eleys, f. 28r and that in suche perell the dede is requesite | and not to counseill, also that he with þe helpe of right fewe wolde take vpon hym, whan other yave theim to slogysshnes, to make distresse vpon the Senate in their counseill howse. A wylde and ferse nature, sharpe and redy to stryke, he iuged all thinges best `do′ne in haste.

[44] Bvt the ambassatoures of Fraunce, according to the commaundment of Cicero, by the meanes of Gabinius had metyng with the oder of the rebellyon where they requyred of Lentulus, Cethegus, Statilius, and Cassius also to haue theim sworne faithfull to theim and their promyses to be wryten vnder their seales, to haue home with theim to their contrey, for oderwise they cowde not lyghtly bryng their noble men to entrepryse vpon so greate a matere. They mystrustyng nothinge graunted therto and sea`l′ed to their covenauntes. But Cassius `a′unswerd that it nedyd not, for shortly he wolde com theder hymsilff, also he wolde take his iourney thederward somwhat afore theim. Lentulus appoynted redy oone Titus Wolturcius to go with the ambassatoures, that afore they shuld com home they myght mete with Catelyne and with faithfull promyses betwixt theim

999 C`icer′os] icer *over eras. letters* 1006 `d′eleys] d *over eras. stroke or letter* 1011 `do′ne] do *over eras. letters* 1019 sea`l′ed] l *over* c `a′unswerd] a *retouched from one- to two-compartment* a

to conferme and stabelissh their amytie and frendshippe. | He sendith let- f. 28v ters also by Wolturcius to Catelyne after this manere that folowith: ‘Who I am ye shall know of hym that I haue sent vnto you. Now take hede to do lyke a man and thinke into what place ye be com into and loke abowte what is nedefull now vnto you and endevour you to gete the helpe of all men, ye also of men of the lowiste degre.’ Moreouer by message he sendith vnto hym that he mervelith vpon what reson he refusith the favour of the vile and banesshed men, where the Senate hathe iuged hym their rebell and put hym from his honour there, ˋaˊlso that in the cite all was redy as he had commaunded and therfore that he haste hym to drawe nerre thedirward.

[**45**] These thinges thus done, whan the nyght cam that was agreed emonxte them for their goyng to Catelyne, Cicero lernyd all thinges by þe ambassatoures. He yeveth in commaundment to Lvcius Valerius Flaccus [and] Caius Pontinus, the pretores, that they do besett the brygge cal-lid Milvius and ther to attache the hole company of the Frenchmen. To them he openyth all the matere, for what intent they were sent theder, and for that they shuld do all thinges accordyng as it was full | requy- f. 29r site. He assigned to theim a certen cumpany of men of armys, so withoute rumour they laid their strenghthis and pryvely besett the brygge as it was commaunded.

Affterwardes whan the ambassatoures with Wolturcius cam to that place and of bothe parties togader the scrye was made, the Frenchmen, per-cevyng anon the dryffte of the matere, yeldyd them incontinent to the pretores. But Wolturcius fyrste cheryd his company to fyght and with his sworde began to diffend hym from the multitude. Afterward whan he sawe the ambassatoures forsake hym, than he made entrety and many requestes for his lyffe to Pomtinus the pretor, that was his olde acqueyntaunce. At the laste, ryght dredfull and mystrusting his lyffe, he was fayne to yelde hymsilff to the pretores as vnto his enmyes.

[**46**] The which thinges accomplisshed, streight the knolege of all maters was broughte to Cicero by the messangers.

Bvt than was he gretly accombred with exceding charge and grete gladnes, for he ioyed moche perceving that the cite, the treson openyd, shulde be deliuerd from the perellz, but yet he was full of thoughte, dowting moche what shulde be mooste expedient for hym to doo, so grete men of the cite founden in the mooste grevous offensis. Their punishment he thought shuld be to hym greate burdyn, | and to suffre theim vnpunysshed he f. 29v

1032 ˋaˊlso] a *retouched from one- to two-compartment* a   1037 and] *om.*

iuged it wold be the daunger of the vndoyng of the comen wele. Therfore with a stronge and faithfull stomake he commaundeth to be broughte afore hym Lentulus, Cethegus, Statilius, Gabinius, and Ceparius also, the which had made hym redy to go into Appulia to reyse the vile people there. These men without tarying be comen thedyr except Ceparius, that fortuned a lytill afore to goo from home and had vnderstonding of the detectyng of theire matere, and thervppon he fled the towne. The consull toke Lentulus and lad hym by the arme bycause he was þe pretor. The other with their kepers he commaunded to be brought also to the convocacion howse of Concordia. Thedyr Cicero called the congregacion of the Senate, of which compan`y′ come a greate nombre, where he brought before them Wolturcius with the ambassatoures of Fraunce and commaunded Flaccus, the *pretor vrbanus*, to fetche thedyr the caskett with the wrytinges that he had taken from the ambassatoures.

[47] Wolturcius than was examynid of his iourney, of his wrytinges, moreouer what mater he was abowte and who were the doers. Fyrst he aunswerd of his iourney, fenyd excusis, and all oder thinges of the rebellyon he dissimulid. After whan the Senate vpon theire promyse of his pardone willid hym to shew the trothe, than he declarid all thinges vnto theim as was done and | [f. 30r] shewed theim that a few dayes afore Gabinius and Ceparius callid hym to their counseill, and more he knew not, he said, than the ambassatoures had shewed, excepte that he had harde oftetymes Gabinius say that Pvplius Antronius, Servius Yla, Lvcius Varguteius, and many other were in that rebellion. The Frenchmen also in lyke wise knoleged the same. But Lentulus denyed and colored all thinges. Than they laid to his charge, besides his lettres, his sayinges that he was wont to haue, that it was proficied in the bokys of Sibilla that thryes the howse of Cornelius shuld subdew the impire of Rome, of the which Cynna was oon and Sulla the oder and that it was his dest`e′ny to be þe third, moreouer that this was the xx^{ti}. yere synnes Capitolium was brent and that the augures had oftetymes aunswerd that that yere there shuld be the grete mordre emonxte the citezens.

But aftir this, the lettres were shewed forthe vnder theire sealis and red afore the Senate, the which they denyed not for theire sealis. Than it was decreed by the Senate that incontinent Lentulus shulde be deposid from his auctoryte and after he and the oder to be commytted into honeste kepynge and places accordyng to their honour, wheruppon Lentulus was deliuerd to the handes of Lentulus Spinter, than beyng *edilis*, Cethegus

1071 compan`y′] y *over two minims* 1089 dest`e′ny] e *over the first stroke of a* y to Qvintus Cornificius, Statilius | to Caius Cesar, Gabinius to Marcus f. 30v Crassus, Ceparius, that was but lytill afore takyn on his wey fleing fro the cite, to Gneius Therencius.

[48] Now the people, this treson pupplisshed, that afore was gretly desirous to haue a chaunge and favored excedingly to haue bataill, chaunged anon their myndes and cursid Catelyne and his mischevous purposis. Than they lyffte vp Cicero in laude and prayses vp to the hevyns. There they made ioye and myrth as and the cite had ben deliuerd from tribute and bondage. Than they talkyd and rehersid what prayes and other harmes and wykked dedys shuld haue folowed vpon the bataill, the cruell fyring withoute mercy, and that they iuged to their vndoyng mooste of all, for why all their substaunce and lyving stode allonly vpon their dayly laboure and occupacion within the cite.

[48.3] Affter that day oon Lvcius Tarquinius was broughte afore the Senate, whome they toke, as was said, vpon his iourney goyng to Catelyne. This man, whan he said he wolde shew theim of the treson yf they wolde promyse hym theire pardone, wheruppon he was commaunded by the consull to declare those thinges that he knew, | than he shewed to the f. 31r Senate in maner the same thinges that Wolturcius did, of the fyres that they had prepared, of the mordre þat they were abowte of diuers noble men, and of the appoyntment of the iourney of Catelyne with his hooste. Moreouer he said he was sente from Marcus Crassus with message to Catelyne that Lentulus, Cethegus, and other that were taken shuld not fere hym of his commyng vnto Rome, but therfore the more rather to make hasty spede thedyr to comfort the stomakes of other his frendys, and they that were takyn to be the more easely deliuerd from their perelles.

But where that Tarquinius named Crassus, that excellent and n`o´ble man of so grete habundaunce in richesse and of so grete myght and power, many men demyd it incredible. Other men ther were þat, though they iuged it trothe, yet the grete power of so myghty a man was rather they thoughte to be peasid than to be agrevid in so daungerous a tyme, many also that Crassus afore had done m`o´che fore in their causis and were gretly bounden vnto hym. They cryed all that he was a falsse accuser and askid of iustice that there shulde be had dewe examynacion vpon hym for the tryall in þe matere, wherin Cicero askyd the counseill of the Senate, and the hole multytude of them anon determyned his saying to be a false surmyse and

1116 knew] *precedes crossed-out* of the fyres 1125 n`o´ble] o *over* e 1127 though] *initially* thoughte, *with* te *eras.* 1130 m`o´che] o *over* i

f. 31v commaunded | that he shulde be kepte in prison and duraunce and iuged forthermore that he shuld no more be herd speke withowte he shewed vpon whose counsaill he ymagenyd suche a lye in so grete a cause.

It was thoughte of many men at that tyme þat that detectyng was ymagenyd by the dryffte of Puplius Antronius, that by the appeling of that grete man Crassus, he taken for their felowe in the matere, the perell of oder men shuld be bolstred by his grete power. Oder men there were that said it was Cicero doyng that Crassus, aftir his olde custome takyng vpon hym the diffence of the wronge partie, shuld not be suffred in this cause to troble the comen wele.

[**48.9**] I mysilff afterward herd Crassus openly shew that all that wrongefull sclaunder was laid vnto hym by Cicero. Howbeit yet the same tyme Qvintus Catullus and Caius Piso, two of the cheffe noble men, nethir by prayer nor for fauour nor yet for rewarde cowde they dryve Cicero vnto it that, edyr by the ambassatoures or by any other of the accusers, Cesar shuld haue any vntrothe laid vnto hym. Eyder of them bare Cesar extreme malice, for Pyso was condempned by his meanes vpon his extorcion done in the contreys to make restitucion to all the parties by reason of his wrongfull execucion vpon oon of the Frenchmen in the tyme of his
f. 32r commyssion. Catullus vpon the eleccion of | the grete dignitie of their religion was sett in grete hate bycause that he, beyng in grete age and in his days had occupied the hye honoures, was ove`r´come and caste by, Cesar beyng but a yonge man. The matere yet was thoughte ryght mete than, bycause he by his excellent liberall mynde and by his grete and large gyftes had so entertayned the favour of the people.

[**49.4**] But where they cowde by no meane brynge the consull to so grete a matere, they went eche of theim abowte the counseill howse to every of the senatouris with talys and lyes the which they herd, they said, of the ambassatoures and of Wolturcius, wherby they resyd ayenst hym grevous hate and put hym to a grete plunge, insomych that the garde of gentilmen, the which for the se`ur´t`y´ of the Senate were sett abowte the temple of Concordia, eyther for the gretene`s´ of the perell that they sawe or ellys styrrid vpon a faithfull mynde that the Senate shulde more evydently se the proofe of their assured stomake, whan Cesar come forthe from the Senate, they wolde haue sett `v´pon hym with theire weypons and had slayn hym yf Cicero asspying it had not takyn hym in his armys and so brought hym thorow theim into saffe places.

1156 ove`r´come] r *over another stroke* 1165 se`ur´t`y´] *initially* senate, *with* r *written over* a *and* y *over* e 1166 gretene`s´] s *over* o 1169 `v´pon] v *over* o

[50] Wyle these maters be in doyng in the Senate and while the rewardes be assigned to the ambassatoures and to Tytus Wolturcius, accordyng as the Senate had | alowid their shewinges, a certen of theim that were f. 32v manymysid and otherwise holpen by Lentulus had made messangers into diuers angylles abowte the towne to reyse the crafty men and vile people in every of the lanes, for rewardes, to haue deliuerd Lentulus, and some of theim had soughte owte the capytayns of the sowgers that were wonte for money to make trouble in the cite. Cethegus moreouer had sent forthe messangers with requestes that his howseholde men and oþer that he had done fore, the which had ben styrred in the matere, shuld gader theim togader and, beyng a multitude, to breke into hym with theire wepons.

The consull, whan he vnderstode those thinges, made anon redy and ordenyd grete watche and warde, as the thing and the tyme requyred, and called forthe hastely the convocacion of the Senate and askyth theire mynde what they will haue done with theim that were commaunded to pryson. But the Senate a lytill afore in their congregacion had iuged that they had offended and rebellid ayenst the comen wele.

Than Decius Iunius Syllanus, bycause of his dignite that he was chosen to be consull the nexte yere folowyng, was askyd fyrst of his sentence, and he iuged as well theim that were kepte in pryson as Lvcius Cassius, Puplius Furius, P. Vmbrenus, and Qvintus Annius, ˋyˊf they coude be taken, all to suffre deth. Yet aftirward he was so styrred with the oracion of Cesar that he yaue his voyce withoute ferther speche, for lett of tyme, to Tiberius Nero. | He said he thoughte it right to revoke his sentence, and the more f. 33r boldly bycause ther was so grete savegarde layd within the citee.

But Cesar, whan it cam to hym, was askyd of the consull his sentence, than he had thise wordes after the manere as folowith:

[51] It is requisite, mooste honourable Faders, to all men that shall yeue good counseill in doutefull causes to be clene, withoute hate, favour, wrathe, and mercy, for that mynde that is accloyed with any of those cannot lightly fynde the ryght, ner no maner man cannot togader serue bothe to his awne apetytis and to þe comen wele also. But alweys wherto a man holy gevyth hym, thervnto his reson will serue hym. Yf wilfulnes haue the possession and rewle of the mynde, his reason is nothing worthe.

I can wele remembre in many causis that oftetymes kynges and peoples styrrid with angre and mercy hathe done many greate folys. But

1192 ˋyˊf] y *over eras. letter*

I had rather speke of those thinges that oure auncetoures dyd, ayenst theire wilfull apetytis, full nobly and rightwesly.

[51.5] In the grete bataill ayenst the Macedones, the which was foughten with kynge Persa, the riche cite of the Roodes, the which was greatlye avaunced and sett in grete welth by vs, was in that bataill f. 33v ryght malicious and extreme ayenst vs. | Whan in grete warre we had subdewed theim it was questioned what shuld be done to theim. Oure forefaders than determyned that they shulde be restored `h´ome withoute any maner of ponysshment, that it shuld not be said that the Romaynys dydde make bataill more for richesse or other pleasure than for the revengyng of their ryghte.

Also in all the batailles ayenst the *Pœnos*, whereas they oftetymes brake the peasis and agrementes and vnder the trewsis dyd many and grevous offensis, yet for all þat they neuer dyd suche thinges by any occasyon. They regarded more what shuld becomme theim and theire honoure than what they myght haue done by right `v´nto theim.

[51.7] This same thing is now to be considred to you, that the grete and horrible dedys of Lentulus and other way not more with you than youre awne honour and that ye applie rather to youre angre than youre noble fame. Certenly, to assigne as grete a payn as theire desertes require, I cowde agre well to theim that hathe geven theire sentence afore me of a new maner ponishment not herd of aforetyme to be done to a senatoure. But notwithstandyng, yf their horrible dedys excede oure reason to yeue theim according ponishment as they be worthy to haue, it is my mynde that your honour may execute allonly those that there be lawes fore.

f. 34r Diverse of you that haue spoken afore | me bemoned right goodly and gretly the ruyne of the comen wele and rek`e´nyd vp what mischeffis shuld folowe vpon the bataill, what perelles to theim that were overcomme: the ravishment of virgins, the yonge children to be pullid from theire moders brestes and slayne, the worshipfull women to suffre by force the wykked lustis of theim that had the victory, the temples and mennys howsis spoiled, the mordre `o´f the noble men, the fyringes within the cite, also what with armour, what with ded corsis, what with `blodshede ⟨and⟩´ wayling all thinges overturnyd and vndone.

[51.10] But, by the hye goddys, wherto belongid that saying for to make vs angry and ferse with theire treson? Forsothe, where so grete

1216 `h´ome] h *over* r 1224 `v´nto] v *over* o 1236 rek`e´nyd] e *over* o
1240 the victory] the *initially* they, *with* y *blacked out* 1241 `o´f] o *over* i
1243 blodshede ⟨and⟩] *in right-hand margin;* and *presumed lost to trimming*

a thing and so horrible shall not move a man, that saying I trowe shall sette hym on fyre. Is it not so? But who is he that thinkes his wronges a lytill matere? Many men moreouer take theim more fersely than \`is′ the desert. Notwithstandyng, moste honourable Faders, to diuers men is divers libertie, for private persones in lowe degre \`that′ ledith their lyffe in hyd places, yf they do trespasis in their angre, few knowith of it: the fame and the fortune of theim be alyke. But they that in greate dignitie be sett vpon hight be loked on of all men. Thaire fame rennyth over all the worlde, wherfore in grete auctoryte may be leste escape ether of favour or hate, but moste speciall it becometh theim not to execute angre, for that that in men of lowe degre is callid wrathe, in the hye | governoures is called pryde and cruelnes. f. 34v

Certanly I, mooste honourable Faders, thinke thus that all maner ponishment is moche lesse than their grevous offensis. But many men here loke allonly vpon the extreme ende of all and forgeting all theire wykked and horrible dedys they discusse of their payne, the which thowe after the sentence of divers it was somwhat to felle, yet I am sewre that Decius Sillanus, that noble and valeant man, that that he said he spake of a faithfull mynde to the comen wele. Ner he intendid not in so greate a cause to do shew ethir favour or rygure. I haue knowen well suche condicions and discrete maner of that man. Truly his sentence semeth me not cruell, for what mey be done cruell vnto suche men? But methinkith it is ferre straunge from oure comen wele, and sewre it was ethir drede or grete wronge that drove the, Sillanus, elected to succede to the dignite of consull, to iuge a newfounde punishment. But to speke now of fere, it is but voyde where moste of all thorowe the provision of that moste noble man, the consull, ther be so greate saffegarde in harnes. And of the payne I mey well say, as the matere is in the selff, to them that be in mesery and sorow deth is theire rest and not the pyne, for she dischargith mortall folkes from all evilles. Afterward is there nother ioye nor care.

[51.21] But by the hygh godys, man, what causid the that thow dydist not commaunde also that fyrst they shuld be scourged with sore strokys? Was it not because | that the lawe made by Porcius Cato forbedith it? But are ther not othir lawis also that haue ordenyd that no senatour shal be putt to deth, but to be sufferd to take banyshment? Or was it not bycause it is sorer to be betyn than to be slayne? But what can be sherpe or to grevouse to men provid in so greate offensis? f. 35r

1248 is] *interlineated, marked with caret* 1250 that] *interlineated, marked with caret*
1256 in the] *follows crossed-out majuscule* I 1274 not] *follows crossed-out* payne

Or yf thow thoughtest it the lighter ponyshment, yet how agrethe it to drede the brekyng of the lawes in a lesse matere, for their scourgyng, where thow rekkyst not therof in a depper cause to iuge theim deth? But who will reprove any maner thing that shal be iuged vpon rebelles and conspirers ayenst the comen wele? Neuerthelesse the tyme, processe of yeris, chaunce of fortune oweth to be considred, the which will haue hir will amonges pe`o´ple.

To these men whatsomeuer shall happen, it is of ryght and deseruyd. But ye, moste honourable Faders, take hede what iugement ye yeve vpon other men. All evill exsamples be sprongyn owte of good thinges. But when gouernaunce is comen to vnlernyd and evill dissposed men, than that new exsample is put from the gydyng of the worthy and discrete men and servith to the wilfulnes of theim that be vnworthy and vnmete to haue rewle.

[51.28] The Lacedemones, whan they had wonne the cite of Athenis, apoynted xxx[ti] rewlers to governe the citee. They in the begynnyng began to putt to dethe every of the mooste wikked disposicion that was in the hate of all good men withoute processe of lawe, the which the people a grete seson gladded with, and they said it was
f. 35[v] done | accordyng to ryght of their desertes. After whan wilfulnes of power by litill and lytill was growen they slew all alyke, the good and the badde, after their willis and appetitis. The remnaunt the[y] kepte in awe of drede and crewelnes. So that cite, oppressid with bondage, recevid for their folissh gladnes intollerable paynes. And of late in oure remembraunce, whan Lvcius Sylla was dryven owte of the cite by the power of Danasippus and other that toke partie with Marius, the which were growen to grete myght thorow evill customes in the comen wele, and afterward by assistans of good men recoveryd in the cite, and havyng the victorye he commaunded to deth Danasippus and suche other, who is he that praysid not his dede? It was of ryght done, they said, that suche wikkyd people that trobled the cite in makyng parties and discencion shuld haue suche execucion. But that same thing was the begynnyng of moche mischeffe, for sone after wheras any of his company covetid howse or land, plate or clothing, or other goodes of any mannys, he made sore warke to gete that man into the nombre of them that were attented. So the same persons þat were glad of th'execusion of Danasippus were sone after pullid forthe to the same. Ner erst had we ende of puttyng men to deth tyll Sylla had fylled vp his company with richesse.

1290 pe`o´ple] o *over another letter* 1305 they] the

[**51.35**] Bvt yet I fere no suche thinges to be done in Marcus Tvllius ner in these tymes, but in so greate a cite be many and right diveˋr´s myndes. It may fortune | another tyme and vnder another consull, havyng in lyke wise power of armour in his hand, somme false matere to be belevid for a trothe. Where than vpon this exsample by the decree of the Senate the consull drawith forthe his sworde of execusion, who shall mesure hym or who shall byd hym sease? f. 36r

Oure elders nethire had lakke of wisdome ner of boldenes at any tyme, and yet pryde dyd not lett theim that they shulde folowe the lesse the direccions of straungers yf they were good and behoffull for theim. Of the Samnytes they toke vp the armour and many wepons for our sowgers, and of the Tusces many signes for dignities to be knowen by, and allweis in any place wheresoeuer they asspied any convenyent maner whether of their frendys or of their fooes, home it shuld be brought and here moste diligently executed. It was gladder to theim to folowe the good men than to invie and malice theim.

[**51.39**] But in the selfe same tyme, folowing the maner of Grece, in theire mooste extreme iugement they ponyshed the citezens condempned in moste ˋgreu´ouse offensis allonly with scoureges and betenynges. After whan the comen wele waxed large and myghty, and parties were gretly taken among theim in so grete a multitude of citezens, they beganne to deceve and oppresse innocentes and many other suche thinges. Than the lawes of Porcius and suche other were ordenyd redy by the which it was sufferd that they that were condempned myght take | banishment and exile. f. 36v

This therfore I trowe is right a greate cause, moste honourable Faders, that we shulde take no new weyse, for be ye well assured, in theim was more noblenes and wisdome that of small substaunce made so greate and so myghty an impire than is in vs that, having it lefte vnto ˋv´s in good condicion, can skante kepe it.

But what therfore? Shall they than be turnyd forthe and so encrese the hoste of Catelyne? Nay not so, but this shal be my iugement: all theire goodes to be attentyd and them to be putt in durans in strongeholdes in the owte parties from the cite, and suche as be of moste power and defence, and that no man be suffred to make sewte for them to the Senate, ner the people to haue any medelyng with theim, and whosoeuer attempte the contrary the Senate to take hym for oon that intended the distruccion of the comen wele and of theim all.

1324 diveˋr´s] *long* r *written over start of an* s *following partly eras. and partly crossed-out strokes* 1341 ˋgreu´ouse] greu *over eras. letters,* 1352 ˋv´s] v *over eras. letter*

[52] Whan Cesar had made an ende of his saying, all other there thorowe his wordes were chaunged and dyversly mynded. But Marcus Porcius Cato, whan he was axed of his sentence, had his oracion after this manere:

Off a ferre contrary mynde, moste honourable Faders, I am whan I consider our matere and our perelles, and whan I remembre in mysilff the sentence of summe men methynkith they questioned and argued of the maner of peyne of them that hathe made redy bataill ayenst their contrey, ayenst their faders, ayenst the go`d´dys and theire temples. | f. 37r But the thing byddith vs rather to beware of theim than to counseill what maner iugement we yeue vpon theim.

But consull, what standist þou thus? As for all other thyn harmys, thow shuldest pursew and ponish after whan the trespasis ben done. This thing, but yf thow provide for it that it happe not whan it is fortuned, to call for our iugementes is but voyde. The cite subdewed and taken, ther is nought leffte to theim that be ouercomen. But by the hye goddys, you syrris, I call forthe that haue allweys sett more by youre fayre howsis, youre grete possessions, your notable pictures and ryche ymages than by the comen wele. Yf ye thinke to kepe those maner thinges the which ye loue and halse so desirously, and yf ye will haue your pleasures in reste, now at the laste aryse and kepe the comen wele, for now it is nott in question of extorcion of the payment of sowgers ner yet of wronges done to our felawys, but our wele and oure lyves also be now in dowte and ieopardy.

[52.7] Many tymes, mooste honourable Faders, I haue had many sayinges in this company and sore I haue complenyd and often of the foule lustis and covetousnes of our citesens, for the which cause I haue many men myn aduersaries. But I, that neuer pardoned mysilff ner my mynde to fall into any trespas, cowde not easely suffer other mennys mischevouse dedys in their lustis and wilfulnes. But thowgh ye did sett lytill by these thinges at that tyme, yet than the comen wele was stronge and sewre and plentiousenes myght well bere your lewdnes. But now I am not abowte to question whether we lyve after good maners or badde, f. 37v nor to talke | of how grete auctoryte and noblenes the impere of Rome is of, but to beholde, whatsoeuer they be thoughte, whether they shal be comen to vs and to our enmyes togader. Here somme men bryngith forthe pite and gentilnes. Nowe of late certenly we haue loste the trew namys of thinges, for free yevyng of other mennys goodes we call it

1369 go`d´dys] d *over* o

liberalite and boldnes to do evill and wikked dedys is called manhode, by the which our comen wele is broughte to the laste caste.

But syrres lett theim be—for suche are your maners—liberall vpon theire felowis goodes, and lett theim be mercifull in saving the mooste erraunt thevis that sparis not to robbe the comen hutche, so they yeue not awey to theim our blode, and by thair sparyng of a few mischevouse men all good men do perissh.

[**52.13**] Ryght well and goodly Caius Cesar a lytill here afore hathe declaryd th'effectes of lyffe and deth. I trow he be vexed and thinkes it false talys that be spoken of hellys, that the evill people be sondred from the goode and caste into fowle, dyrke, horrible, and right dredfull places. Therfore he iuged their goodes to be attenˋtˊyd and them to be kepte in the strongeholdes from the cite, ye forsothe feryng theire kepyng in Rome that yf the people did make insurreccion or a grete strengith were resyd, by force they myght so be taken awey, as thowe iwis all the mischevouse and perlowse people be allonly in this towne and non thorow all Italye and the contreys rounde abowte vs, or ellz that hardynes may not so well ther where is moche lesse helpe to defende it. Wherfore that counseill | sewrely is nought yf he dredith the perelles f. 38r
of theim, or yf he in so grete drede to all men allone is not aferde. The more therfore it is convenient for me to be in fere of mysilff and of you all.

Therfore whereas ye shall yeue iugement of Lentulus and other here, thinke it in certen right necessarye also to yeue lyke sentence of Catelyne and his hoste and of all other the rebelles. The more discretely that ye do it, so moche shall their stomake be the weyker. Yf they se you langere any maner thing in it, than they all incontinent comme on fersly. ˋAndˊ think it not that our forfaders of a lytill thing did make by thair warres a grete impere. Yf the matere were so we shuld haue the comen wele moche more welthye, for why of our felowis, of citezens, also of armoure and horsis, we haue gretter multitude than they had. But other thinges there were that made theim greate men the which we haue non of: at home pollice, owtewarde rightwese gouernaunce, non oppression, the mynde in gevyng counseill free, nether in bondage to offense ner plesure. For these, we haue superfluouse lustis and covetousenes; in the causes of the comen wele, nedynes; in our howses, plentiousnes; we yeue the prayse to richesse and seeke ease; betwene the good and the badde no difference; all the gyftes that belonge to vertew

1410 attenˋtˊyd] t *over minim*   1426 And] *written out in full over eras. Tironian et*

f`l'ateryng requestes now occupieth. And no marveyle where, ye, every man by hymsilff takith his waye, where at home ye serue to youre apetitis and plesures. Here ye do all for mony or favour, of the which is commen
f. 38v that distresse | is laid ayenst an empty and naked comen wele.

[52.24] But I leve these maters. Here be citezens of the mooste noble byrth that haue conspired to fyre their contrey. They haue callid to them to make bataill the Frenchmen, the mooste malicious nacion ayenst the name of Rome. The capytayn of our enmyes with his hoste is over oure hedes. Ye tarye, and that in this tyme, and make dowtes what ye may do to your enmyes taken within youre wallis. I thinke it best ye haue pite vpon theim—they are yonge men that haue offended, it was but a lytill covetousenes of honour that blynded theim—ye, and turne theim forthe also in theire harnesse. I fere me leste this pyte and foryeving, yf they gete to harnes, will turne vs all to wret`c'hednes and mischeffe. Forsothe it is a sherpe and a dredfull matere, but ye fere it nott? Yes certenly, and that mooste of all. But of lewdenes and faynt stomake oone herkenyth vpon another, ye, trewly trustyng in the godys immortall, the which haue saved this comen wele oftetymes in mooste perelles. Nay, the helpe and strengith of goddys is not geten by womanly vowes and wayling prayoure; with wise condytte, noble actes, good counseill, welth and prosperite is obtenyd. Where thow yevist thysilff to slouthe and cowerdnes, aske nothing of the goddys: they are angre and hate the.

f. 39r [52.30] Be oure elders, Aulius Manlius Torquatus, | in the bataill ayenste the Frenchmen, commaundyd his owne son to execucion bycause he faughte with his enmyes contrary to the commaundment of his soueraigne. So that excellent yonge man, for his noble—but in owterage—corage, suffred the paynes of dethe.

Ye, of the moste cruell rebelles ayenst theire contre, what maner iugement ye shall yeue ye stonde in a dowte because, I trowe, theire good levyng in all other thinges dothe recompense this offence. Trothe, spare the grete honour of Lentulus yf he ethir spared for his honesty or good fame, or yet regarded att any tyme the goddys or any maner man. `Par'don the tendre age of Cethegus but yf now ayen he hathe made warre ayenst his owne cuntre. And what shall I say of Gabinius, Statilius, Ceparius, to the which yf anything had euer ben regarded or considred they wolde neuer haue taken suche wayes ayenst the comen wele? Fynally, moste honourable Faders, yf there were place to offende,

1437 f`l'ateryng] l *over the start of another letter* 1450 wret`c'hednes] c *over the start of an* h 1470 `Par'don] *barred* p *written over another letter*

I cowde lightly suffer you to be chastesid with the selfe same thing bycause ye repute my wordes for noughte. But we are sett fore rounde abowte. Catelyne with his hoste is besy enforsyng in the borders and passages. Other oure enmyes be within the wallis in the bosum of the cite. Ther can nothing be made redy, ne | yet counseld that can be f. 39v secrete, for the which the more hasty spede is to be made.

Therfore this is my iugement, where that thorow the wycked meanes of the myscheuose citezens the comen wele is comen almoste into the moste daungerous perelles, and these men by the appeching of Wolturcius and of the ambassatoures of Fraunce be convicte and haue confessed that they had made redy mordour, fyringes, and other horrible and moste cruell dedys ayenst the citezens and ayenst their contre, of these maters confessid as of opyn dedys that deserue dethe, after the custome of oure elders, execucion to be done.

[53] Whan Cato had fynished his sayinges and was sett downe, all the honourable men and the grete parte of the Senate lawded gretly his sentence and praysid th`e' noblenes of his mynde vp to the hevyn. Other, oon blamyng anoder, callid theim kowardes. Cato was had the noble and greate man. The decre of the Senate is gevyn according to his iugement.

Bvt to me, that haue redde and herde many right noble and excellent actes the which the Romaynes haue doen as well at home in tyme of peas as in the warris vpon the londe and vpon the sees, it was peradventure accordyng to consider diligently what | thing dyd mooste cheffely menteine f. 40r and beyre vppe so greate enterpryses. I haue vnderstonde offte and many tymes the Romayns with a small strength make warre with many legyons of their enmyes. I haue knowen theim havyng small substaunce make bataill with the mooste welthy and myghtiest kynges, and moreouer oftetymes paciently suffer and ouerpasse the distresse of fortune: the Grecyans in eloquencye, the Frenchmen in the glorye of bataill were above the Romayns.

[53.4] And to me, b`e'holding many thinges, it was evident to perceve that the excellent noblenes of a few of our citezens did all, and by this it apperith that poverty did better than richesse and the few company ouercame the multitude. But after whan the cite was infected with superfluouse lustis and slothefull ease, yet the comen wele thorow the greate myght therof bere vp the vices of the governoures and of the greate men. But lyke as she had bene baren and faderlesse, many yeris certenly in Rome was

1491 th`e'] *initially* this, *with* s *blacked out and* i *retouched as* e   1504 b`e'holding] e *over* o

ther neuer a greate man. But in my tyme were two men of grete noblenes of diuers and contrary maners, Marcus Cato and Caius Cesar, the which bycause the mater ˋhathe offe⟨rd⟩ˊ it it were not convenient for me to overpasse theim onspoken of, but that I shuld also declare, as ferforthe as my reason will geve, the nature and the maners of ether of theim. [**54**] So,
f. 40ᵛ theire byrth, theire age, their eloquence were nygh egall, | the valeantnes of their stomakes lyke and theire honour and glorye also, but to ether of theim contraryly, Cesar by his noble actes and liberalite had the renome of a grete man, Cato by his clene and perfyte lyving. The oon for his curtesye and mercy was made notable and excellent. The other, his faste and substanciall wey wanne hym the grete honour. Cesar by his gyfftes and helping men owte of daungour and lightly foryeving offensis, Cato sekyng non of those wayes, geving nothing, purchased hym glorye. In the oon was socour for men in perell and mysery, in the oder extreme execucion vpon trespasers. His gentilnes, this mannys constancye and iustice was praysed. Moreouer Cesar gave his mynde to greate laboure and contynuall watche and diligens, and bestowing hymself in the causes of his frendys lytill regardid his owne. Nothing denyed he to man that was worthe the gevyng. He desirid ferventlye to haue greate gouernaunce, a myghty hoste of sawgers, and nˋeˊwe bataill such as manlynes myght shyne in. But Cato, laboure and study was in good and honeste behauour, but mooste speciall in sadnes and gravite. He strove not with the riche man for his richesse ner with a besy quarelous felowe for the maistre, but with the manly man in vertew and valiauntnes, with the temperate man in drede of shame, with the innocent in iustice and abstinence. He wolde rather be good than seme good, wherfore the lasse he asked glorye, the more it folowed hym. |

f. 41ʳ [**55**] After as I said the Senate had happely applied to the sentence of Cato, the consull, demyng it best to be done to prevente the nyght that drew nerer on, leste any new besynes shuld ryse in that space, commaunded the doers of execucion to prepare those thinges that belonge thervnto. He bestowed the saffegardes in the cite and broughte Lentulus into the pryson. Lykewise was done to the residew by the pretores. There is a place in the pryson that is callid Tullyanum, where ye shall go forthe a few stayris on the lefte hand abowte xij fote depe downe vnder the grounde, the which is strongly wallid rownde aboute, and ouer it also a chamber wowted of myghty ston, bvt fowle, deformyd, horrible, derke, and stynkyng, and the sight of the house is right dredfull. Into that place after that Lentulus was putt downe, the doers of execucion, to the which it was gevyn in com-

1513 hathe offe⟨rd⟩] hathe *over eras. word and* offerd *supplied in right-hand margin;* rd *lost to trimming* 1530 nˋeˊwe] e *over* o maundment, with a rope brake his nek. So this Lentulus, a senatour of the mooste noble howse of the Cornelius, the which had occupied the hye gouernaunce of the consull in Rome, founde ther the departing of the lyffe accordyng to the deserte of his maners and of his dedys. To Cethegus, Statilius, Gabinius, Ceparius in lyke wise the execucion was done.

[56] While these thinges be doyng in Rome, | Catelyne, of all the mul- f. 41^{v}
titude that he resid and drew forthe with hym and that Manlius had, he ordenyd two legiones in his hoste that he myght garnish the wardes after the nombre of his sowgers. Also, as any man vpon his owne mynde or any of his felowis came into the felde, he bestowed hym egally in the ordre of his wardes, and in shorte space he furnyshed the legyones with nombre of men to the mustre of xij^{Ml}. ij^{C}. fotemen and M^{l}. iiij^{c}. and iij^{xx} horsemen, howbeit in the begynnyng he had not above ij M^{l}. sowgers. But of all that multitude, abowte the fourth parte stant was diffensible arraid in warly armour; the other, every of them as fortune dyd arme. At all adventures, some caryed sperys or sithes, other but sharpe swordes.

But after þat Antonius the consull came nere on with his hoste, Catelyne toke his iourney over the mounteyns and sett forward his tentys and caryage now to Rome, now towardes Fraunce. He offerd non occasion to fight with his enmyes. He trustid to haue hymsilffe within few days grete multitudes after that his affinite had done their mischevous purposes in Rome. In the meanetyme he shoke of bondemen and haskerdes of the which in the begynnyng greate multitude ranne to hym, trustyng to the helpe of them that were in the conspirise, thynkyng it also not agreable to his ententys to entirmedle the cause of the citezens with vile men owtelawed.

[57] But after that there was comen a messangere into their hooste shewing their treson was publisshed in Rome and execucion | done vpon f. 42^{r}
Lentulus, Cethegus, and other the which I rehersid afore, many than that afore hope of greate prayes or desir of a chaunge had sett vppon bataill fled faste into dyvers parties. The remnaunt Catelyne brought forthe thorow the herde mountayns, with grete iourneys, into þe felde of the cite of Pistoie in this entent, that he might secretly haue fled by the strayte passages into the hye contrey of Fraunce callid *Transalpina*. But Qvintus Metellus Celar, having the hye auctorite, laye with thre legyones in the felde afore the cite of Picenum, demyng vpon the herd chaunce of their maters the self same thinges of Catelyne as I said afore, \`to the entent′ to pursew an\`d′

1569 after] *follows crossed-out* of 1585 to the entent] *interlineated, marked with caret*
an\`d′] d *added retrospectively*

vex`e´ Catelyne and his company. So where he vnderstode his iourney of them that fled, incontynent he sett forthe his hoste and commyth to the same mowntayns fote and satyld his company, to the which necessarely he must com downe goyng into Fraunce. Notwithstondyng all that, Antonius yet was not ferre of, the which had sett his grete hoste in the playnes in a redynes mete to folowe the chase.

But after that Catelyn sawe hymsilf closed in with mowntayns and multitudes of his enmyes, his maters in the cite dasshed, no maner hope eyder in fleyng or of socoure, thinkyng it beste to be done in suche a thing to prove the fortewne of bataill, [he] determyned (f. 42v) | streight to fyght with Antonius. Wheruppon his company was callid abowte hym, `wher´ he had an oracion vnto them in suche wise as folowith:

[58] I know it in certayn, my sowgers, that wordes encressys not manlynes to men, `ner by´ the speche of the governour can be of a dulle felowe made a quykke, ner a valeant man of a kowarde. How moche boldenes is in the stomake of any man, edyr `by´ nature or `by´ maners, so moche will evidently appere in bataill. He that nedyr glorye ne p`a´relles stirrith, it is folye for the to exhorte hym: the dredfulnes of that stomake is noyouse to be herd of. But I haue callid yow togader to putt you sumwhat in remembraunce as to open the cause of my daungere. Ye vnderstand syrrs, I am sewer, howe grete a ruyne the cowardnes and slouthe of Lentulus hathe broughte vs in, also howe that while I abyde vpon grete socour from the cite I am put by to goo into Fraunce. And nowe what place and condicion our state is in ye perceve as well as I. There be two hostes of our enmyes: the oon from the cite, the oder from Fraunce dothe lett vs. Longer yf oure mynde covetid to be in these parties, the lakke of vytaill and other thinges will not suffre vs. Whedyrsoever it lystith vs to goo, by handstrokys oure way muste be made. Wherfore I warne you that ye be of a manly stomake and a redy. (f. 43r) | And whan ye shall entre into the felde, bere in y`our´ mynde ye carye in your ryght handes richesse, worshippe, glorye, fredome also and your contre. Yf we haue the victory, all thinges shal be sewer to vs; the greate companyes abundantlye, the inhabitantes in the citees, the contrees vnder the iurisdiccion of Rome shal be open to vs. Yf we yelde for cowardnes, the self same thinges shal be mooste ayenst vs. Neyder place ner any maner frende shall hide hym that his harnesse

1586 vex`e´] e *added retrospectively* 1595 he] *om.* 1596 wher] *over eras. word* 1599 ner by] *interlineated, marked with caret, following crossed-out* of 1601 by] *over* in by] *over* in 1603 p`a´relles] a *over* r 1615 y`our´] *initially* ye, *with* e *crossed out and superscript* r *added* dothe not defende. [58.11] Moreouer syrris, it is not lyke necessite that restith vpon vs and vpon theim. We fyght for our contre, our fredome, our lyves. To them it is but a voyde mater to fyght for, `th′e powere of a few men, for the which sett on the more boldlye, remembryng your olde approved manlynes. Ye myght with mooste shamefull vilanye haue led your lyffe in exile. Summe of you, dispoyled of your goodes, myght haue byden in Rome trustyng to other mennys eyde. But because they semed to vile and to grevouse to men to suffer, ye haue determyned to folowe these wayes. Yf ye will leve and ouercome those thinges, hardynes necessarely muste be had. No man but he had the victorye leffte bataill trustyng to haue peas, for to beleve to sa`v′e thy lyff in fleyng where þou castyth awey thy armour with the which the body is kepte in saffegarde, that is a verrey madnesse. Allweis in a felde to theim is mooste daunger | that be in mooste drede. Hardynes is a fense (f. 43v) worth a wall. Whan I considre you, my sowgers, and whan I waye your valiaunt dedys, a right greate hope assurith me of the victorye. Youre stomake, your yeris, your manlynes dothe exhorte me, also necessite, the which makith kowardes in trowthe to be bolde. And the straytnes of the place dothe lett that the multitude of oure enmyes cannott com abowte vs. But yf fortune be sett in hate ayenst your vertew, take hede diligently that ye lose not your lyffes vnrevenged, or yet taken more lyke bestys slaughterd than fighting as men, to leve to your enmyes a blody and wofull victorye.

[59] Whan Catelyne had thus spoken, after a lytill tarying he commaunded the standers to blowe vppe the trumpettes and other melodies and than he ledith downe the wardes of his hoste, sett in dew ordre to a playne. After that, all the horsis putt by from the fotemen that vpon the open perell theire stomake shuld be moche the more fer`s′er, he hymsilff, on foote, ordred his hooste accordyng to the place and the rate of his company. For whereas betwene the mountayns on the leffte hand was a playn and on the right hand a rokke of sherppe stonys, he ordenyd in the fronte .vj. cohortes, abowte the nombre of our accompting `V′. M[l]. i. C. and xxij men. The banerrers and standers of the residew he settith | mete for their (f. 44r) socoure in straite rome. From theim he chose owte all the cheffe capytayns that belonged to the retynew of Rome. Also, of sowgers of the comyns, every of the best that was armed he puttith into the forefronte. To Caius Manlius he assigneth the gyding on the right hand, to oon Fesulanus the

1624 `th′e] th *over eras. letter or letters* 1632 sa`v′e] v *over* u 1649 fer`s′er] s *over* r 1653 V] *over eras. letter* (?) 1655 From] *follows crossed-out* Also of sowgers leffte hand. He hymsilf with his sonnys and with the plowmen standith nere to the egell the which Caius Marius, as was said, had in his hoste in the bataill of Cymbris.

[**59.4**] Off the odere party, Caius Antonius the consul, sore diseasid in his leggys, bycause he myght not be present at the felde, deputed the gouernaunce of the hoste to Marcus Petreius, that grete capytayn. He appoynted the garde of the olde sowgers of Rome called *cohortes veterane*, as they be allweis accustomed vpon any soden perell, to the forward. The oder company of his hoste he lays byhynd them in the rerewarde for their reskew. He hymsilff on horsebak, ryding abowte, callid to every man by his name exhorting and praying them to haue in mynde that they shall fyght ayenst thevis, onharnessid `men′, | for their contre, for theire children, for the temples and their sacrifices. This noble man of warre that more than xxx[ti] yere afore was allweis in the hoste cheffe capitayn or vndyr hym his depute with grete glorye—callid in the Laten tonge *tribunus* or *prefectus* or *lygatus* or *pretor*, the which had the hole governaunce—knew many of theim well and their valeaunt dedys. Rehersyng the same, he sett on fyre the stomakes of the sowgers.

f. 44v

[**60**] But w`h′ere all thinges were accordyng`ly′ overlokyd and putt in a redynes, Petreius with a trumpett gave warnyng. The wardes of the hoste callid *coh`o′rtes* he commaundyd easely to goo forwardes. Lykewise dothe the hoste of his enmyes, and after they com so nere to the ioynyng that the light-harnessed men called *ferentarii* myght make bataill, than with the mooste excedyng crye they ranne bothe parties fersly togader with their standers: their gonnys and dartes be shotte, the mater is in doyng with swordes of handstrokes. The olde accustomed sowgers callyd *veterani*, remembryng their old manhode, laid fersly abowte them, as well on them that were nere as ferder of. The other, nothing aferde, withstode theim. It is foughten to the vttremost. Catelyne was than besy among the feble-harnessed men in the forefront. He socourerd them that had the sore fyght and labour, callid in hole and fressh men for them that were hurt, provided for all thinges. He foughte moche, oftetymes ouerturnyd his enmye. He executed togader as well the offices of a bolde sowger as of a good gouernoure.

Petreius where he seith Catelyne make sore fyght

1665 *cohortes veterane*] *underlined in MS* (*see n.*) 1670 men] *added retrospectively a line below the ruled textblock, preceded by a paraph* 1675 valeaunt] *initially* valeauntnes, *with* nes *crossed out* 1677 w`h′ere] h *interlineated, marked with caret* accordyng`ly′] *initially* accordynge, *with* l *written over* e *and* y *added* 1679 *coh`o′rtes*] o *retouched*

SUPPLEMENT TO *THE CONIURACION*

As given in the Loeb translation,* the *Bellum Catilinae* concludes as follows:

When, contrary to his expectation, Petreius saw Catiline putting up a strong fight, he led his praetorian cohort against the enemy's center, and having broken their close order, he slew those who resisted in various parts of the field; then he attacked the rest on both sides at their flanks. Manlius and the man from Faesulae fell fighting in the front ranks. When Catiline saw that his troops had been routed and that he had been left with a few comrades, mindful of his birth and his former standing, he plunged into the thickest of the enemy and while fighting there was run through.

[61] Now when the battle was ended, truly then you might have beheld what boldness and resolution had been present in Catiline's army. For nearly every man covered with his body, when life was gone, the position he had taken while alive and fighting. On the other hand, a few whom the praetorian cohort had scattered in the center, lay a little apart from the rest, but nevertheless all had fallen with wounds in front. Catiline, it is true, was found far from his men, amid the bodies of the foemen, still breathing slightly and showing on his face the fierceness of spirit that he had possessed when alive. Finally, out of the whole force, neither in the battle nor in flight, was a single freeborn citizen taken prisoner; thus had all been no less sparing of their own lives than their enemies'.

Nevertheless, the army of the Roman people had gained no joyful or bloodless victory. For all the most resolute had either fallen in the battle or come away with severe wounds. Many, too, who had gone out from the camp to have a look or to pillage, on turning over the bodies of the enemy found now a friend, now a guest or kinsman; some also recognized their personal enemies. Thus the whole army was variously affected with exultation and mourning, lamentation and gladness.

* SALLUST, VOL. I, translated by J. C. Rolfe, revised by John T. Ramsey, Loeb Classical Library Volume 116, Cambridge, Mass.: Harvard University Press, Copyright © 2013 by the President and Fellows of Harvard College. Loeb Classical Library ® is a registered trademark of the President and Fellows of Harvard College. Used by permission. All rights reserved.

APPENDIX

Incunables Containing the *Bellum Catilinae* Consulted for This Edition

All extant incunables that contain the *Bellum Catilinae* were consulted for this edition, except for an imprint issued at Milan by Leonardus Pachel and Uldericus Scinzenzeler (4 May 1485; *ISTC* is00072300, *USTC* 991415) and a Leipzig imprint issued by Martin Landsberg ([after 1492]; *ISTC* is00088570, *USTC* 748698); in both cases, multiple other versions of each edition were consulted (see below). In dating editions, the new year is assumed to start on 1 January. Shelfmarks are underlined if annotations by one or more readers indicate Tudor provenance. The editions are grouped into six categories according to shared textual characteristics; the bracketed abbreviations within their headings are used for reference purposes in the Explanatory Notes. Copies were consulted either in person or via digital facsimiles. Books which are mentioned only here and nowhere else in this edition do not appear in the Bibliography.

1. Incunables without commentary (*IncT*)

1470.1 Venice: Vindelinus de Spira, 1470. *ISTC* is00051000, *USTC* 991435. Copies consulted: BL, C.2.b.4; BL, IB.19523; BodL, Auct. L 5.20; Cambridge, King's College, Bryant.XV.2.18; Cambridge, Trinity College, Grylls 3.281; JRL, 3488.

1470.2 [Italy: printer of Sallustius *Opera*], 1470. *ISTC* is00052000, *USTC* 991434. Copies consulted: BL, C.2.b.5; BL, G.9127; JRL, 3489.

1471.1 Venice: Vindelinus de Spira, 1471. *ISTC* is00054000, *USTC* 991433. Copy consulted: BodL, Auct. L 5.17.

1473.1 [Rome]: A[dam] R[ot], [*c*.1473]. *ISTC* is00055000, *USTC* 991432. Copy consulted: JRL, 3490.

1474.1 Milan: Antonius Zarotus [for Marco Roma], 4 Aug. 1474. *ISTC* is00058500, *USTC* 991429. Copies consulted: BL, C.2.b.6; BodL, Auct. N 3.22; BodL, Auct. Q inf. 1.38.

1474.2 [Fivizzano: Jacobus de Fivizzano, Lunensis], 1474. *ISTC* is00057000, *USTC* 991430. Copy consulted: BodL, Auct. Q 3.7.

1474.3 Venice: Johannes de Colonia and Johannes Manthen, 23 Mar. 1474. *ISTC* is00056000, *USTC* 991431. Copies consulted: BodL, Auct. O 5.35; Cambridge, Trinity College, Grylls 2.130A; JRL, 10547; Oxford, The Queen's College, Sel.a.271.

1475.1 [Barcelona: Johannes de Salsburga and Pablo Hurus], 1475. *ISTC* is00060300, *USTC* 333061. Copy consulted: BL, IB.52502.

1475.2 Brescia: Eustacius Gallus (Statius Gallicus), 26 Aug. 1475. *ISTC* isooo60000, *USTC* 991428. Copies consulted: BodL, Inc.c.I22.1475.1; JRL, 17283.

1475.3 Valencia: [Lambert Palmart], 13 July 1475. *ISTC* isooo59000, *USTC* 765175. Copy consulted: Madrid, Biblioteca Nacional de España, INC/496.

1476 Milan: Philippus de Lavagnia, 27 Nov. 1476. *ISTC* isooo61000, *USTC* 991427. Copy consulted: BodL, Auct. O 5.37.

1477 Milan: Jacobus de Marliano, [10 Nov. or 22 Dec.] 1477. *ISTC* isooo62000, *USTC* 991426. Copy consulted: BL, IB.26403.

1478.1 Florence: apud Sanctum Jacobum de Ripoli, 1478. *ISTC* isooo64000, *USTC* 991423. Copy consulted: BodL, Auct. P inf. 2.12.

1478.2 [Venice]: Filippo di Pietro, 22 June 1478. *ISTC* isooo63000, *USTC* 991425. Copies consulted: BL, 167.c.18; BodL, Auct. P 5.2; CUL, Inc.3.B.3.16[1415]; Edinburgh, National Library of Scotland, Inc.157.5; Oxford, All Souls College, b.5.4(1); Oxford, Corpus Christi College, *ϕ*.C.2.6.

1478.3 [Torrebelvicino: Giovanni Leonardo Longo, after 22 June 1478]. *ISTC* isooo63500, *USTC* 991424. Copies consulted: BL, IB.31787; BodL, Auct. O 2.21(3); BodL, Auct. Q 2.25.

1479.1 Milan: Antonius Zarotus, 3 Nov. 1479. *ISTC* isooo66500, *USTC* 991422. Copies consulted: BL, IB.25996; Cambridge, King's College, Bryant.XV.6.16.

1480.1 [Milan: printer of Riccius, *c.*1480]. *ISTC* isooo67500, *USTC* 991420. Durham, Ushaw College, XVIII.B.2.5.

1480.2 Venice: [Nicolaus Girardengus, de Novis], 1480. *ISTC* isooo67000, *USTC* 991421. Copies consulted: BL, IB.20780; BL, IB.20780a; JRL, 3439.

1480.3 [Milan: Leonardus Pachel and Uldericus Scinzenzeler, about or before 1480]. *ISTC* isooo88300, *USTC* 991401. Copy consulted: Göttingen, Staats- und Universitätsbibliothek, 4 AUCT LAT II, 5780 INC.

1481 Venice: Baptista de Tortis, 23 Dec. 1481. *ISTC* isooo68000, *USTC* 991419. Copies consulted: BL, IB.21326; BodL, Auct. N 3.25.

1482.1 Milan: Leonardus Pachel and Uldericus Scinzenzeler, 24 Jan. 1482. *ISTC* isooo69000, *USTC* 991418. Copy consulted: Stuttgart, Württembergische Landesbibliothek, Inc.fol.14212.

1482.2 Rome: [Eucharius Silber], 17 Apr. 1482. *ISTC* isooo70000, *USTC* 991417. Copy consulted: BL, IA.18813.

1485 Venice: Bernardinus Benalius et socii, 23 Apr. 1485. *ISTC* isooo72000, *USTC* 991416. Copies consulted: BL, IB.22309; BodL, Auct. P 3.24.

1486–90 [Venice]: Johannes Rubeus Vercellensis and Franciscus de Madiis, [not after 1490]. Ed. by Justinianus Romanus. *ISTC* isooo74200, *USTC* 991413. Copy consulted: BL, IB.23114.

1487–90 [Venice]: Johannes Rubeus Vercellensis and Franciscus de Madiis, [between 1487 and 1490]. Ed. by Justinianus Romanus. *ISTC* is00074000, *USTC* 991414. Copies consulted: BodL, Auct. Q 3.31; CUL, Inc.3.B.3.90[1687].

1492.1 Deventer: Jacobus de Breda, [not before 16 Nov. 1492]. *ISTC* is00088550, *USTC* 438770. Copy consulted: Allendale, MI, Seidman House, PA6653.A4 1492, A48.

1494–6 Zwolle: Peter van Os, [*c.*1494–6]. *ISTC* is00088600, *USTC* 436238. Copy consulted: CUL, Inc.5.E.7.2[3094].

1497.1 Zwolle: Peter van Os, [1497]. *ISTC* is00089000, *USTC* 438772. Copy consulted: CUL, Inc.5.E.7.2[3097].

1497.2 Deventer: Jacobus de Breda, [after 10 Apr. 1497]. *ISTC* is00088650, *USTC* 438771. Copy consulted: BodL, Auct. Q inf. 1.18.

2. Parisian and Paris-derived incunables (*ParisT*), without commentary

1471.2 [Paris: Ulrich Gering, Martin Crantz, and Michael Friburger, Jan. 1471?]. *ISTC* is00053000, *USTC* 202920. Copies consulted: BL, C.2.a.19; BL, IA.39004; BodL, Arch. G e.46; JRL, 3519.

1473.2 Paris: [Petrus Caesaris and Johannes Stol, *c.*1473]. *ISTC* is00055500, *USTC* 200706. Copy consulted: JRL, 10647.

1474.4 [Basel: Martin Flach, *c.*1474]. Based on **1471.2**. *ISTC* is00058000, *USTC* 748695. Copies consulted: BL, G.9163; BL, IB.37224; BL, IB.37226; BodL, Auct. O 4.22; Edinburgh, University Library, CRC Inc.F.46; JRL, 7683; Oxford, The Queen's College, Sel.a.284.

1475.4 [Paris: in vico S. Jacobi (Au Soufflet Vert [Louis Symonel et socii]), *c.*1475]. *ISTC* is00060500, *USTC* 202872. Copies consulted: BL, IA.39236; CUL, Inc.4.D.1.4[2418](1).

1478.4 Paris: Ulrich Gering, [not after 1478]. Ed. by Filippo Beroaldo. *ISTC* is00065000, *USTC* 761617. Copies consulted: BL, IA.39187; Cambridge, King's College, Bryant.XV.3.25/1; Cambridge, Trinity College, VI.13.187; Edinburgh, University Library, CRC Inc.S.56.

1479.2 Paris: in vico S. Jacobi (Au Soufflet Vert [Louis Symonel et socii]), 1479. *ISTC* is00066000, *USTC* 200797. Copy consulted: Paris, Bibliothèque Sainte Geneviève, OEXV 328 RES.

1483 Paris: Ulrich Gering, [1483?]. Ed. by Filippo Beroaldo. *ISTC* is00071000, *USTC* 761618. Copies consulted: BL, IA.39195; BodL, Auct. N 5.29; CUL, Inc.5.D.1.2b[4463].

1492–6 Paris: Georg Mittelhus, [between 1492 and 1496]. Ed. by Filippo Beroaldo. *ISTC* is00077300, *USTC* 201183. Copy consulted: Roanne, Médiathèque municipale, Inc. 56.

1497.3 Paris: André Bocard, 20 Dec. 1497. Ed. by Filippo Beroaldo. *ISTC* is00082550, *USTC* 761621. Copy consulted: Orléans, Bibliothèque municipale, Rés.E1736.

3. Imprints of Pomponio Leto's edition (*LaetT*) without commentary

1490 Rome: Eucharius Silber, 3 Apr. 1490. *ISTC* is00075000, *USTC* 991412. Copies consulted: BL, IA.18913; Cambridge, King's College, Bryant.XV.3.3.

1491–2 [Deventer: Richardus Pafraet, between 21 June 1491 and 25 Jan. 1492]. *ISTC* is00088500, *USTC* 436151. *IncT* readings are often preferred over *LaetT*. Copy consulted: Berlin, Staatsbibliothek Preußischer Kulturbesitz, 8° Inc 4869.

1495.1 [Leipzig: Martin Landsberg, *c.*1495]. *ISTC* is00088620, *USTC* 748699. Copy consulted: Munich, Bayerische Staatsbibliothek, 2 Inc.s.a. 317.

1500.1 [Leipzig: Martin Landsberg, *c.*1500]. *ISTC* is00090000, *USTC* 748700. Copy consulted: Munich, Bayerische Staatsbibliothek, Res/2 A.lat.b. 750.

4. Imprints of Pomponio Leto's edition (*LaetT*) with the Valla commentary

1491 Venice: Philippus Pincius, 11 May 1491. *ISTC* is00076000, *USTC* 991411. Copies consulted: BL, IB.23618; BodL, Auct. P inf. 2.1; Chicago, Newberry Library, Inc. 5287; Oxford, New College, BT1.10.35(3).

1492.2 Venice: Theodorus de Ragazonibus, 9 July 1492. *ISTC* is00077000, *USTC* 991410. Copies consulted: BL, IB.23556; BodL, Auct. O inf. 2.6; Cambridge, St John's College, Ii.2.27(1); Oxford, Corpus Christi College, ϕ.C.4.6(2).

1493.1 Milan: Uldericus Scinzenzeler, 31 Jan. 1493. *ISTC* is00077500, *USTC* 991409. *IncT* readings are occasionally preferred over *LaetT*. Copy consulted: BL, IB.26745.

1493.2 Venice: Johannes Tacuinus, de Tridino, 5 Aug. 1493. *ISTC* is00078000, *USTC* 991408. Copies consulted: BL, IB.24021; BodL, Auct. P 5.1(1); Cambridge, Peterhouse, O.6.31; JRL, R106193.

1493.3 Venice: Bernardinus Benalius, *c.*1493. *ISTC* is00079000, *USTC* 991407. Copies consulted: BL, IB.22351; BodL, Auct. P 3.18(1); JRL, 3418.1.

1494 Turin: Nicolaus de Benedictis and Jacobinus Suigus, 25 Nov. 1494. *ISTC* is00080000, *USTC* 991406. Copies consulted: Madrid, Biblioteca del Palacio Real, I/62; Baltimore, MD, Walters Art Museum, 91.1061.

1495.2 [Lyon: Gaspard Ortuin, *c.*1495]. *ISTC* is00082350, *USTC* 761619. Copy consulted: Zaragoza, Biblioteca Universidad de Zaragoza, I 258.

1497.4 Lyon: Jean de Vingle, 7 Jan. 1497. *ISTC* is00082500, *USTC* 761620. Copy consulted: Edinburgh, University Library, NCL Inc.28.

1497.5 [Lyon: Pierre Mareschal and Barnabé Chaussard, *c.*1497]. *ISTC* is00082700, *USTC* 761622. Copy consulted: Paris, Bibliothèque nationale de France, RES-J-614.

5. Britannicus's revision of Leto's edition (*BritT*), with the Valla commentary

1495.3 Brescia: Bernardinus de Misintis, for Angelus and Jacobus Britannicus, 13 Jan. 1495. *ISTC* is00082000, *USTC* 991405. Copies consulted: BL, IB.31233; BodL, Auct. N inf. 2.17; London, Lambeth Palace Library, L40.4/38 01.

1495–1500.1 [Venice: Christophorus de Pensis, de Mandello, after 14 Nov. 1495]. *ISTC* is00084000, *USTC* 991403. Copies consulted: BL, IB.23526; BodL, Auct. N 3.23; BodL, Auct. N 3.24(1); Shrewsbury School, F.VI.5.

1495–1500.2 [Venice: Christophorus de Pensis, de Mandello, after 14 Nov. 1495]. *ISTC* is00082300, *USTC* 991404. Copies consulted: BL, G.9162; BodL, Inc.c.I4.2.

1498 Paris: André Bocard, for Jean Petit, and Jean Alexandre and Charles de Bougne at Angers, 13 Jan. 1498. *ISTC* is00083000, *USTC* 201369. Copies consulted: Cambridge, Trinity College, VI.13.130; CUL, Inc.4.D.1.26[2562]; Oxford, Exeter College, 9F 1497.

6. Britannicus's revision of Leto's edition (*BritT*), with the Valla and ps.-Omnibonus commentaries

1500.2 Venice: Johannes Tacuinus, de Tridino, 20 July 1500. *ISTC* is00085000, *USTC* 991402. Copies consulted: BL, IB.24104; BodL, Auct. P 3.19; Durham, Palace Green Library, SA 0101; Oxford, Magdalen College, Arch.B.I.5.1(3).

EXPLANATORY NOTES

Longer passages from *Sal* are abbreviated since the Latin is readily found in modern editions. Passages from *Val* are quoted in full since the commentary lacks a modern edition and can be difficult to navigate in contemporary copies. Emendations of *Val* are in square brackets. Textual variants are only discussed when they may have affected *Con*'s translation choices. '.i.' stands for *id est*, '.s.' for *scilicet*. References to groups of incunables use abbreviations explained in the Appendix (*IncT*, *ParisT*, *LaetT*, *BritT*). All *OED* and *MED* citations were checked in October 2024.

2–4 *Qvintilianus declarith . . . Herodotvs or Livius*. *Con* supplies details from *Val*: 'In quo genere quintiliani iudicio: qui eum Thucydidi in historia eminentissimo opposuit præcipuam inter eos . . . Et enim quo thucydides est Herodoto maior: cui secundæ tribuuntur partes eo certe hic noster Liuio præstantior' (sig. a2[r]). In contrast with *Con*, which follows *Val*, Quintilian says that he does not hesitate to match ('opponere') Sallust with Thucydides, 'nec indignetur sibi Herodotus aequari Titum Liuium' (Quintilianus, *Institutionis oratoriae libri duodecim*, ed. Winterbottom, 10.1.101).

4–6 *Marcialis also, that . . . glorie to avaunce*. *Con* follows *Val*: 'Accedit et martialis urbanissimi poetæ carmen. Hic erit ut perhibent doctorum corda uirorum. Primus romana crispus in historia: quo haud dubie apparet doctorum hominum iudicio Crispum cæteris romanarum rerum scriptoribus prælatum' (sig. a2[r]). The epigram ('Hic erit ut . . . crispus in historia') is Martialis, *Epigrammata*, ed. Lindsay, 14.191.

6–8 *But Saynt Augustine . . . of the historye*. Cf. 'nobilitate veritatis historicus' in Augustine, *De ciuitate Dei libri XXII*, ed. Dombart and Kalb, 1.5. Not in *Val*, but quoted in paratexts in several other incunables, as e.g. by Filippo Beroaldo: 'vir ille egregius nobilitate ueritatis historicus/ut inquit Augustinus' (**1478.4**, sig. 18[v]).

13–14 *in owre wolgare . . . Englisshe tonge declared*. 'declared' most obviously means 'related' or 'told' (*MED*, s.v. 'declaren', v., sense 1[a]), but may also suggest 'made clear', 'explained', or 'interpreted' (*OED*, s.v. 'declare', v., sense 1). The latter sense would resonate with *Con*'s approach to translation as interpretive.

14–18 *I dar not . . . so to wryte*. Knotty syntax. 'wher' makes most sense as a conjunction, i.e. 'I dare not claim—when I am not about [to do so]—to assume the duty of an interpreter, due to my great lack of knowledge of both of those languages, nor do I intend [to assume] so great a responsibility or attentiveness, but instead it will be enough for me', etc. 'interpreter' is a calque of *interpres*, on which, see Introduction, p. xliv. On 'overrunne', see further Introduction, pp. xliv–xlv, xlix.

28 *ascape*. This sense antedates 1st citation in *OED*, s.v. 'escape', n.[1], sense 6.

37 *It is expedyent*='decet' (*Sal* 1.1). See further Introduction, p. xlviii.

47 *actes of vertew*='uirtus' (*Sal* 1.4). *Virtus* is also translated once each as 'wisdome' (51), 'wyse and vertuouse' (64–5), 'vertewis and noblenes' (102), 'vertew and polecy' (186–7), 'vertew and noblenes' (225–6), 'vertew and valiauntnes' (1534), and 'manhode' (1685), three times as 'valyantnes' (170, 196, 212), and five times each as 'vertew' (73, 95, 262, 1436, 1641), 'manlynes' (468, 1530, 1599, 1626, 1638), and 'noblenes' (490, 1350, 1491, 1505, 1511).

51 *wisdome of the soule*='uirtute animi' (*Sal* 1.5).

53–4 *the actuall dede of þe body*. *Sal*: 'mature facto' (1.6). *Con* follows *Val*: 'nam sine consilio factum nihil ualet: nec consilium sine facto multum prodesse potest: et consilium ad uires pertinet: et factum ad corpus' (sig. a2^{v}).

56 *rewle and power*='imperi' (*Sal* 2.1).

59 *Lacedemones*='Lacedaemonii' (*Sal* 2.2). This word's earliest appearance is dated to 1489 in *OED*, s.v. 'Lacedaemonian | Lacedemonian', n. and adj.

60 *Athenienses*='Athenienses' (*Sal* 2.2). The earliest appearance of 'Athenians' is dated to 1526 in *OED*, s.v. 'Athenian', adj. and n. Skelton's *Bibliotheca* similarly renders Lat. *athenienses* as 'Athenyensis' (Skelton, *Bibliotheca*, i. 40).

62 *impere*. Probably meant here as elsewhere (and, sometimes, anachronistically) specifically as 'empire' rather than e.g. 'dominion' (cf. *MED*, s.v. 'empire', n., sense 4). On this and the etymologizing spelling, see further Introduction, p. lii.

64 *improwrys*='imperatorum' (*Sal* 2.3). Probably meant here as elsewhere as 'emperors' (often anachronistically; cf. 'impere', 62*n*). On this and the etymologizing spelling, see also Introduction, p. lii.

64–5 *of as wyse and vertuouse disposicion*='animi uirtus' (*Sal* 2.3).

68 *the hye dignyte*='imperium' (*Sal* 2.4).

72–3 *imperys be translatyd . . . to better men*. *Sal*: 'imperium semper ad . . . minus bono transfertur' (2.6). *LaetT* (and subsequently *BritT*) flip the prepositions, giving 'ab optimo' and 'ad minus', but *Con* follows 'ad optumum' and 'a minus', as given in *IncT* and *ParisT*. John Claymond in his copy also—like our translator, presumably—writes 'ad optumum' and 'a minus' as a correction in the margin (Oxford, Corpus Christi College, *ϕ*.C.4.6(2) [**1492.2**], sig. a3^{r}). Aldus would later address this very mistake in the preface to his 1509 edition: see Manutius, *Humanism and the Latin Classics*, 88–91. On the history of this variant, see also Osmond and Ulery, 'Pomponius Laetus, Editor of Sallust', 173–4.

74 *be subiecte and obeysant*='parent' (*Sal* 2.7). On the doublet, see Introduction, p. liv.

dyspysing vertu. Not in *Sal* but follows *Val*: 'contempta uirtute' (sig. a3^{r}).

75 *in mete, drynke*='uentri' (*Sal* 2.8), amplified via *Val*: 'Nam hi uentri dediti dicuntur esse qui suos omnes appetitus sequuntur uel edendi uel bibendi uel alterius uoluptatis comparandæ' (sig. a3[r]).

76 *their body vnexcersi*[*s*]*id*. *Sal*: 'incultique' (2.8). *Con* may follow *Val*: 'Inculti: id est sine exercitio' (sig. a3[r]).

77 *vnknowen men and vnspokyn of* = 'sicuti peregrinantes' (*Sal* 2.8), amplified via *Val*: 'Peregrinantes: sicut homines incogniti' (sig. a3[r]).

81 *occupieth reason* = 'frui anima' (*Sal* 2.9).

83 *good science and faculte* = 'artis bonae' (*Sal* 2.9), amplified via *Val*: 'Bonæ artis: scientiæ et eruditionis' (sig. a3[r]).

84 *to wynne honour by*. Not in *Sal* but follows *Val*: 'Sed cum multæ sint res: quibus homines sibi laudem possint comparare' (sig. a3[r]). 'honour' translates *Val*'s 'laudem' here and is a word that *Con* uses throughout, in a range of senses, as part of translations of *ambitio* (106, 260, 1448), *clarus* (84), *dignitas* (822, 829, 1032, 1224, 1227, 1468, 1521), *gloria* (201, 302, 1517), *honor* (107, 109, 262, 289, 609, 1156), *honos* (487), and *magnitudo* (897).

99 *in tendre age and in my begynnyng* = 'ego adulescentulus initio' (*Sal* 3.3), amplified via *Val*: 'Adolescentibus: admodum adolescens: adhuc teneræ ætatis'; 'Initio: id est in principio' (sig. a3[v]).

100 *I lefte lernyng*. *Sal*: 'studio' (3.3). *Con* follows *LaetT* 'a studio' (as also in *ParisT* and *BritT*); *Val* further glosses as 'A studio litterarum' (sig. a3[v]).

101–2 *for abstinence and doyng no violence* = 'pro abstinentia' (*Sal* 3.3).

102 *for vertewis and noblenes* = 'pro uirtute' (*Sal* 3.3).

103 *pompowsnes* = 'largitio' (*Sal* 3.4), which *Val* glosses as 'opponitur abstinentiæ' (sig. a3[v]), hence 'magnificent living', not a sense currently covered by *OED*, s.v. 'pompousness', n., or *MED*, s.v. 'pompousnesse', n. Cf. 324, where 'pompowsnes' translates 'sumptui' (*Sal* 13.5).

105–6 *the corrupcion of desyre of honour* = 'ambitione corrupta' (*Sal* 3.4), via *Val*: 'Corrupta ambitione: quia ego quoque mihi quærebam honores: quemadmodum cæteri' (sig. a3[v]).

108–9 *as well in . . . honour of it* = 'fama atque inuidia' (*Sal* 3.5), amplified via *Val*: 'Fama: propter famam: quia fama mea pro inuidia sæpe laborauit. Inuidia: quia quærebam mihi famam: odium et inuidiam populi fugiebam: ut suffragiis eius possem ad hunc honorem peruenire quem ego quærebam' (sig. a4[r]).

114 *in the vile offices* = 'seruilibus officiis' (*Sal* 4.1). 'vile' probably fails to capture the precise sense of the Lat.: cf. 598, 697, 712, 1030, 1064, 1176, 1573; see also Introduction, pp. l–li.

115–16 *retornyd and dryven* = 'regressus' (*Sal* 4.2).

117 *`not' of all . . . actes at length*. Not in *Sal* but follows *Val*: 'Nolui inquit ab urbe condita historiam sumere et perpetuam scribere historiam' (sig. a4^{r}).

118–19 *do . . . is*. *Sal* 'erat' (4.2). *Con* uses present for Lat. past tense.

123 *for the gretnes . . . the parell also*. *Sal*: 'sceleris atque periculi nouitate' (4.4). *Con* misses the idea of novelty ('nouitate') on account of *Val*: 'Nouitate magnitudine: nam nouus dicitur magnus: inde nouitas .i. magnitudo' (sig. a4^{r}).

124 *afore I begynne my `t'rayties*. *Sal*: 'prius . . . quam initium narrandi faciam' (4.5), where '`t'rayties' follows 'historiam' in *Val*: 'Initium narrandi: priusquam incipiam narrare historiam eius' (sig. a4^{r}).

125 *of a right noble `ly'n`age'* = 'nobili genere natus' (*Sal* 5.1). The scribe apparently wrote 'kynne' before correcting to *Con*'s more Latinate 'lynage'. 'kynne' was a more obvious word choice here. E.g. 'nobili genere natus' at *Sal* 5.1 is glossed 'of a nobull kyne' in Shrewsbury School, F.VI.5 [**1495–1500.1**], sig. a4^{r} (on which book, and its annotations, see Introduction, p. xxxii). The same phrase is also similarly glossed—as 'nobyll kyndred', and as 'stoke or kynred'—in two other, anonymously annotated copies of Ascensius's 1504 edition of the *BC*: see BodL, Broxb. 79.3, sig. a4^{v}; BodL, DD 20 Art., sig. a4^{v}. *Con* adopts similar language when translating 'nobilis', elsewhere, as 'of noble kynred' (427–8; cf. *Sal* 18.4).

126 *stomake* = 'animi' (*Sal* 5.1). The first of almost twenty instances where *Con* translates *animus* as 'stomake'. This was a relatively common early Tudor translation of *animus*, also appearing as a gloss in *BC* copies annotated by later Tudor readers (cf. BodL, DD 20 Art., sigs. e1^{r}, f4^{r}; CUL, Tc.54.58, sigs. c5^{r}, c5^{v}, d5^{v}, d6^{r}). This translation also appears in other early Tudor translations, e.g. Paynell's *Conspiracie of Lucius Catiline* (1541) and John Blount's early 16th-c. translation of Nicholas Upton's *De studio militari*: see Paynell, *The conspiracie of Lucius Catiline*, sigs. D2^{v}, L4^{v}, S4^{r} (cf. Felici, *De coniuratione L. Catilinae*, sigs. C3^{v}, H3^{v}, N2^{v}); Blount, 'An Edition with Introduction and Commentary of John Blount's English Translation of Nicholas Upton's *De studio militari*', ed. Walker, ii. 28 (line 548) (cf. Upton, *De studio militari libri quatuor*, ed. Bysshe, 23).

127–8 *ravisshment of women* = 'rapinae' (*Sal* 5.2).

128 *debates and stryves* = 'discordia ciuilis' (*Sal* 5.2).

128–9 *therin excersysid hymselffe*. *Sal*: 'ibique iuuentutem suam exercuit' (5.2). 'iuuentutem' not translated.

129 *abyde and suffre* = 'patiens' (*Sal* 5.3).

130 *bolde and hardy* = 'audax' (*Sal* 5.4).

132 *appetitis*. Perhaps the scribe originally wrote 'desyrous': 'appetitis' is the first word on a new line of text and the line immediately above starts with 'desirous'.

133–4 *coveting hye thinges . . . reason or mesure*. Slightly condensing *Sal*, 'inmoderata incredibilia nimis alta semper cupiebat' (5.5), but 'without reason or mesure' amplifies from *Val*: 'Incredibilia: quæ nulla ratione consequi posset (sig. a4^{v}).

135–6 *after he had . . . hole comen welle*='post dominationem L. Sullae' (*Sal* 5.6), amplified via *Val*: 'Dominationem L. Syllæ: qui motis partibus rei publicæ aduersariis perpetuam dictaturam assecutus est' (sig. a4^{v}).

137 *the cite*='rei publicae' (*Sal* 5.6).

139–40 *by his fallyng . . . meynteine his pleasures*='inopia rei familiaris' (5.7). 'to meynteine his pleasures' follows 'tueri magnificentiam' in *Val*: 'Inopia rei: nam cum magnificus esset et inopia premeretur: quia suis rebus non poterat tueri magnificentiam: alienis necesse erat conseruaret' (sig. a4^{v}).

140 *of his horrible offencis*='scelerum' (*Sal* 5.7).

142–3 *the which with . . . lustis, and covetyse*. *Sal*: 'quos pessuma ac . . . luxuria atque auaritia' (5.8). 'diuorsa inter se' not translated.

144 *The very thing and the tyme . . . I haue spoken*. *Sal*: 'Res ipsa . . . tempus' (5.9). *Con* misconstrues the syntax, necessitating the interpolation of 'I haue spoken'. Sg. verb ('requyrith') may reflect the fact that *Con* translates a sg. verb ('uidetur'), even though a sg. subject in the Lat. has been substituted with 'very thing and the tyme' (and so we might expect a pl. verb in the Engl.); a similar explanation makes sense of 'occupieth' (='possidet', *Sal* 52.22) at 1437. Alternatively, however, the translator may sometimes imitate a possibility in Lat. by employing a sg. verb in sentences that have multiple third-person objects (cf. 'hangith', 483; 'oweth', 1289). On this Lat. usage, cf. Kennedy, *Revised Latin Primer*, §199.1

146–7 *in tyme of . . . in their warrys*='domi militiaeque' (*Sal* 5.9), amplified via *Val*: 'Domi: in pace. Militiæ: in bello' (sig. a5^{r}).

147 *by lytill and lytill*='paulatim' (*Sal* 5.9). An idiom: cf. *OED*, s.v. 'little', pron., sense P.2.a.iii. Cf. 256–7, 573, 1304.

152 *fled from ferre contres*='profugi' (*Sal* 6.1), amplified via *Val*: 'Profugi: procul fugati a domo sua' (sig. a5^{r}).

153 *a people of . . . ther callid* latini='Aborigines' (*Sal* 6.1), amplified via *Val*: 'aborigenes populi dicti sunt latini prisci' (sig. a5^{r}).

rewde. I.e. rural, rustic;='agreste' (*Sal* 6.1). This sense neither in *OED*, s.v. 'rude', adj. nor *MED*, s.v. 'rude', adj., but cf. e.g. Reuchlin, *Vocabularius*, s.v. 'agrestis' (n.): '.i. agricola. quasi stans in agro' (sig. b1^{v}).

154 *withoute any correccion*='solutum' (*Sal* 6.1), via *Val*: 'solutum quia sine imperio' (sig. a5^{r}).

156–7 *it is incredeble . . . lightly they encresid*='incredibile memoratu est quam facile coaluerint' (*Sal* 6.2). Unusual phrasing results from studiously close translation; see also Introduction, p. xlviii.

157–8 *and howe, shortly . . . made a citee*. *Sal*: 'ita breui multitudo . . . ciuitas facta erat' (6.2). See Introduction, pp. xxx–xxxii.

159 *incresyd and* \`*semyd*'*myghty* = 'aucta' (*Sal* 6.3).

161 *incontinent*. Not in *Sal* but suggested by *Val*: 'inuidia repente orta est contra eos' (sig. a5^r^).

162 \`*the*' *invy of theire neighboures* = 'inuidia' (*Sal* 6.3).

Wheruppon. Could, grammatically, be either an adv. or subordinating conj. This edition treats *wheruppon* as an adv. where, as here, features of MS punctuation and/or layout suggest the start of a new sentence, and otherwise as a conj.

166 *ryght dyligent bothe . . . tyme of peas* = 'domi militiaeque intenti' (*Sal* 6.5), amplified via *Val*: 'Domi militiæque intenti .i. bello et pace diligentes' (sig. a5^v^).

168 *to deffend* = 'tegere' (*Sal* 6.5), perhaps via *Val*: 'Tegere .i. defendere' (sig. a5^v^).

169 *their faders and their moders* = 'parentis' (*Sal* 6.5).

170–1 *dryven fer from themselffes* = 'propulerant' (*Sal* 6.5), amplified via *Val*: 'Propulerant: procul pepulerant' (sig. a5^v^).

171 *their frendys causis* = 'sociis atque amicis' (*Sal* 6.5). 'sociis' or 'amicis' not translated, perhaps because *Con* interprets as hendiadys.

172 *by their gyftes . . . to other men* = 'dandis' (*Sal* 6.5).

174 *a rewler whome . . .* \`*nami*'*d a kyng*. *Sal*: 'Imperium . . . nomen imperi regium habebant' (6.6). 'rewler' = 'Imperium'. *Con* follows *LaetT* 'nomen regium habebat', i.e. 'imperi' om. (as also in *BritT*).

175 *brayns*. Seemingly means 'talent' or 'ability', in the vein of *OED*, s.v. 'brain', n., sense II.3.b, though appearance here as pl. antedates *OED* (which comments that this sense appeared in the plural 'From the 16th cent.'). One of the words used to translate *ingenium* and *ingenia*: cf. 211, 471.

177 *for theire auctoryte* = 'curae similitudine' (*Sal* 6.6).

180–1 *yerely two governours . . . of oon yere* = 'annua imperia binosque imperatores' (*Sal* 6.7), amplified via *Val*: 'Annua imperia .i. quæ tantummodo anno uno permanerent. nam consules uno tantum anno permanebant in imperio' (sig. a5^v^).

182 *cowde not*. Slightly modifying *Sal*: 'minume posse' (6.7).

182–3 *fall into pryde*. *Sal*: 'insolescere' (6.7), where the idea of falling follows *Val*: 'Insolescere: in superbiam et in insolentiam posse recidere' (sig. a5^v^).

184–5 *manlynes and wisdo*\`*me*' = 'ingenium' (*Sal* 7.1).

186–7 *vertew and* \`*polecy*' = 'uirtus' (*Sal* 7.2).

190 *Than þe youth in their begynnyng*. *Sal*: 'Iam primum iuuentus' (7.4). *Con* misinterprets 'primum'.

191–3 *streight were putte . . . men of warre*=‘in castris per laborem usum militiae discebat’ (*Sal* 7.4), amplified via *Val*: ‘Per laborem usu militiam .i. laborando et militando militiam gerere: et laborem pati assueti erant: quia per laborem et continuum usum fiebant belli peritiores’ (sig. a5[v]). ‘tentys’ is a common fifteenth- and sixteenth-century translation of *castra*.

195–6 *with strengith of armour*=‘armatus’ (*Sal* 7.5). The first of five times that *Con* collocates ‘strengith’ with ‘armour’ or ‘armes’. Also a common collocation in Barclay’s Sallust, including as a translation of *arma* and its cognates: see Barclay, *Famous Cronycle*, ed. Waite, 45, 104, 122, 181.

197 *stryffe and besynes*=‘certamen’ (*Sal* 7.6).

198 *scaled fyrst þe . . . at a sege*=‘murum ascendere’ (*Sal* 7.6), amplified via *Val*: ‘Murum ascendere: properabat unusquisque in oppugnandis urbibus primus esse uolebat qui murum ascenderet et muralem coronam assequeretur’ (sig. a6[r]).

197–8 *every man that . . . vpon his enmy*. *Sal*: ‘quisque hostem ferire’ (7.6). ‘fyrst’ follows *Val*: ‘Ferire: non expectabant alii alios ut hostes inuaderent: sed unusquisque primus esse uolebat’ (sig. a6[r]).

200 *lawde and prayse*=‘Laudis’ (*Sal* 7.6).

201 *exceding*. Antedates 1st citation in *OED*, s.v. ‘exceeding’, adj.
competent. *Sal*: ‘honestas’ (7.6). *Con* misinterprets due to *Val* gloss, ‘Honestas: mediocris’ (sig. a6[r]).

204 *mooste strongly warded and fensyd*=‘natura munitas’ (*Sal* 7.7). ‘natura’ not translated.

204–5 *toke and subdewed*=‘ceperit’ (*Sal* 7.7).

208 *settyth all thinges . . . downe full lowe*=‘celebrat obscuratque’ (*Sal* 8.1). *Con* introduces the spatial metaphor.

210–11 *were bredde*. *Sal*: ‘prouenere’ (8.3). *Con* follows *Val*: ‘Prouenere: nati sunt progeniti sunt’ (sig. a6[r]).

211 *the*[*r*]=‘ibi’ (*Sal* 8.3).
brayns. On the sense, cf. 175*n*.

214 *by wordes cowde sett theim*. *Sal*: ‘eam uerbis potuere’ (8.4). *Sal*’s ‘eam’ refers to *uirtus*, but *Con*’s ‘theim’ refers to ‘actes’. *Con* translates ‘ea uerbis potuere’, as is printed in all incunables.

216–17 *To study allonly . . . the warris also*=‘ingenium nemo sine corpore exercebat’ (*Sal* 8.5), amplified via *Val*: ‘nemo se dederat studiis litterarum sine exercitatione corporis’ (sig. a6[r]).

218 *to teche and speke*=‘dicere’ (*Sal* 8.5).

225 *had but oon stryffe*. *Sal*: ‘certabant’ (9.2). ‘oon’ follows *Val*: ‘Cum ciuibus unum certamen erat’ (sig. a6[v]).

226 *In thaire sacrifices*='In suppliciis' (*Sal* 9.2), perhaps following *Val*: 'In suppliciis: in sacrificiis' (sig. a6[v]).

228 *Manlynesse . . . Iustice*='audacia', 'aequitate' (*Sal* 9.3). Both words are engrossed in MS.

231–3 *oftetymes*; *than they that . . . by the signes*='saepius'; 'quam qui signa relinquere' (*Sal* 9.4). Having mistranslated 'saepius' as 'oftetymes', the translator then misunderstands the contrast introduced by 'quam'. To fit his mistaken interpretation, he subsequently twists the meaning of 'relinquere', contrives the direct object 'them', and treats 'signa' as abl. agent rather than, correctly, as acc. pl.

231–2 *contrary to þe . . . of their soueraigne*='contra imperium' (*Sal* 9.4), amplified via *Val*: 'Contra imp[er]ium: contra iussum imperatoris' (sig. a6[v]).

235 *the impire was gouerned*='imperium agitabant' (*Sal* 9.5). *Con* renders Lat. active as Engl. pass. to suit the translation of *imperium* as 'impire'.

236 *coarcion of fere*='metu' (*Sal* 9.5). 'coarcion' antedates 1st citation in *OED*, s.v. 'coercion', n.

239 *their rewle spred . . . all the worlde*. *Sal*: 'res publica creuit' (10.1). 'rewle'='res publica'. *Con*'s amplification follows *Val*: 'Res publica .i. postquam omnia imperio suo subegit romanus populus' (sig. a6[v]).

240 *wilde*='ferae' (*Sal* 10.1), perhaps via *Val*: 'Feræ: sæuæ: uidelicet barbaræ ut sithe: ut Tracenses: ut Parthi' (sig. a6[v]).

241 *þat grete cite Cartago in Grece*='Carthago' (*Sal* 10.1). *Con*'s geographical mishap here (Carthage was on the north coast of Africa) is not suggested by *Val*, nor explained by the fact that contemporaries generally knew of two Carthages, 'cartago in affryca and cartago in spayne' (Higden, *Polycronicon*, f. 58[v]); cf. also, e.g., 'Cartage in Aphrike' in Skelton, *Howe the Douty Duke of Albany*, line 196, in *Complete English Poems*, ed. Scattergood. The Carthage meant here by Sallust is indeed Carthage in Africa, as fifteenth-century writers could have known e.g. from the description of war between Rome and Carthage in Book V of Lydgate's *Fall of Princes*.

243 *open and obesaunt*='patebant' (*Sal* 10.1).

243–4 *to wex wode*='saeuire' (*Sal* 10.1).

244 *easely and paciently*='facile' (*Sal* 10.2).

247 *moste coveted and desyred*='optanda' (*Sal* 10.2).

248 *those two thinges*='ea' (*Sal* 10.3).

249 *of all evilles and mischeffis*='omnium malorum' (*Sal* 10.3).

250 *and all other vertewis maners*='ceterasque artis bonas' (*Sal* 10.4).

251–2 *for mony to . . . all maner thinges*. *Sal*: 'omnia uenalia habere' (10.4). 'for mony' follows *Val*: 'Habere omnia uenalia: facere omnia propter pecuniam' (sigs. a6^{v}–b1^{r}).

252 *fervent desire of dignite* = 'Ambitio' (*Sal* 10.5).

254 *not ac*[*c*]*ording to right* = 'non ex re' (*Sal* 10.5).

256 *These two thinges*. *Sal*: 'Haec' (10.6). *Con* follows *LaetT* 'Haec utraque'.

256–7 *by lytill and lytill* = 'paulatim' (*Sal* 10.6). An idiom: cf. 147*n*.

258 *had infected theim* = 'inuasit' (*Sal* 10.6).

260 *þe desir of honour* = 'ambitio' (*Sal* 11.1), amplified via *Val*: 'honoris cupidi erant' (sig. b1^{r}).

263–4 *he . . . the oþer*. I.e. the former; the latter.

263 *by trew and right weyse* = 'uera uia' (*Sal* 11.2).

265 *fervent desire*. *Sal*: 'studium' (11.3). *Con* follows *Val*: 'Studium: desiderium et uoluptatem' (sig. b1^{r}).

266–7 *makyth . . . right vyle* = 'effeminat' (*Sal* 11.3).

270 *after that the . . . of Lvcius Sulla*. *Sal*: 'postquam L. Sulla armis recepta re publica' (11.4). Abl. absol. 'recepta re publica' is summarized as 'victorye'.

271 *evill chaunces and mischevous maners* = 'malos euentus' (*Sal* 11.4).

271–2 *all they fyll to oppression* = 'rapere omnes, trahere' (*Sal* 11.4).

276 *was suffred by . . . and were kepte*. Thus trying to capture the meaning of 'habuerat' (*Sal* 11.5), which in this usage is 'virtually equivalent to *tractare*' (Ramsey, 72).

277 *prodygally*. See Introduction, p. lii. Cf. 323–4, 378.

278 *swete and plesaunt howsis* = 'Loca amoena' (*Sal* 11.5).

280 *love* = 'amare' (*Sal* 11.6). I.e. lust, with sexual sense suggested by *Val*: 'Amare .s. mulieres' (sig. b1^{v}).

to haue their greate bankettes = 'potare' (*Sal* 11.6), with amplification suggested by *Val*: 'Portare [*sic*] uinum: cum antea semper sobrii fuissent et continentes: nunc amœnis locis corrupti: et mulieres amare: et uinum superfluum. nimis luxuriose sumere cœperunt' (sig. b1^{v}).

281 *goodly pictures*. *Sal*: 'signa' (11.6). *Con* follows *Val*: 'Signa: statuas. Nam signum statuam dicimus' (sig. b1^{v}).

ymages sett with . . . and precious stones. *Sal*: 'tabulas pictas' (11.6). *Con* follows *Val*: 'Tabulas pictas: imagines tabulis preciosis depictas aureas uel argenteas' (sig. b1^{v}).

282 *fressh facions of plate* = 'uasa caelata' (*Sal* 11.6).
they dred not to stele = 'rapere' (*Sal* 11.6).

283 *spoylid the temples*. *Sal*: 'delubra spoliare' (11.6). *LaetT* gives 'delubra deorum spoliare' (as does *BritT*). So, either *Con* or the scribe omitted a translation of 'deorum' here, perhaps accidentally, or perhaps *Con* followed the variant reading 'delubra spoliare' as transmitted via *IncT* and *ParisT*. 'temples' follows *Val*: 'Delubra: templa deorum' (sig. b1 v).

283–4 *spared not to . . . in theim `all'* = 'sacra profanaque omnia polluere' (*Sal* 11.6).

286 *prosperity and welth* = 'secundae res' (*Sal* 11.8).
oppressith and werith = 'fatigant' (*Sal* 11.8).

287–8 *vicious maners of the wilfulnes of victorye* = 'corruptis moribus uictoriae' (*Sal* 11.8). *Con* takes 'corruptis moribus' as the object of 'temperarent' rather than, correctly, as abl. of quality. 'wilfulnes of victorye' = 'uictoriae'.

291 *for reproffe and shame* = 'probro' (*Sal* 12.1). *Con* follows *LaetT* 'pro probro'.
innocency and pleyn levyng = 'innocentia' (*Sal* 12.1).

292 *hate and dispyte* = 'maleuolentia' (*Sal* 12.1).
vpon this ease and welth = 'ex diuitiis' (*Sal* 12.2), with 'ease' translating 'ocio' in *Val*: 'Igitur ex diuitiis ergo quia ocio et ignauiæ se dedere' (sig. b1 v). Cf. 'ease' as translation, or in translations, of *otium* at 245, 406, 851, 880.

293 *oppression*. I.e. extortion, following *Val*'s gloss of *Sal* 'superbia' (12.2): 'Nam qui diuites sunt omnia sibi licere arbitrantur' (sig. b1 v).

300 *moste devoute and religious* = 'religiosissumi' (*Sal* 12.3).

301 *they anournyd the . . . holynesse and sacrifice*. *Sal*: 'delubra deorum pietate . . . decorabant' (12.4). 'deorum' is not translated, probably because this gen. pl. is wanting in *LaetT* (though most *BritT* and all *IncT* and *ParisT* have 'deorum' here). 'with holynesse and sacrifice' = 'pietate'.

302 *with honour and glory* = 'gloria' (*Sal* 12.4).

303–4 *liberty and power to wronge theim* = 'iniuriae licentiam' (*Sal* 12.4), perhaps via *Val*: 'Et iniuriæ licentiam . . . quæ libertatem faciunt iniuriæ' (sig. b1 v).

304 *moste vyle men*. *Sal*: 'ignauissumi homines' (12.5). *Con* follows *Val*: 'Ignauissimi: uilissimi homines (sig. b1 v).

305 *toke* = 'adimere' (*Sal* 12.5), with past tense following *Val*: 'Adimere: pro adimebant' (sig. b1 v).

305–6 *the moste valeant men our eldres* = 'fortissumi uiri' (*Sal* 12.5), amplified via *Val*: 'fortissimi uiri .s. maiores nostri' (sig. b1 v).

307 *by power dyd oppression and wronge* = 'iniuriam facere' (*Sal* 12.5).

308–9 *their lustis and plesures the which*. *Sal*: 'ea . . . quae' (13.1). *Con* expands 'ea' as 'lustis and plesurs', but 'ea' correctly looks ahead to 'quae'.

310 *Many meane men*. *Sal*: 'a priuatis compluribus' (13.1). *Con* erroneously treats this phrase as the start of a new sentence and misconstrues the acc.–inf. construction of which it is part.

310–12 *drye groundes* [*with*] . . . *the fresshest maner* = 'maria constrata esse' (*Sal* 13.1). *Con* amplifies with a description of the Gardens of Lucullus from *Val*: 'amœnitate omnibus præstantia: quæ usque in medium mare porrigebantur: ita ut ubi maria fuerant: ibi stratum erat solum ueluti in terra continenti fabricasset' (sig. b2^r^). '[with] ferre compas' is interpolated (and 'ferre' starts a new line of text, which helps to explain the erroneous om. of 'with'). For the phrase 'ferre compas' used in a similar sense, cf. 'ere euer he had fette any farre compasse', in Cope, *The historie of two the moste noble capitaines of the worlde*, sig. Z4^r^, where the Engl. amplifies Livy, *Ab Urbe condita*, ed. Briscoe et al., 27.18.15.

314 *in foly and vylenes* = 'per turpitudinem' (*Sal* 13.2).

315–16 *advoutre, comyn women* . . . *moste vylonowse offensys*. *Sal*: 'stupri ganeae ceterique cultus' (13.3). 'advoutre' and 'comyn women' follow *Val*'s glosses 'Stupri adulterii' and 'ganeæ .i. meretricis' respectively (sig. b2^r^). 'bawdre' is an interpolation, though cf. 329, where it also appears in a translation of *ganeum* (a variant of *ganeae*).

316–17 *The women were* . . . *to desyre it*. *Sal*: 'uiri muliebria pati . . . in propatulo habere' (13.3). *LaetT* (like most incunables) gives 'uiros', but regardless *Con*'s translation is still inaccurate, perhaps because *Con* confuses *pateo* and *patior*. Alternatively, *Con*'s inaccuracy may be coyly deliberate because the Lat. alludes to sodomy. *Val* also self-censors here: 'uiros pati muliebria tangit rem obscœnam' (sig. b2^r^).

320 *after their appetytis and lustis* = 'luxu' (*Sal* 13.3).

323–4 *the more excedyngly and more prodygally* = 'profusius' (*Sal* 13.5). 'excedyngly' antedates 1st citation in *OED*, s.v. 'exceedingly', adv., sense 2. Cf. 1103. On 'prodygally', see Introduction, p. lii.

326–7 *Catelyne, thinkyng to* . . . *lyght to do*. *Sal*: 'Catilina, id quod factu facillumum erat' (14.1). 'to wynne the rewle' follows *Val*: 'Id quod erat facillimum .s. posse usurpare rem publicam' (sig. b2^r^). 'thinkyng' probably follows the *LaetT* variant 'Catilina ratus id quod' (as also in *BritT*); *Con* need not have known the 'Catilina existimans' variant, as in most *IncT* editions.

329–31 *paste shame, adwoutrer* . . . *rappe and rynde*. *Sal*: 'inpudicus adulter ganeo . . . bona patria lacerauerat' (14.2). 'comen hasarder' idiomatically translates 'alea', which appears in *LaetT* between 'ganeo' and 'manu' (as also in *IncT*, some *ParisT*, and *BritT*). 'all that he myght rappe and rynde' offers a strikingly vernacular translation of 'bona patria' (cf. Loeb, 'his family's property'): see further *MED*, s.vv.

'repen', v.², sense 1(b), 'rinen', v.¹. 'levyd by bawdre' (='ganeo') follows *Val*: 'Ganeo: in lupanari: nam ut paulo ante diximus ganeum dixerunt locum abditum' (sig. b2r).

331–2 *for the redemyng . . . his wykkyd dedys*='flagitium aut facinus redimeret' (*Sal* 14.2).

332 *that had kyld thair fadres*. *Sal*: 'parricidae' (14.3). *Con* follows *Val*: 'Parricidæ: quasi parentes interfecerunt' (sig. b2r).

334–5 *their hand had . . . wytnes or periurye*. *Sal*: 'manus atque lingua . . . sanguine ciuili alebat' (14.3). *Con* misconstrues the functions of 'periurio' and 'sanguine' as instrumental abl. and leaves 'ciuili' untranslated. 'thefte or m\u/rder'='sanguine'. 'false wytnes or periurye'='periurio'.

337 *after he had wasted all*. Not in *Sal*.

340 *with his flatery and pleasures*. *Sal*: 'inlecebris' (14.4), perhaps following *Val*: 'Illecebris: uoluptatibus' (sig. b2v).

342 *theire age freyll*. *Sal*: 'fluxi' (14.5). *Con* follows *LaetT* 'aetate fluxi' (as in most *IncT* and all *BritT*).

343 *theire nature*. *Sal*: 'studium' (14.6). *Con* follows *LaetT* 'ingenii'. Contrast John Claymond, who in his copy subpuncts *LaetT* 'ingenii' and interlineates 'studium', the variant in all previous incunables (and also *BritT*) (Oxford, Corpus Christi College, *ϕ*.C.4.6(2) [**1492.2**], sig. b2v).

346 *mesure*. *Con* does not translate 'suae' (*Sal* 14.6), which would make better sense of this sentence; cf. Loeb, 'spared neither expense nor *his own* sense of decency' (emphasis added).

348–9 *the which was . . . or spoken of*. *Sal*: 'sed ex aliis . . . haec fama ualebat' (14.7). *Con* misinterprets, failing to take 'haec fama' as the subject of the main clause here. 'puplished or spoken of'='fama ualebat'.

350 *In the begynnyng of his yeris*. *Sal*: 'Iam primum adulescens' (15.1). *Con* misconstrues the adverbial phrase 'Iam primum'.

350–1 *wikkyd and fowle ravishmentes and adwowtrees*='nefanda stupra' (*Sal* 15.1). Pl. forms of *avoutri* with sg. meaning are precedented by *OED*, s.v. 'adultery', n., sense 1.a, γ forms, albeit only from 1568 onward; for a mid-fifteenth-century example, see the quotations for *MED*, s.v. 'avoutri(e', sense 1(a). *Con* probably opts for pl. rather than sg. here (contrast 315) because 'adwowtrees' is part of a translation of neut. pl. 'stupra'.

351–2 *with a mayde professid to perfeccion*='cum sacerdote Vestae' (*Sal* 15.1).

352–3 *ayenst the lawys . . . and of man*='contra ius fasque' (*Sal* 15.1), amplified via *Val*: 'Ius contra ius humanum. Fas: contra ius diuinum' (sig. b2v).

353–4 *with the love of Avrelia Orestella* = 'amore Aureliae Orestillae' (*Sal* 15.2), i.e. an objective gen., 'love for' (Loeb), as *Con* seems to realize.

356–7 *he sparid not . . . his awne son* = 'necato filio' (*Sal* 15.2), amplified via *Val*: 'Neccato [*sic*]: ueneno interfecto' (sig. b2^{v}). The Valla commentary probably takes this detail from Valerius Maximus, *Factorum et dictorum memorabilium libri IX*, ed. Briscoe, 9.1.9.

357 *mete*. *Sal*: 'uacuam' (15.2). *Con* follows *Val*: 'Vacuam: expeditam' (sig. b2^{v}).

359–60 *his mynde, beyng . . . malicious to men*. *Sal*: 'animus inpurus, dis hominibusque infestus' (15.4). *Con* follows the punctuation as given in most incunables, here quoted from **1491**: 'animus impurus diis: hominibusque infestus'.

361 *wilde* = 'excitam' (*Sal* 15.4), perhaps via *Val*: 'Excitam pro excitatam: commotam' (sig. b2^{v}).

362 *bl`odye´*. *Sal*: 'foedi' (15.5). *Con* follows *Val*: 'Fœdi: cruenti: sanguine pleni' (sig. b2$^{v}$). 'bl`odye´' probably corrects a more obvious word that could follow 'eyn', perhaps 'bleere'.

363 *fersenes and mischeffe* = 'uecordia' (*Sal* 15.5).

366 *prosperous fortune* = 'fortunas' (*Sal* 16.2).

369 *to worke apon his horrible dedys* = 'peccandi' (*Sal* 16.3).

372 *the hand ner . . . the yonge men* = 'manus aut animus' (*Sal* 16.3), amplified via *Val*: 'Manus animus: illorum iuuenum' (sig. b3^{r}).

376–7 *all the contreys . . . oppressid with dett*. *Sal*: 'aes alienum per omnis terras ingens erat' (16.4). 'contreys abow`t´e the citee' and 'in þe warrys oppressid with dett' follow *Val*: 'omnes finitimæ ciuitates'; 'propter assidua bella quibus oppressæ fuerant' (sig. b3^{r}).

378 *prodygally*. See Introduction, p. lii.

379 *bataill among the citezens* = 'ciuile bellum' (*Sal* 16.4).

381 *senator of strengith of armes* = 'exercitus' (*Sal* 16.5). On 'strengith of armes', cf. 195–6*n*. For a similar translation of *exercitus*, cf. 1326.

382 *He hymselfe*. Sc., Catiline.
stode in the . . . be chosen consul = 'consulatum petenti' (*Sal* 16.5).

384–5 *mete and accordyng . . . appetyte of Catelyne* = 'opportuna Catilinae' (*Sal* 16.5), amplified via *Val*: 'Opportuna: ualde accommodata ad id quod Catilina exoptabat' (sig. b3^{r}).

386 *aboute the begynnyng of Februarii*. Working from *Val*, 'Kalend. Ianuarias: circa principium mensis februarii' (sig. b3^{r}). See also Introduction, p. xxxvi.

387–8 *callid his company to his counseill*='appellare' (*Sal* 17.1).

389–90 *what assistaunce he . . . not to haue*='opes suas' (*Sal* 17.1).

391 *that wolde take . . . in the rebellion*='coniurationis' (*Sal* 17.1).

391–2 *whan he had . . . after his mynde*='Vbi satis explorata sunt quae uoluit' (*Sal* 17.2). 'compassid' used thus, transitively, antedates *OED*, s.v. 'compass', v.[1], sense I.3.a, 'To consider, ponder, meditate, "go through"'. *Con*'s usage here resonates with both transitive and intransitive usages in Douglas's *Eneados*, e.g. 'Within my mynde compasyng', 'That with hym self can mony thing cumpas', in *Eneados*, ed. Bawcutt with Cunningham, VII.prol.151, X.3.96. Cf. also *MED*, s.v. 'compassen', v., sense 3.

394 *of the noble degre of senatouris*='senatorii ordinis' (*Sal* 17.3).

395–9 *Puplius Lentulus Sura . . . P. Capito*. This list of names proved troublesome for early editors: there were extensive variations between, and errors in, early editions here. Errors were especially rife in *LaetT*. Hence Parrasio, in his heavily annotated copy of the *Bellum Catilinae*, adds a full suite of corrections for these names (see Cambridge, King's College, Bryant.XV.3.3 [**1490**], sig. b2[v]); on Parrasio, cf. Introduction, p. xxxiv. In contrast, our translator seems to have made only occasional corrections to these names in his copy of *LaetT*; these corrections (or lack thereof) are detailed in the following notes.

395 *Puplius Lentulus Sura*. *Sal*: 'P. Lentulus Sura' (17.3). *LaetT* gives 'P. Lentulus' then 'P. F. Sura', or 'P. L.' then 'P. F. Sura' (as does *BritT*). *Con* may correct *LaetT* via *ParisT* or *IncT*, which give 'P. Lentulus Sura' or close variants thereof.

P. Antronius. *Sal*: 'P. Autronius' (17.3). Variants in *LaetT* commentary editions include 'P. Antronius' (**1492.2**, following **1490**), 'P. Antonius' (**1493.1**, **1493.2**, **1494**, **1495.2**, **1497.4**, **1497.5**), and 'P. Atronius' (**1491**, **1493.3**). If **1491** or **1493.3** were the translator's source, *Con* may correct to 'Antronius' from Beroaldo's edition (where that reading appears) or from later in **1491** or **1493.3** where the name is correctly printed with medial **n** after **A**, or with a macron to signal **n** (cf. 418, 430, 1083, 1139). No incunable ever spells the name 'Autronius', which is why this edition always transcribes the name as 'Antronius', even though the second letter could be interpreted in MS Nn.3.6 as either **n** or **u** (two minims).

Lvcius Cassius Longinus. *Sal*: 'L. Cassius Longinus' (17.3). All *LaetT* commentary editions give 'L. Cassius' and then 'L. F. Longinus', or close variants thereof (as does *BritT*). *Con* may correct from the reading 'lucius cassius longinus' that was transmitted via *IncT* and *ParisT*. NB. John Claymond in his copy subpuncts the 'F.' (Oxford, Corpus Christi College, ϕ.C.4.6(2) [**1492.2**], sig. b3[r]).

395–6 *Marcus Cethegus*. *Sal*: 'C. Cethegus' (17.3). *Con* follows *LaetT* 'M. Cethægus' (as also in *BritT*). Only *IncT* and *ParisT* (and, thereafter, only Aldine editions onward) give 'C. Cethegus' or 'G. Cethegus', or close variants. John Claymond in his copy subpuncts 'M.' and supplies 'C' in the margin (Oxford, Corpus Christi College, ϕ.C.4.6(2) [**1492.2**], sig. b3[r]).

396 *P. Servius Sila*. *Sal*: 'P. et Ser. Sullae Ser. filii' (17.3). A crux for early editors and printers, attracting an especially wide range of variants. Among *LaetT* editions, *Con*'s solution is closest in content and orthography to **1491** and **1493.3**, which are the only two imprints to give 'P. Seruius. Sila. F. filius' (*Con* does not translate 'F. filius').

L. Vargenteius. *Sal*: 'L. Vargunteius' (17.3). *LaetT* commentary editions vary between 'L. Vargunteius' and 'L. Varguteius' (incl. **1491**, **1493.3**). If **1491** or **1493.3** were *Con*'s base text, the translator could have corrected with medial **n** from e.g. Beroaldo's edition, which gives the reading 'vargunteus'. A spelling with medial **n** is also transmitted via most *IncT* editions. No incunable prints medial **en**, which probably results in *Con* from an error in scribal transmission. John Claymond in his copy interlineates **n** to correct 'Varguteius' to 'Vargunteius' (Oxford, Corpus Christi College, ϕ.C.4.6(2) [**1492.2**], sig. b3[r]). On this name, cf. 661*n*, 1083*n*.

396–7 *M. Porcius Leca*. *Sal*: 'M. Porcius Laeca' (17.3). *LaetT* commentary editions give 'M. Porcius' then 'M. F. Læca', or close variants (as does *BritT*). *Con* may correct from the reading 'marcus porcius lecca' as was transmitted via Beroaldo's edition and several *IncT* editions. NB. John Claymond in his copy subpuncts 'M.F.', leaving 'M. Portius Læca' (Oxford, Corpus Christi College, ϕ.C.4.6(2) [**1492.2**], sig. b3[r]).

397 *Lvcius Calphurnius*. Om. in *Sal*, *IncT*, and *ParisT*. This name is new to *LaetT* and persists in editions until it was (correctly) deleted in the 1509 Aldine edition. Of the two readings in *LaetT* commentary editions, *Con* follows 'Calphurnius' (as in **1491**, **1493.1**, **1493.3**, **1495.2**, **1497.4**) rather than 'Calphurinus' (as in **1492.2**, **1493.2**, **1494**, **1497.5**). John Claymond in his copy subpuncts 'Calphurinus' (Oxford, Corpus Christi College, ϕ.C.4.6(2) [**1492.2**], sig. b3[r]).

L. Bestia. *Sal*: 'L. Bestia' (17.3). *LaetT* and *BritT* give 'L. F. Bestia' or close variants. *Con* may drop the 'F.' in deference to the reading transmitted via *ParisT* ('lucius bestia'), or the 'F.' may accidentally have been om. by the translator or scribe. Historically, this refers to the same individual who has already been identified in this list of names as 'Lvcius Calphurnius'.

397–8 *of the degre of meane gentilmen*='ex equestri ordine' (*Sal* 17.4). *Sal* refers to *equites*, the second tier of ancient Rome's property-based classes, as explained e.g. in Soldus's 1495 commentary on *BJ*: 'Tres ordines erant Rome. Ordo Senatorius. Ordo equestris. Ordo plebeius' (**1495.3**, sig. f1[v]). *Val* twice distinguishes between the *ordo senatorius* and *ordo equestris* (sigs. b4[r], c4[v]), and perhaps the inherent class implications inspire *Con*'s use of 'meane gentilmen' to translate the latter (as also at 660). 'gentylmen' was likewise used to translate *equites* in Paynell's *Conspiracie* (*Conspiracie*, sig. T2[v]; cf. Felici, *De coniuratione*, sig. N4[r]). The phrase 'meane gentilmen' could also more generally describe men below the rank of lords and princes: cf. e.g. Starkey, *A Dialogue between Pole and Lupset*, ed. Mayer, 64. Cf. *Con*'s translations of *equites* elsewhere as men of 'low degre' (956) and 'the garde of gentilmen' (1164–5).

398 *Marcus Fulvius*. *Sal*: 'M. Fuluius Nobilior' (17.4). 'Nobilior' not translated, though all incunables have the cognomen 'Nobilior' (variously with upper- or lower-case **n**). *Con* may not have understood what 'Nobilior' meant (*Val* does not gloss it).

398–9 *P. Gabinivs*; *P. Capito*. *Sal*: 'P. Gabinius Capito' (17.4). The duplication of one historical individual into two is explained by the *LaetT* (and *BritT*) variant 'P. Gabinius' followed by 'P. F. Capito', or close variants thereof (except for **1498**, which gives 'P. Sabinus' then 'P. Fuluius Capito'). *IncT* and *ParisT* give 'P. Gabinius Capito', or close variants. The 'F.' in 'P. F. Capito' may accidentally have been om. by the translator or scribe. John Claymond in his copy, correctly, subpuncts 'P. F.', leaving 'P. Gabinius Capito' (Oxford, Corpus Christi College, *ϕ*.C.4.6(2) [**1492.2**], sig. b3^{r}).

400 *but of low and symple degre*='ex coloniis et muncipiis' (*Sal* 17.4).

400–1 *noble and wors`h'ipfull*='nobiles' (*Sal* 17.4).

402 *after a more secrete manere*. *Sal*: 'paulo occultius' (17.5). 'paulo' not translated, perhaps accidentally om. by the translator or scribe.

405–6 *the which covetid . . . plesauntly and pompously*. *Sal*: 'quibus in otio . . . uiuere copia erat' (17.6). Inaccurate translation, suggested by a misinterpretation of *Val*: 'In ocio uel molliter: et ideo cupiebant aliquem regem qui suis cupiditatibus concederet' (sig. b3^{v}).

406–7 *to aventure vpon . . . leve the certayn*='incerta pro certis . . . malebant' (*Sal* 17.6).

408 *Marcus Lucius Crassus*. *Sal*: 'M. Licinium Crassum' (17.7). *IncT*, *ParisT*, and *LaetT* give 'Lucinium' or 'Licinium', or close variants. *Con*'s mistake could result from scribal transmission if the translator or scribe abbreviated Licinium as 'L.', since this letter was conventionally expanded to 'Lucius', as noted e.g. in a glossary owned by Richard Bole: 'per l. lucius' (Oxford, Balliol College, MS 121, f. iv^{v}). Some *BritT* editions make this mistake, printing 'M. L. Crassum'.

410 *invyed and bare hym malice*='inuisus ipsi' (*Sal* 17.7).

410–11 *was of so . . . powere of `a'rmys*='magnum exercitum ductabat' (*Sal* 17.7).

411–12 *he . . . his*. Sc., Crassus; Pompey's.

415–16 *the destruccion of the comen wele*='contra rem publicam' (*Sal* 18.1).

418 *Marcus Lepido*. *Sal*: 'M'. Lepido' (18.2), i.e. Manius Lepidus. *Con*'s expansion as 'Marcus' correctly expands 'M.', as was printed in all incunables. Ramsey explains that the M'. praenomen was 'invariably corrupted to M. (=Marcus) in the MSS' (Ramsey, 110).

Puplius Antronius. *Sal*: 'P. Autronius' (18.2). *LaetT* commentary editions give either 'P. Atonius' (**1491**), 'P. Atronius' (**1492.2**, **1493.1**, **1493.2**, **1493.3**), or 'P.

Antonius' (**1494**, **1495.2**, **1497.4**, **1497.5**). *Con* may correct *LaetT* from the 'antronius' reading as transmitted e.g. via Beroaldo's edition, or from elsewhere in *LaetT* when the same name is printed with medial **r** and either medial **n** or a macron to signal **n** (cf. 395, 430, 1083, 1139).

420–1 *in the lawis . . . corrupcion of money*='legibus ambitus' (*Sal* 18.2), amplified via *Val*: 'Ambitus: lex ambitus erat ut qui consulatum uel magistratum quempiam uel largitionibus corrupto populo cum secuti essent ipsi punirentur' (sig. b3[v]). McGushin explains that '*Leges ambitus* were laws passed to put down corrupt practices, bribery in particular, at elections' (McGushin, 124). 'ambitus' is engrossed in the MS and italicized in this edition on the assumption that *Con* (correctly) quotes the word as a Lat. common noun; alternatively, the translator or scribe may erroneously have interpreted *ambitus* as a person's name.

421 *opyn punyshment*='poenas' (*Sal* 18.2). A common collocation: cf. e.g. Elyot, '*The Image of Governance' and Other Dialogues of Counsel*, ed. Carlson, 196; Udall, *Apophthegmes*, sig. b6[v].

423–4 *because he was . . . þe iurisdiccion of* ='pecuniarum repetundarum reus' (*Sal* 18.3), amplified via *Val*: 'Pecuniarum: quia prouinciam pecuniam expoliasset: ille dicebatur reus pecuniarum qui prouinciam cum magistratum gereret pecunia spoliasse diceretur' (sig. b3[v]).

425–6 *and had not . . . of the consulles*='quod intra legitumos dies profiteri nequiuerat' (*Sal* 18.3). On Catiline's disqualification, see McGushin, 126–8; Ramsey, 111. 'tryall' antedates 1st citation in *OED*, s.v. 'trial', n.[1], sense 5, but cf. *MED*, s.v. 'trial', n.[1], sense 1(a).

430 *Antronius*. *Sal*: 'Autronius' (18.5). *Con* follows *LaetT* commentary editions that give 'antronius' (**1491**, **1492.2**, **1493.2**, **1493.3**); other *LaetT* commentary editions give 'atronius' (**1493.1**) or 'antonius' (**1494**, **1495.2**, **1497.4**, **1497.5**). On this name, cf. also 395, 418, 1083, 1139.

made apoyntment. *Sal*: 'circiter Nonas Decembris consilio communicato' (18.5). 'circiter Nonas Decembris' not translated, perhaps because *Con* did not understand the Roman date: cf. 433, 437, 694.

431 *Cota*. *Sal*: 'Cottam'. Cf. e.g. **1491** 'cotam', **1493.3** 'co.tam' (*sic*).

431–3 *in the convocacion . . . their congregacion thether*='in Capitolio' (*Sal* 18.5), amplified via *Val*: 'in capitolio: cum senatus eos conuocassent consules' (sig. b3[v]). 'convocacion' is suggested by *Val*'s 'conuocassent', but may also suggest 'convocations' or gatherings of medieval English clergy. 'congregacion' could perhaps echo the *congregatio magna* of the University of Oxford, the University's chief governing body since the thirteenth century: see *MED*, s.v. 'congregacioun', n., sense 3(c); *OED*, s.v. 'congregation', n., sense 3.b; Brockliss, *The University of Oxford: A History*, 19–20. *Con* misunderstands both *Capitolium* and the Lat. preposition 'in'; correctly, the plot is to murder the consuls *on* the Capitoline Hill.

433 *in the* kalendas *of Ianuary*. *Sal*: 'Kalendis Ianuariis' (18.5). I.e. on the first of January. On the untranslated '*kalendas*', cf. Introduction, pp. lii–liii; see also 430*n*, 437, 694.

433–4 *by suche forse . . . auctoryte of* `*c*'*onsulles*. *Sal*: 'fascibus conreptis' (18.5). 'auctoryte of `c'onsulles' follows *Val*'s gloss of 'fascibus' as 'insignibus consulum' (sig. b3^{v}). 'by suche forse' not in *Sal*.

435 *with strengith of armour*='cum exercitu' (*Sal* 18.5). Cf. 195–6*n*.

the contreys of Speyne. *Sal*: 'duas Hispanias' (18.5). I.e. the two provinces of Spain, as *Val* later explains in its gloss of 19.1: 'duplex est hispania .s. hispania citra hiberum fluuium: quæ citerior appellatur: et hispania ultra hiberum quæ ulterior appellatur' (sig. b4^{r}). 'contreys' here means 'provinces' or (more generally) 'regions', depending on the extent of *Con*'s contextual knowledge: cf. 446, 532.

436 *asspied and knowen*='cognita' (*Sal* 18.6).

437 *the* nonas *of February next folowing*. *Sal*: 'in Nonas Februarias' (18.6). I.e. the fifth of February. On the untranslated '*nonas*', cf. Introduction, pp. lii–liii; see also 430*n*, 433, 694.

439–40 *preventid and to . . . appoynted amonges theim*='maturasset . . . signum . . . dare' (*Sal* 18.8). 'appoynted amonges theim' not in *Sal*.

440–1 *afore the counseill house*. *Sal*: 'pro curia' (18.8). See Introduction, p. l.

442–3 *the greate company . . . men of armes*='armati' (*Sal* 18.8).

443–4 *not than gadred . . . at his calling*='nondum . . . conuenerant' (*Sal* 18.8), where 'nor all thing redy at his calling' is *Con*'s interpolation. On 'all thing', cf. *MED*, s.v. 'al-thing, al(le thing', n., sense 1(a).

444 *all theire purpose and intent*='consilium' (*Sal* 18.8).

445 *commyssion graunted hym to be pretor*. *Sal*: 'quaestor pro praetore' (19.1). 'quaestor' is not translated, probably because this noun is om. in all *LaetT* commentary editions (as in *BritT*, though it appears in *IncT* and *ParisT*). 'commyssion graunted hym' not in *Sal*.

446 *into the nerer contrey of Spayne*. *Sal*: 'in citeriorem Hispaniam' (19.1). On the amplification and meaning of 'contrey', cf. 435*n*.

thorow the laboure of Marcus Crassus. *Sal*: 'adnitente Crasso' (19.1). *Con* follows 'adnitente M. Crasso', as in all *LaetT* (as also in *BritT* and most *IncT*).

452–3 *in his iourney*='iter faciens' (*Sal* 19.3). 'iourney' probably means 'march' in a military sense, as suggested by *Val*: 'Iter faciens: agmen exercitus ducens in hispaniam occisus est' (sig. b4^{r}).

453 *of the gentilmen horsemen*='ab equitibus' (*Sal* 19.3). Idiosyncratic translation of *equites*. The class implications suggested by 'gentilmen' are misleading in this context; the word probably arises here from *Val*'s gloss of *eques* elsewhere as 'equestris ordinis', which *Con* twice renders as 'degre of meane gentilmen': cf. 397–8*n*, 660*n*.

457–8 *by his `advises'*=‘uoluntate’ (*Sal* 19.5). This odd pl. may only be used because the addition of word-final **s** helped cover up the partially erased word over which ‘advises’ is written. Cf. *MED*, s.v. ‘avis’, n., sense 6(c).

466 *ferre from the heryng of straungers*. *Sal*: ‘omnibus arbitris procul amotis’ (20.1). *Con* renders the abl. absol. as an adverbial phrase. ‘straungers’ does not fully capture the sense of *arbitri*, despite *Val*’s helpful explanation: ‘arbitri proprie dicuntur qui alienæ rei quasi testes intersunt’ (sig. b4[r]).

466–7 *aftyr this maner folowing*. Written a line below the ruled text block, preceded by a paraph.

481 *of myght and power*=‘potentium’ (*Sal* 20.7).

482 *kynges and prynces*=‘reges tetrarchae’ (*Sal* 20.7). *Tetrarchae* are ‘petty monarchs or rulers (*tetrarches*, a Greek term, is lit. the ruler of the quarter part of a country)’ (Ramsey, 119).

482–3 *mennys wages and their rewardes*=‘stipendia’ (*Sal* 20.7). Cf. e.g. Reuchlin, *Vocabularius*: ‘Stipendium . . . dicitur lucrum. precium. fructus laboris. Proprie quidem stipendium dicitur quod datur militibus soldariis pro precio’ (sig. w5[r]).

484 *comons of lyke reputacion*=‘uolgus’ (*Sal* 20.7), with ‘comons’ influenced by *Val*: ‘Fuimus uulg. reputati fuimus quasi uulgus ignobile’ (sig. b4[v]).

486–7 *power, honour, richesse*. *Sal*: ‘gratia potentia honos diuitiae’ (20.8). ‘gratia’ not translated.

493–4 *We haue youthe . . . stomake and hardynes*=‘uiget aetas, animus ualet’ (*Sal* 20.10).

498 *these excedyng habundaunces of goodes*=‘diuitias’ (*Sal* 20.11).

498–9 *to bylde pompouse . . . in the sees*. *Sal*: ‘in extruendo mari’ (20.11), where ‘howsis’ follows *Val*: ‘Extruendo mari: in ædificandis ædificiis in ipso mari: quia sicut superius dictum est in ipso mari ædificia condita sunt’ (sig. b4[v]). This expression ‘appears to refer to the same practice of building houses over the water *molibus iniectis* that was described at 13.1 by the words *maria constrata*’ (Ramsey, 121).

499–500 *to make for . . . the hye mountaynes*=‘montibus coaequandis’ (*Sal* 20.11), amplified via *Val*: ‘Montibus coæquandis: explanandis montibus: ut ibi ædificia faciant amœnitate plena’ (sig. b4[v]). On ‘pleasures’ as being suggested by ‘amœnitate’, cf. e.g. the gloss of ‘Amenium’ as ‘locus pulcer et delectabilis’ in Reuchlin, *Vocabularius*, sig. b5[v].

501 *they also haue . . . how`sh'oldes or moo*. *Sal*: ‘Illos binas aut amplius domos continuare’ (20.11). *Con* misinterprets ‘continuare’ as ‘contynually’, perhaps because the translator only looks so far as the first half (‘Continue’) of *Val*’s gloss of ‘continuare’ as ‘Continue iugiter’ (sig. b4[v]).

501–2 *we to haue . . . of our awne*. *Sal*: ‘nobis larem familiarem nusquam ullum esse’ (20.11). *Con* mistranslates ‘nusquam’ as ‘neuer’. ‘chamber’ translates *lares* as a metonym for *domus*, as is suggested e.g. in Reuchlin, *Vocabularius*, sig. n5[v]. *Lares* is also glossed metonymically, as 'a lytell cotage', by a Tudor annotator of a Lyon 1512 edition (BodL, 8° H 183 Art., sig. B8[v]).

502–3 *goodly pictures, fressh and shynyng ymages*. *Sal*: 'tabulas signa toreumata' (20.12). For 'pictures', see *Val*: 'Tabulas pictas' (sig. b5[r]). For 'ymages', see *Val*: 'Signa: statuas uel marmoreas uel eburneas uel argenteas uel aureas' (sig. b5[r]). 'toreumata' (='fressh and shynyng') is translated as an adj. modifying 'signa' when it should correctly be taken as a noun, as *Val*'s gloss clarifies: 'Toreumata: uasa torno facta ut sunt pateræ pulcherrimæ cathedræ: et alia huiusmodi' (sig. b5[r]).

503 *The olde maners they disspise*. Not in *Sal*. *Con* follows *LaetT* editions, all of which (except **1490**) interpolate 'uetera negligunt' between 'emunt' and 'noua diruunt' in *Sal* (20.12).

504–6 *But all maner . . . ouercome their richesse*. *Sal*: 'postremo omnibus modis . . . suas uincere nequeunt' (20.12). *Con* misconstrues 'summa ludibine' (='mooste bysely') as modifying 'uexant' when correctly the phrase is part of a new clause after 'tamen'.

508 *So, in the extreme of it*='denique' (*Sal* 20.13). Absolute use of 'extreme' antedates 1st citation in *OED*, s.v. 'extreme', n., sense 1. Cf. e.g. a more standard translation of *denique* as 'in conclusyon' in Elyot, *Dictionary*, sig. F2[r]. Translations of 'denique' in Barclay's *BJ* most frequently include '(and/but) finally' and 'at (the) last', but also 'And so', 'And shortly', 'Anon after', 'But whan', 'And also', 'But brefely to speke', and 'At conclusyon' (Barclay, *Famous Cronycle*, ed. Waite, 50, 54, 86, 95, 106, 107, 122, 136, 143, 144, 169, 171, 181, 184, 185, 188, 194).

509–10 *Wherfore now aryse and bestyrre you*. *Sal*: 'Quin igitur expergiscimini?' (20.14). The sense of *quin* is not correctly captured. 'aryse and bestyrre you'= 'expergiscimini'.

510–11 *gretly desyred*='optastis' (*Sal* 20.14).

514 *chose you*='uos hortantur' (*Sal* 20.15). **1491**='hortentur'. Not glossed in *Val*, though *Asc* glosses the phrase as 'incendant vos magis quam oratio mea' (sig. c3[v]). Seemingly an idiosyncratic use of 'chose' to mean 'encourage', perhaps suggesting that Catiline's speech could make people self-select to join his cause. Cf. Reuchlin, *Vocabularius*, s.v. 'hortor': '.i. suadere . confortare . instigare . vel instigari' (sig. z7[r]).

517 *with your helpe togader*='uobiscum una' (20.17).

youre mynde. *Sal*: 'animus' (20.17). Misleading, since sg. 'animus' implies Catiline's own mind.

518 *to be in bondage and thraldome*='seruire' (*Sal* 20.17). The senses in which these nouns are intended depends on *Con*'s understanding of Roman slavery (cf. 'vile' [114*n* etc.], 'bondemen' [1570*n*]); see also Introduction, pp. l–li. 'bondage' may especially seem to overlay the idea of Roman slavery with medieval feudalism: cf. *OED*, s.v. 'bondage', n.; *MED*, s.v. 'bondage', n.

519 *in auctoryte and rewle*=‘imperare’ (*Sal* 20.17).

521–2 *ne nought they . . . good hope in*=‘neque spes bona ulla’ (*Sal* 21.1), amplified via *Val*: ‘Mala spes nihil habebant. et nihil sperabant quod deterius est’ (sig. b5[r]).

522–3 *thowe they sawe . . . was in quyete*. *Sal*: ‘tametsi illis quieta . . . magna merces uidebatur’ (21.1). *Con* follows the *LaetT* variant ‘quietam rem publicam’ (as in *BritT*). ‘prayes’=*Sal* ‘merces’, i.e. ‘value’ in this context, in line with *Val*’s (accurate) explanation of ‘merces’ as a non-monetary reward: ‘Magna merces: uidebatur tametsi loco mercedis ponebant ocium et quietem rei publicæ perturbare’ (sig. b5[r]).

525–6 *for that they . . . make suche warre*=‘armis’ (*Sal* 21.1).

528 *new grauntes in wryting of possescions*. *Sal*: ‘tabulas nouas’ (21.2). On the amplification, see Introduction, p. xxxvii. ‘wryting’ refers to the making of deeds: cf. *MED*, s.v. ‘writing(e’, ger., sense 2(a).

529 *the riche mennys goodes to be attaynted*. *Sal*: ‘proscriptionem locupletium’ (*Sal* 21.2). The interpolation of ‘goodes’, and the consequent meaning of ‘attaynted’ as ‘subject to attainder’ or ‘forfeited’, misses the correct sense of ‘proscriptionem’.

529–30 *the hye dignyties . . . and welthy offices*=‘magistratus sacerdotia’ (*Sal* 21.2). ‘welthy’ in this sense, meaning ‘valuable’, antedates 1st citation in *OED*, s.v. ‘wealthy’, adj., sense 4.

531–2 *the nerrer contrey of Spayne*=‘in Hispania citeriore’ (*Sal* 21.3). On the amplification and meaning of ‘contrey’ here, cf. 435*n*.

532 *Puplius Siccio Nucerius*. *Sal*: ‘P. Sittium Nucerinum’ (21.3). See Introduction, pp. xxix–xxx.

in Mauritania in Affrica=‘in Mauretania’ (*Sal* 21.3). *Con*’s interpolation draws on elementary geographical knowledge. E.g. Mauritania’s location in Africa is clear in Higden, *Polycronicon*, trans. Trevisa, ff. 24[r], 173[v]. Cf., however, *Con*’s earlier mishap re the location of Carthage (241*n*).

533 *the which*. Sc., Piso and Puplius.

535–6 *verrey famyliar and frendly to hym*=‘familiarem’ (*Sal* 21.3).

536 *with all displeasures and necessities*=‘omnibus necessitudinibus’ (*Sal* 21.3).

537 *to sett vpon bataill*. *Sal*: ‘agundi’ (21.3). *Con* follows *Val*: ‘Agendi .s. ciuilis belli’ (sig. b5[v]).

539–40 *he instructed and yaue theim monycions*=‘admonebat’ (*Sal* 21.4).

545 *his sewte for þe dignyte of consull*=‘petitionem suam’ (*Sal* 21.5), amplified via *Val*: ‘Petitionem suam. scilicet consulatus ut suffragia uestra sint mihi parata’ (sig. b5[v]).

550–1 *after they had . . . promys of confeddresye*=‘post execrationem’ (*Sal* 22.2), amplified via *Val*: ‘Post execrationem etc. post maledictionem qua execrati sunt multa mala in seipsos uertere si non effecti essent fideliter ea quæ promiserant' (sig. b5[v]).

555 *wykked and horrible dede*='facinoris' (*Sal* 22.2).

557–8 *those men that . . . afterward ayenst Cicero*. *Sal*: 'qui Ciceronis inuidiam . . . est, leniri credebant' (22.3). *Con* misses or misinterprets the acc.–inf., misconstruing the grammatical roles of 'inuidiam' and 'leniri' and treating pass. inf. 'leniri' as though it were an active inf.

562 *censores*. If this is intended as an Engl. word rather than untranslated Latin (cf. *Sal* 'censores', 23.1), it antedates 1st citation in *OED*, s.v. 'censor', n.

deprivid. *Sal*: 'mouerant' (23.1). *Con* translates 'amouerant', as printed in all Sallust incunabula; *Val* glosses as 'remouerant' (sig. b6[r]).

563 *for greate vylony and shame*='probri gratia' (*Sal* 23.1), perhaps via *Val*: 'Probri: uituperii' (sig. b6[r]).

567 *that had a . . . name in vice*. *Sal*: 'muliere nobili' (23.3), interpreted via *Val*: 'Nobilis: famosa et clara: dicitur non solum uirtute insignis: sed uitio cognitus ille qui uel uirtutibus uel uitiis ingentibus omnibus cognitus est: nobilis appellatur: unde nobile scortum: quia multis cognitum est' (sig. b6[r]).

570 *he thretenyd to sley hir*='minari . . . ferro' (*Sal* 23.3).

571 *applied and obeyd*='sibi . . . foret' (*Sal* 23.3).

571–2 *fowler and more dredfully*='ferocius' (*Sal* 23.3).

572–3 *this straunge and prowde dealyng*='insolentiae' (*Sal* 23.4).

573–4 *be lytill and . . . all the matere*='causa cognita' (*Sal* 23.4). On 'be lytill and lytill', cf. 147*n*.

575 *whan his bakke . . . hit vnto hir*. *Sal*: 'sublato auctore' (23.4). *Con* introduces the metaphor of a turned back, working from *Val*'s (misguided) gloss of *sublatus* as 'discedente': 'Sublato autore: discedente autore coni[u]rationis qui autor fuerat aperiundæ coniurationis: scilicet Curius' (sig. b6[r]).

582 *yet he was . . . vp to worshippe*='homo nouos' (*Sal* 23.6), amplified via *Val*: 'Nouus homo dicitur qui paulo ante ab infimo gradu ad summum officium ascenderit: ut tribunatus et consulatus ut Cicero fuit' (sig. b6[r]).

583–4 *in the day of the commyssyon*='comitiis habitis' (*Sal* 24.1). Cf. 'day of the commyssion' (633), translating 'dies comitiorum' (*Sal* 26.5).

585 *dede*. I.e. deed.

587 *strengith of armour*='arma' (*Sal* 24.2). Cf. 195–6*n*.

587–8 *in the mete . . . for his bataill*='locis opportunis' (*Sal* 24.2).

588–9 *vpon his owne credens*=‘sua’ (*Sal* 24.2).

589 *Fesulanum*. *Sal*: ‘Faesulas’ (24.2). *Con* translates using a form given later in *Sal*, at 43.1, and is either unaware of or chooses not to use the (correct) nom. form given in *Val*’s gloss at 24.2: ‘Fesulas: fesulæ oppidum est’ (sig. b6ᵛ). *Con* later refers to this town (the modern Fiesole) with the accusative form ‘Fesulas’, including when his copy text gives ‘Fesulanum’ (639, 692, 700, 990; *Sal* 27.1, 30.1, 30.3, 43.1). Cf. *Con*’s misunderstanding of ‘Faesulanum’ at 1658.

592–3 *bothe men and women*. *Sal*: ‘homines’ (24.3). ‘and women’ pre-empts ‘mulieres etiam’ (*Sal* 24.3).

596 *desyris of lecherye and covetousnes*=‘luxuriae’ (*Sal* 24.3).

598 *the vile men*=‘seruitia’ (*Sal* 24.4). On ‘vile’, cf. 114, 697, 712, 1030, 1064, 1176, 1573.

603–4 *by hirsilff oone . . . and right fortunate*. ‘right fortunate’=‘fortunata’ (*Sal* 25.2); ‘by hirsilff oone of all the worlde’ is not in *Sal*, and adopts the intensifying use of ‘one’ as in the type ‘one the best man’. The sense is that Sempronia is the world’s best in ‘byrth’ and ‘bewty’, rather than one of the best. See further Introduction, p. liv.

607–8 *the instrumentes and . . . lustis and pleasaunce*=‘instrumenta luxuriae’ (*Sal* 25.2).

609 *honour*=‘decus’ (*Sal* 25.3), perhaps *Val*: ‘Decus honor’ (sig. b6ᵛ). The Engl. is gendered: cf. *MED*, s.v. ‘honour’, n., sense 2(c), ‘feminine repute, reputation for purity’; *OED*, s.v. ‘honour’, n., sense 7.a.

the. I.e. thee.

610 *they were so comyn*. Not in *Sal*, but cf. 567.

613–14 *to forswere hir . . . in truste of*=‘creditum abiurauerat’ (*Sal* 25.4), with amplification suggested by *Val*: ‘Creditum abiurauerat: depositam et commendatam ei rem iure iurando negauerat. Nam abiurare est rem creditam periurio negare’ (sig. b6ᵛ).

614–15 *to helpe forwarde . . . dyvers men also*=‘caedis conscia’ (*Sal* 25.4), amplified via *Val*: ‘Cædis conscia: sibi communicata fuerat cædes hominum’ (sig. b6ᵛ).

615–16 *But with thise . . . mesery and nede*=‘luxuria atque inopia praeceps abierat’ (*Sal* 25.4). ‘luxuria atque inopia’ is condensed as ‘with thise craftes’. ‘into greate mesery and nede’ amplifies ‘ad inopiam’ in *Val*: ‘Luxuria atque inopia: nam quia luxuriæ et uoluptati operam dederat: ideo ad inopiam redacta erat: ut suas cup[i]ditates expleret’ (sig. b6ᵛ).

616–17 *to make solace . . . whansoeuer they lustyd*=‘iocum mouere’ (*Sal* 25.5), perhaps via *Val*: ‘Iocum mouere .i. ridicula uerba proponere et iactare quibus ad risum sodales mouerentur’ (sig. b6ᵛ).

619 *moche myrth, deyntynes, and fressh disporte*='multae facetiae multusque lepos' (*Sal* 25.5). 'myrth' and 'disporte' collocate elsewhere: cf. e.g. Lydgate, *Siege of Thebes*, ed. Erdmann, i. 3035–6; Berners, *The thirde and fourthe boke of Sir Iohn Froissart*, sig. BBB2^r. 'deyntynes' antedates 1st citation in *OED*, s.v. 'daintiness', n.

621 *for the eleccion of consulles*='consulatum' (*Sal* 26.1).

624 *he devysed and . . . destruccion of Cicero*='insidias parabat Ciceroni' (*Sal* 26.1).

625 *he*. Sc., Cicero.

crafte. Probably pejorative since it translates 'dolus' (*Sal* 26.2); cf. *Val*, 'Dolus: est mali ingenii cogitatio' (sig. c1^r).

626 *by hys greate gyftes and promyses*='multa pollicendo' (*Sal* 26.3).

628 *all the counseill and dryfte*='consilia' (*Sal* 26.3). On 'dryfte', see further Introduction, p. liv.

629–30 *in their covenaunt . . . of the citee*. *Sal*: 'pactione prouinciae' (26.4). *Con* interpolates 'for the savegarde of the citee' and otherwise amplifies from *Val*: 'Pactione prouinciæ. nam conuenerat inter eos ut prouincia extrema contingeret Antonio quæ nobilior erat: hoc autem fecit Cicero ut uoluntati Antonii morem gereret: et ipse urbis uni periculum coniurationis iminebat. Nam mos erat ut consules inter se prouincias sortirentur' (sig. c1^r). Cicero 'purchased his colleague's cooperation, or at least his neutrality, in the struggle against Catiline by offering to exchange the provinces that had been allotted to them. According to this arrangement, Antonius received the more lucrative province of Macedonia in place of Gallia Cisalpina' (Ramsey, 135).

631 *in þe parties*. Not in *Sal*.

632 *seruauntes*. *Sal*: 'clientium' (26.4). *Con* follows *Val*, 'Clientum: minorum: Nam clientes dicuntur qui sub maioris imperio sunt constituti' (sig. c1^r). NB. *Asc* explains correctly, though, that 'clientum' means 'eorum qui se colebant quod patronus eorum esset' (sig. c5^v).

634–5 *his besynes that . . . to dystroy Cicero*. *Sal*: 'insidiae quas consulibus in Campo fecerat' (26.5). Most *LaetT* (incl. **1491** and **1493.3**) give sg. 'consuli', hence 'Cicero' (as do all *IncT* and most *BritT*). *Con* also amplifies via *Val*: 'Neque insidias .i. cum nihil contra Ciceronem molliri posset ad ipsius Ciceronis perniciem' (sig. c1^r). 'in Campo' is not translated, probably because this detail is om. in *LaetT* (as also in *BritT*).

637 *vnder subtell and prevy meanes*='occulte' (*Sal* 26.5).

639–42 *sent . . . his waye aboute*. I.e. sent on his way.

639–40 *the same party of Tvscan*. *Sal*: 'eam partem Etruriae' (27.1). 'Tuscan' (i.e. *Etruria*) is also spelled thus in the description of Catiline's conspiracy in Lydgate, *Fall of Princes*, VI.3038.

640–1 *Lucius Septimius towarde the marchesses of Italye*. *Sal*: 'Septimium quendam Camertem in agrum Picenum' (27.1). *Con* translates *LaetT* 'L. Septimium' (as also in *BritT*), hence 'Lucius'. 'quendam Camertem' is not translated. 'marchesses' echoes 'marchiam' in *Val*'s gloss, 'In agrum picenum: in marchiam anconitanam' (sig. c1[r]). 'Picenum' may not be translated here because *Con* struggled with the word: cf. 707*n*.

644–5 *prevy sawtes to . . . distroyed the consull*. *Sal*: 'consulibus insidias' (27.2). *Con* follows *LaetT* 'consuli' (also the usual reading in *BritT*), hence sg. 'consull'. 'prevy sawtes' = 'insidias'. 'to haue distroyed' is interpolated to translate the sense of *insidias*+dat.

645 *crewell fyres* = 'incendia' (*Sal* 27.2).

646–7 *ware prevy weypon* = 'cum telo esse' (*Sal* 27.2).

650–1 *in the dede of the nyght*. *Sal*: 'intempesta nocte' (27.3). Phrase antedates 1st citation in *OED*, s.v. 'dead', n., sense 2. Cf. 764.

651–2 *by Marcus Porcius than his messangere*. *Sal*: 'per M. Porcium Laecam' (27.3). *Con* follows *Val*: 'hic hoc tempore præconis fecit officium' (sig. c1[r]). 'Laecam' om., perhaps because *Val* sows confusion by garbling its lemma as 'per marcum porcūlētā' (as printed in **1491**; cf. *Val* in **1493.3**, 'marcum porcum lentam').

652 *and att their metyng*. *Sal*: 'ibique' (27.4). *Con* follows *Val*: 'Ibi in concione eorum' (sig. c1[r]).

657 *was þe greate hynderans and lett* = 'multum officere' (*Sal* 27.4).

660 *of the degre of meane gentilmen* = 'eques' (*Sal* 28.1), via *Val*'s (accurate) gloss, 'Eques: quia equestris ordinis cuius erat' (sig. c1[r]). On 'meane gentilmen', cf. 397–8*n*, 453*n*.

661 *Varguteius*. *Sal*: 'Vargunteius' (28.1). No medial **n**, perhaps because certain *LaetT* editions (incl. **1491**, **1493.3**) print this name without either medial **n** or a macron: cf. also 396*n*, 1083*n*. Note in contrast, for example, that Parrasio in his copy corrects here (as elsewhere) by adding a macron above **u** (Cambridge, King's College, Bryant.XV.3.3 [**1490**], sigs. b2[v], b7[v], c7[v]); on Parrasio, cf. Introduction, p. xxxiv.

661–2 *at the same tyme* = 'ea nocte' (*Sal* 28.1).

668 *in Tushan*. *Sal*: 'in Etruria' (28.4). Cf. 639–40*n*, 990.

671–2 *thevis and vagaboundes* = 'latrones' (*Sal* 28.4).

673 *of the olde . . . then were laborers*. *Sal*: 'ex Sullanis coloniis' (28.4). 'olde frendys' follows *Val*: 'Ex syllanis colonis: ex illis qui amici fuissent syllæ' (sig. c1[v]). 'laborers' here means agricultural workers (cf. *MED*, s.v. 'labourer(e', n., sense 1[b]) and follows *LaetT* and *Val* 'colonis' (not 'coloniis'); cf. e.g. the gloss of *colonus* as 'terrae cultor' in Reuchlin, *Vocabularius*, sig. f6[r].

674–5 *of their prayes and spoylinges*=‘ex magnis rapinis’ (*Sal* 28.4).

676–7 *his mynde was . . . of bothe handes*=‘ancipiti malo permotus’ (*Sal* 29.1). ‘of bothe handes’ (=‘ancipiti’, literally ‘two-headed’) is an idiosyncratic way of saying ‘twofold’, anticipating the phrases ‘on (the) one hand’ and ‘on the other hand’, which are dated 1581 onwards by *OED*, s.v. ‘hand’, n., sense P.1.i.v.

678 *of his awne police and wisdome*=‘ab insidiis’ (*Sal* 29.1).

682–3 *that the consulles . . . do their dyligence*=‘darent operam consules’ (*Sal* 29.2). *Con* misses the significance of *Sal*’s wording, as does *Val*, who glosses ‘darent operam’ as ‘laborarent’ (sig. c1^v^). *Sal* in fact alludes to the *senatus consultum ultimum*, a decree that ‘served as a substitute for the dictatorship . . . It invested the consuls with exceptional powers (29.3) and effectively suspended a citizen’s right of *provocatio*, which ordinarily protected him from coercion by a magistrate . . . if the consul judged the state to be threatened’ (Ramsey, 140–1).

684 *of mooste myght and gretest auctoryte*=‘maxuma’ (*Sal* 29.3).

687–8 *the royall poour and extreme iugementes*=‘imperium atque iudicium summum’ (*Sal* 29.3). On the anachronism of ‘royall poour’, see Introduction, p. li. ‘extreme iugementes’ (i.e. the ability to pass sentences of execution) is a misleading translation of ‘iudicium summum’, since the *senatus consultum ultimum* did not obviously permit the execution of Roman citizens without proper trial. Indeed the fact that such executions took place under cover of this decree, as during the events of 63 BCE, was a source of fierce debate in late Republican Rome (see Momigliano and Lintott, ‘senatus consultum ultimum’). *Con*’s misinterpretation here simply follows the initial gloss offered in *Val* (‘I[u]dicium: sumere capitalem pœnam’), except that our translator either fails or elects not to incorporate the nuance that *Val* subsequently provides: ‘I[u]dicium: sumere capitalem pœnam: cum essent in castris imperatores licebat eis quemquam noxium capite uel alio supplicio afficere: sed in urbem nihil tale permittebatur: nisi hoc decretum factum fuisset’ (sig. c1^v^).

691 *Servius*. *Sal*: ‘Saenius’ (30.1). *Con* follows the *LaetT* variant ‘Seruius’ (as also in *ParisT* and *BritT*).

692 *from Fesulas*. *Sal*: ‘Faesulis’ (30.1). Cf. 589*n*.

694 *vj. dayes afore the begynnyng of Novembre*. *Sal*: ‘ante diem vi Kalendas Novembris’ (30.1). *Con* translates *Val*’s gloss, ‘ante sextum diem principii nouembris’ (sig. c1^v^), but neither *Con* nor *Val* is quite right, because Roman dates are counted inclusively; the correct date is 27 October. For the translator’s other difficulties with dates, cf. 430*n*, 433, 437.

695 *somme tolde signes and pronosticates*. *Sal*: ‘alii portenta atque prodigia nuntiabant’ (30.2). Most *LaetT* editions (incl. **1491**, **1493.3**) omit ‘atque prodigia nuntiabant’, so *Con* probably translates both ‘portenta’ and ‘prodigia’ here from the appearance of both nouns in *Val* (sig. c1^v^). On ‘pronosticates’, see Introduction,

p. xliii. *Portenta* and *prodigia* are more mundanely glossed as 'maruelles' and 'wonders', for example, in a Lyon 1518 edition of the *BC* that was signed by several sixteenth-century pupils of Eton College: see BodL, 8° F 75 Linc., sig. b4[v].

697 *vile persones*. Part of a translation of 'seruile bellum' (*Sal* 30.2); on 'vile', cf. 114, 598, 712, 1030, 1064, 1176, 1573.

699–700 *Qvintus Marcius was . . . auctoryte to Fesulas*. *Sal*: 'Q. Marcius Rex Faesulas' (30.3). *Con* translates 'rex' in line with *Val*, 'hic Martius huic sacerdotio præerat cum fesulis missus esset regio decore' (sig. c2[r]), not realizing that 'Rex' is Marcius' cognomen, as *Asc* notes: 'rex .s. cognomine' (sig. d1[r]). For the same confusion, cf. 772. On 'Fesulas', cf. 589*n*.

702 *from their contreys*. Interpolated.

702–3 *putte by of . . . in their conqueste*='inpediti ne triumpharent' (*Sal* 30.4).

707 *into the marchesse . . . citee callid Picenum*. *Sal*: 'in agrum Picenum' (30.4). 'marchesse' comes from an earlier *Val* gloss (cf. 640–1*n*), but this time *Con* also misunderstands 'agrum' as 'citee', apparently not realizing that 'Picenum' was a region rather than a municipality, town, or stronghold (cf. the available senses in *MED*, s.v. 'cite', n.; *OED*, s.v. 'city', n., sense 2); cf. 977, 1584. 'citee' may alternatively come from a later *Val* gloss: cf. 1580–1*n*.

711 *large rewardes*. *Sal*: 'praemium' (30.6). *Con* probably follows Lat. pl. 'præmia', as in *LaetT* (and *BritT*).

711–12 *to a bond or vile man*='seruo' (*Sal* 30.6). 'bond' and 'vile' both seem to misrepresent the exact sense of the Lat. For 'vile', cf. 114, 598, 697, 1030, 1064, 1176, 1573. For 'bond', cf. *MED*, s.v. 'bond(e', n.[2] and adj. See also Introduction, pp. l–li.

712 *in money CC.l.* libri. I.e. 250. *Sal*: 'sestertia centum' (30.6). *Con*'s calculation is correct based on *Val*'s conversion: 'sequitur ergo ut sestertium sit duarum librarum cum dimidia' (sig. c2[r]). But *Con* and *Val* are both inaccurate: the correct conversion is 250,000 *libri*, since '*sestertia* (neut.) is used as an adj., with *milia* understood, and denotes the sum of 1000 sesterces' (Ramsey, 144).

713 *.v[c].M[l].* libri. I.e. 500,000. *Sal*: 'sestertia ducenta [milia]' (30.6), where *LaetT* includes 'milia'. *Con*'s figure is correct based on *Val*'s conversion: cf. 712*n*.

714–15 *the quarelouse people . . . excersise of wepyns*='gladiatoriae familiae' (*Sal* 30.7), amplified via *Val*, 'Gladiatoriæ familiæ .i. qui gladiis dimicabant in ludis' (sig. c2[r]). 'howseholders' misinterprets 'familiae', which 'is the usual term for a gang of slaves or a troop of gladiators who were trained by a *lanista* [i.e. a gladiator-trainer] and offered for hire at public spectacles' (Ramsey, 144).

715 *holdes*='municipia' (*Sal* 30.7). 'municipia' is also translated as 'strongeholdes' at 1355–6 and 1411 (51.43, 52.14), and 'holdes' here has the same meaning: cf.

MED, s.v. 'hold', n.[2], sense 3(b). Both 'holdes' and 'strongeholdes' are misleading translations, but echo the gloss of 'municipia' as 'castella' which is attested in the Middle Ages, as e.g. (among other places) in the older ps.-Ognibene commentary (**1500.2**, sig. b5^{v}). *Municipia* is also glossed thus in Anonymous Amandensis, a Sallust commentary that survives in two twelfth-century manuscripts (see Turner, 'Reading Sallust in Twelfth-Century Flanders', 206). Cf. also Reuchlin's *Vocabularius*, which gives one meaning of *municipium* as 'castrum munitissimum' (sig. p8^{v}). For a different translation of *municipia*, cf. 1618*n*. NB. *Con* avoids translating *municipia* when the word appears at *Sal* 17.4, which may also suggest some confusion with this word in general.

716–17 *having delyuerd to . . . substaunce and possescions*. *Sal*: 'pro quoiusque opibus' (30.7). 'substaunce and possescions' = 'opibus'. 'having delyuerd to them in goodes' is not in *Sal* and twists *Sal*'s meaning; it may arise from retranslating 'distribuerentur', which *Con* has already translated as 'shuld be sent owte' (715).

717 *watche and warde* = 'uigiliae' (*Sal* 30.7). Idiom, as at 1184. Cf. *OED*, s.v. 'watch', n., sense II.7.a.

718 *t`h'e secondare dignitees* = 'minores magistratus' (*Sal* 30.7).

723–4 *accombred were they . . . they stode on* = 'festinare trepidare' (*Sal* 31.2).

725–6 *the contynewaunce of pease* = 'pacem' (31.2).

730 *prayde lowly to . . . feryd all thinges*. *Sal*: 'rogitare omnia, pauere' (31.3). *Con* follows *LaetT* 'rogitare deos: omnia pauere' (as in *BritT*, occasionally in *IncT*, and usually in *ParisT*).

733–4 *went abowte the . . . he dyd afore*. *Sal*: 'eadem illa mouebat' (31.4). 'as he dyd afore' follows *LaetT* variant 'eadem illa quæ antea mouebat'.

734 *defensys an`d' sauega`r'des* = 'praesidia' (*Sal* 31.4).

735 *that were ordenyd*. Written a line below the ruled text block, preceded by a paraph.

Lvcius Pavllo, the which was tribunus. *Sal*: 'L. Paullo' (31.4). *Con* follows *Val*: 'Lucio pau[l] .s. tribuno' (sig. c2^{r}).

736–8 *required by the . . . to his charge* = 'lege Plautia' (*Sal* 31.4), amplified via *Val*: 'Lege Plautia .i. lege plautii: qui legem tulit aduersus coniuratores ut ipsi responderent si quis coniurationis accusatus fuisset omnibus que sibi obiicerentur' (sig. c2^{r}).

745–6 *with . . . a demure speche* = 'uoce supplici' (*Sal* 31.7), via *Val*: 'Voce supplici .i. oratione plena commiserationis' (sig. c2^{v}). 'speche' = 'oratione', but 'demure' is odd as a translation of 'supplici', especially in the light of *Val*'s gloss, 'plena commiserationis'. Perhaps *Con* did not understand *commiseratio* (the word is not glossed, for instance, in Reuchlin's *Vocabularius*). *Con* could also have known the similar phrase 'demure of speche' from, say, Woodville, *Dictes or sayengis of the philosophres*, sig. [d]1^{v}.

750 *borne of noble senatours*='patricio homini' (*Sal* 31.7), perhaps via *Val*'s gloss: 'Patricio nobili' (sig. c2^{v}).

752 *a man new comen vppe*. *Sal*: 'inquilinus ciuis urbis Romae' (31.7). *Con* follows the variant 'homo nouus', which replaces 'inquilinus . . . Romae' in all *LaetT* (except **1490**) and *BritT*.

753 *To thise*. *Sal*: 'Ad hoc' (31.8). *Con* probably follows *LaetT* 'ad haec', the variant in most incunabula.

754 *rebell*. *Sal*: 'parricidam' (31.8). *Con* (correctly) follows *Val*: 'Parricidam: qui patriam perdere uellet' (sig. c2^{v}). By extension of its basic meaning, *parricida* 'is often used to describe a traitor or rebel against his country' (Ramsey, 96).

755–6 *full of fure . . . thus bysett abowte*. Syntax echoes *Sal*: 'furibundus "quoniam quidem circumuentus" inquit' (31.9). 'full of fure lyke a mad man'='furibundus' (*Sal* 31.9), amplified via *Val*: 'Furibundus: furore plenus' (sig. c2^{v}).

756 *putt to a plunge*='praeceps agor' (*Sal* 31.9). Idiom antedates 1st citation in *OED*, s.v. 'plunge', n., sense II.5. Cf. 1164.

758 *owte of the temple*. *Sal*: 'ex curia' (32.1). *Con* follows the variant 'e templo', as in *LaetT* (except **1493.1**) and *BritT*. Contrast John Claymond, who in his copy subpuncts 'templo' and interlineates 'curia', the variant in all earlier incunables (Oxford, Corpus Christi College, *ϕ*.C.4.6(2) [**1492.2**], sig. c2^{v}).

759 *his sawtes to sley the consull*='insidiae consuli' (*Sal* 32.1), amplified via *Val*: 'Consuli .s. factæ quem interficere parauerat' (sig. c2^{v}).

762 *sowgers*. *Sal*: 'legiones' (32.1). *Con* follows *Val*, 'Legiones: milites' (sig. c2^{v}), though note that Lat. 'legiones' becomes Engl. 'legiones' at 1556 (*Sal* 56.1).

to prevente='antecapere' (*Sal* 32.1), perhaps via *Val*: 'Antecapere. peruenire præoccupare' (sig. c2^{v}).

764 *In the ded tyme of the nyght*='nocte intempesta' (*Sal* 32.1). Cf. 650–1*n*.

766 *boldnes and hardynes*='audaciam' (*Sal* 32.2).

he yeueth in charge. *Sal*: 'mandat, quibus rebus possent' (32.2). 'quibus rebus possent' not translated.

772 *to Qvintus Marcius*. *Sal*: 'ad Marcium Regem' (32.3). On the omission of 'Regem', cf. 699–700*n*. *Con* follows the variant 'ad Q. Martium', as in most *LaetT* (incl. **1491**, **1493.3**) and as also in some *IncT* and *BritT*.

774 *We take recorde . . . of all men*. *Sal*: 'Deos hominesque testamur, imperator' (33.1). All *LaetT* (except **1491–2**) omit the vocative 'imperator', hence *Con*'s omission of this vocative.

776 *daunger or perell* = 'periculum' (*Sal* 33.1).

777 *the which*. *Sal*: 'qui' (33.1). *Con* fails to clarify that *qui*'s antecedent is not 'corpora', but 'must be supplied from *nostra*' (Ramsey, 151).

necessite = 'egentes' (*Sal* 33.1), probably via *Val*: 'Egentes. rebus omnibus necessariis carentes' (sig. c2^v^).

778 *of the inordinate covetise men* = 'faeneratorum' (*Sal* 33.1).

781 *fredome ner liberte* = 'liberum' (*Sal* 33.1).

783 *Oure elders*. *Sal*: 'maiores uostrum' (33.2). *Con* follows 'maiores nostri', the variant in most incunabula (incl. all *LaetT*).

783–4 *by þe graunte of the hole counseill* = 'decretis suis' (*Sal* 33.2), perhaps via *Val*: 'Decretis: suis consultis: nam decretum et consultum senatus idem sunt' (sig. c3^r^).

784–5 *hathe yeven greate . . . necessite of them* = 'inopiae eius opitulati sunt' (*Sal* 33.2).

787 *of their comen hutche*. *Sal*: 'aere' (33.2). *Con* probably translates 'comuni' from its appearance in *Val*, 'Ex comuni ære: ex erario' (sig. c3^r^), or possibly from an earlier incunable, since *IncT* and *ParisT* (as also *BritT*) print 'communi aere' in the main text (all *LaetT* except **1493.1**, however, follow *Sal*). 'comen hutche' is a calque of *aerarium commune* and antedates its 1st appearance in a citation (1536) in *OED*, s.v. 'hutch', n., sense 1a.

quyteth. Primarily meaning 'rescue' but punning on *quit* in the sense of cancelling debt: cf. *OED*, s.v. 'quit', v., senses II.6.a, II.9.

788–9 *bycause they myght . . . of the gouernours* = 'superbia magistratuum' (*Sal* 33.3), amplified via *Val*: 'Superbia magistrat[u]um: quia ipsi insolentiam consulum pati non poterant' (sig. c3^r^).

793 *instance*. Antedates 1st citation in *OED*, s.v. 'instance', v.

795–6 *hathe taken vyolently from vs* = 'eripuit' (*Sal* 33.5).

798 *Marius*. Correctly 'Marcius' (*Sal* 34.1), as at 699, 772; alternatively, 'Martius' (as e.g. in **1491**, **1493.3**). The translator or scribe probably missed the medial **c** or **t** by accident. For the policy of not emending mistakes in the spelling of proper nouns, see Introduction, p. lvi.

800 *with humble supplicacion* = 'supplices' (*Sal* 34.1).

802 *socour or helpe* = 'auxilium' (34.1).

805–6 *myghty power* = 'factioni' (*Sal* 34.2), probably via *Val*: 'Factioni: potentiæ et opibus' (sig. c3^r^).

806–7 *to departe the . . . exile to Manlius*. *Sal*: 'Massiliam in exilium proficisci' (34.2). 'to Manlius' more precisely conveys Catiline's intent and follows *Val*'s gloss: 'In itinere: Cum iret ad manlium litteras quæ continebant hoc quod sequitur' (sig. c3^r^). 'the towne' not in *Sal*.

810 *Catullus*. *Sal*: 'Catulus' (34.3). All *LaetT* give 'Catulus' here, but the majority of *LaetT* (incl. **1491**, but not **1493.3**) then give 'Catullus' at *Sal* 35.1, where *Con* again gives 'Catullus' (813). *Con* also erroneously gives 'Catullus' at 1147 and 1154. The misspelling could have arisen with the translator or the scribe. *Val* only ever gives either 'Catul.' or double l forms, e.g. 'catullus' (sig. d1[r]).

811 *a messanger with lettres*. *Sal*: 'litteras' (34.3). 'lettres' translates 'litteras', though pl. *litterae* here correctly means a single letter. 'a messenger' not in *Sal*.

813 *Lvcius Catelina yeveth . . . to Qvintus Catullus*. *Sal*: 'L. Catilina Q. Catulo' (35.1). *Con* follows 'L. Catilina Q. Catulo S.' (i.e. 'salutem'), as printed in all incunabula. On 'Catullus', cf. 810*n*.

815 *truste and assuraunce*='fiduciam' (*Sal* 35.1).

816–17 *not to question . . . defend to you*. *Sal*: 'defensionem' (35.2). *Con* follows *Val*, 'Defensionem: ut ego meum consilium defendam apud te an sit bonum an sit malum' (sig. c3[r]), but *Con* and *Val* both miss the correct sense of *defensio* (cf. 817–18*n*).

817–18 *Ner I thinke . . . mysilff culpable of*. *Sal*: 'satisfactionem ex nulla . . . culpa proponere decreui' (35.2). 'satisfactionem'='excuse', via *Val*: 'Satisfactionem: excusationem' (sig. c3[r]). 'Ner' misconstrues *Sal*, which distinguishes between *defensio* (a formal defence, which Catiline does not give) and *satisfactio* (an explanation, which Catiline does give).

820 *so sore oppressid . . . that*='concitatus, quod' (*Sal* 35.3). *Con* mistakes 'quod' as part of a result clause.

822–3 *the cause and comyn deffence*='publicam . . . causam' (*Sal* 35.3). On 'comyn deffence', here a calque of *causa publica*, cf. *MED*, s.v. 'commun(e', adj., sense 3(d): 'Shared by, or serving, the members of a community or organization; also, official, public (as opposed to private)'.

826–7 *honoured with þe grete dignyties*='honore honestatos' (*Sal* 35.3).

827–8 *sore hyndered and imparid*='alienatum' (*Sal* 35.3).

831 *that they resyd power ayenst me*. *Sal*: 'uim mihi parari' (35.5). *Con* interpolates 'they' and translates pass. inf. as active.

833–4 *Wryten at the . . . of youre sonnys*. *Sal*: 'per liberos tuos rogatus' (35.6). *Con* contorts the sense of 'per' and interpolates 'Wryten' to fit a mistaken interpretation of the Lat. This phrase also caused confusion in *Li Fet des Romains*, where it becomes 'en te recontendant lestat de ma gent': see *Lucan, Suetone, et Salluste* [i.e. *Li fet des Romains*], sig. a8[v].

835 *in the felde of Arretyn*. *Sal*: 'apud C. Flaminium in agro Arretino' (36.1). 'apud C. Flaminium' is not translated. *Con*'s 'Arretyn' is closest to the spelling in *LaetT* commentary editions ('Arretino'); cf. 'arretino' or 'reantino' (*IncT*), 'reatino' or 'aretino' (*ParisT*), 'Aretino' (*BritT*).

837–8 *with his signes . . . to an emperour*. *Sal*: 'cum fascibus atque aliis imperi insignibus' (36.1). 'other astate that belongith to an emperour' follows *Val*: 'Cæteris insignibus: uidelicet cum prætexta: quæ erat uestis imperatoria' (sig. c3[v]). 'emperour' (='imperi') is probably intended in its most common (and, here, anachronistic) sense of *emperor*: cf. 64*n*. Indeed *Con* could have translated 'imperi' here with a more general (and more historically accurate) word such as 'governour', as *imperium* is translated at 1257. 'with his signes' (='cum fascibus') may follow *Val*'s gloss of *fasces* as *insignia* at sig. b3[v] (cf. 433–4*n*). *Con* misses or disregards the *Val* gloss at 36.1 that interprets 'fascibus' metonymically—'Fascibus .i. lictoribus: nam fasces erant secures: quibus fasciculi uirgarum erant aligati: quas secures lictores imperatoribus perferebant' (sig. c3[v])—perhaps because *Con* was confused by the meaning of 'lictores'. A Tudor annotator of a Paris 1518 edition was also confused here, glossing 'fascibus' as 'tokyns of harms' (BodL, 8° F 75 Linc., sig. b7[r]).

838 *to Manlius*. *Sal*: 'in castra ad Manlium' (36.1). 'in castra' not translated.

841–2 *to come into . . . pardone withoute punysshment*='sine fraude' (*Sal* 36.2), following *Val*: 'Sine fraude. sine pœna' (sig. c3[v]).

842–3 *condempned by the . . . for other offensis*. *Sal*: 'rerum capitalium condemnatis' (36.2). 'capitalium' not translated.

845 *Caius Antonius*. *Sal*: 'Antonius' (36.3). *Con* follows 'C. Antonius', 'C. Anto.', or 'C. Ant.', as given in *LaetT* (among other close variants, and as also *BritT*).

846 *with the strengith of Rome*='cum exercitu' (*Sal* 36.3).

848 *the empire of Rome*='imperium populi Romani' (*Sal* 36.4).

848–9 *in the gretyst . . . it was in*='multo maxume miserabile' (*Sal* 36.4).

850 *obeyd*='parerent' (*Sal* 36.4), perhaps via *Val*: 'Parerent: obedirent' (sig. c3[v]).

853 *iuged themselffes but . . . comen wele also*. *Sal*: 'seque remque publicam obstinatis animis perditum irent' (36.4). *Con* contrives 'iuged' as a main verb, apparently not realizing that the supine 'perditum' connotes purpose, even though *Val* clarifies this: 'Perditum: ad perdendum se' (sig. c3[v]).

856–8 *The gretnes of . . . of the citezens*. *Sal*: 'tanta uis morbi . . . ciuium animos inuaserat' (36.5). *Con* contrives a result clause even though 'inuaserat' is indicative, not subjunctive; 'uti', correctly, introduces a comparison. 'contagiousnes' antedates 1st citation in *OED*, s.v. 'contagiousness', n., though not *MED*, s.v. 'contagiousnesse', n. For the adj. 'contagiouse', cf. 257.

864–5 *with . . . stryves*='seditionibus' (*Sal* 37.3). I.e. civil discord. Cf. e.g. Reuchlin, *Vocabularius*, 'Seditio . . . .i. dissensio ciuium' (sig. v1[v]).

865 *poverty goothe forthe at all adventures*. Idiomatic translation of 'egestas facile habetur' (*Sal* 37.3). 'facile'='at all adventures', a phrase which according to *OED* had only recently entered English from French, via Caxton (s.v. 'adventure', n., sense P.1.b).

866–7 *ryght perelouse and . . . all other people*='praeceps' (*Sal* 37.4). Cf. e.g. Reuchlin, *Vocabularius*: 'Praeceps etiam dicitur homo omnia sine modo. et cum periculo faciens' (sig. s4[r]).

867–8 *Fyrst, for they that in the contreys*. *Sal*: 'Primum omnium qui ubique' (37.5). 'in the contreys' follows *Val*: 'Vbique in omnibus Italiæ locis' (sig. c3[v]). 'omnium' is not translated, probably because most *LaetT* (incl. **1491**, **1493.3**) omit 'omnium'.

869 *also they*. *Sal*: 'item alii' (37.5). *Con* follows *LaetT* 'item qui' (as also in *BritT*).

869–70 *had loste their . . . and were vagaboundes*. *Sal*: 'patrimoniis amissis' (37.5). *Con* translates 'patrimoniis amissis uagabantur', the variant in all *LaetT* (except **1490**) and *BritT*.

870 *moreouer they*. *Sal*: 'postremo omnes' (37.5). 'omnes' is not translated, probably because the word is om. in *LaetT* (as also in *BritT*).

wikkid or myschevouse demenure='flagitium aut facinus' (*Sal* 37.5). 'demenure' antedates 1st citation in *OED*, s.v. 'demeanour', n.

872 *rennyth to the pumppe*='in sentinam confluxerant' (*Sal* 37.5). 'pumppe' in this sense antedates 1st citation in *OED*, s.v. 'pump', n.[1], sense I.2. This sense not currently recorded in *MED*, s.v. 'pumpe', n. A Tudor annotator of Ascensius's 1504 edition similarly glosses this phrase as 'as þe watur runnys in to þe chyffe pumpe' (BodL, DD 20 Art., sig. d4[v]).

873 *of hastardes*='ex gregariis militibus' (*Sal* 37.6), perhaps via *Val*: 'Ex gre. mi. .i. ex ignobilibus: nam gregarii milites dicuntur ignobiles quasi ex grege' (sig. c4[r]). On 'hastardes' see Introduction, p. xliii.

881 *the viciousnes of the cite*='malum publicum' (37.7).

882–3 *so grete hope laid afore theim*='maxume spe' (*Sal* 37.8), amplified via *Val*: 'in maxime spe utilitatis proposita' (sig. c4[r]).

883–4 *dyd thinke that . . . mooste profett by*='rei publicae iuxta ac sibi consuluisse' (*Sal* 37.8).

884 *atteynted*='proscripti' (*Sal* 37.9). Presumably with the sense 'condemned to death' (cf. *OED*, s.v. 'attaint', v., sense II.6), on the assumption that *Con* follows *Val*: 'Proscripti: capite damnati' (sig. c4[r]). Cf. 1318–19*n*, and 529*n* for *Con*'s earlier confusion about *proscriptio*.

886–8 *whosoeuer take vpon . . . of þe Senate*='quicumque aliarum atque senatus partium erant' (*Sal* 37.10), where 'whosoeuer toke vpon . . . party of rewle' follows *Val*'s gloss, 'qui partes sequebantur' (sig. c4[v]).

888 *the decaye of the comen wele*='conturbari rem publicam' (*Sal* 37.10).

890–1 *Gneius Pompeius, Marcus Crassus beyng consulles*. *Sal*: 'Cn. Pompeio et M. Crasso consulibus' (38.1). 'et' is not translated, probably because 'et' is om. in most

LaetT (incl. **1491**) when Crassus is mentioned at all (among *LaetT* editions, 'M. Crasso' is om. here in **1494**, **1495.2**, **1497.4**, and **1497.5**).

896 *with all possibilitie*='summa ope' (*Sal* 38.2), following *Val*'s gloss of 'ope' as 'possibilitate' (sig. c4[r]).

896–7 *as for the . . . their grete honoure*. *Sal*: 'senatus specie pro sua magnitudine' (38.2). *Con* misses the contrast between 'specie' and 'pro'.

898 *vnto you*. Not in *Sal*.

899 *vnder honest colour*. *Sal*: 'honestis nominibus' (38.3). *Con* follows *Sal*, which is also the reading in *IncT*, *ParisT*, and *BritT*. **1491** erroneously has 'ominibus', which some later *LaetT* editions (incl. **1493.3**) emend to 'omnibus'. *Con* probably translates or corrects from *Val*, which correctly gives 'honestis nominibus' (sig. c4[r]).

902 *their awne strengith and power*='potentia' (*Sal* 38.3).

905 *ayenst Metridates the kynge of Pontus*. *Sal*: 'Mithridaticum' (39.1). *Con* follows *Val*: 'contra mithridatem regem ponti' (sig. c4[r]).

906 *the power of . . . a fewe company*. *Sal*: 'paucorum potentia' (39.1). *Con*'s amplification echoes *Val*: 'Paucorum .s. nobilium' (sig. c4[r]). Here as elsewhere the translator associates nobility with Rome's senatorial order, with words for senator, senate, and nobility being used interchangeably: cf. 913*n*, 956*n*.

908 *they dyd no wronges*='innoxii' (*Sal* 39.2).

910 *ponysshed by ryghtfull iugementes*='iudiciis' (*Sal* 39.2).

912 *renewing of doutefull thinges an hope*='dubiis rebus nouandi spes' (*Sal* 39.3). **1491**='innouandis', hence *Con* takes 'innouandis' with 'dubiis rebus' rather than 'nouandi' with 'spes' ('nouandi spes'='hope of revolution' [Loeb]). 'doutefull' could mean 'dangerous' (*MED*, s.v. 'douteful', adj., sense 3[a]), and Loeb renders 'dubiis rebus' as 'in a perilous state of affairs'. *Con*, however, probably intends 'doutefull' in the weaker sense of 'uncertain'. Cf. e.g. Reuchlin, *Vocabularius*, s.v. 'dubius', '.i. incertus' (sig. h5[v]).

913 *the olde stryffe . . . and the people*. *Sal*: 'uetus certamen animos eorum' (39.3). 'animos eorum' is not translated; otherwise, *Con* follows *Val*'s gloss of the 'certamen' as 'inter nobiles et plebem' (sig. c4[r]), again rendering *nobiles* as 'Senate' (cf. 906*n*).

914 *in his bataill*. *Sal*: 'primo proelio' (39.4). 'primo' not translated.

918 *beyng so weyke . . . in the felde*='defessis et exsanguibus' (*Sal* 39.4), amplified via *Val*: 'Defessis .s. uictoribus detrimentis belli lassis. Exanguibus: languidis uulneribus acceptis in bello' (sig. c4[v]).

919 *the gouernaunce of all thinges*. *Sal*: 'imperium atque libertatem' (39.4). 'atque libertatem' not translated.

920 *that were not . . . to the treson*='extra coniurationem' (*Sal* 39.5), amplified via *Val*: 'Extra coniurationem: qui coniurationis conscii non erant' (sig. c4[v]).

925–6 *for their vnthryfty . . . or hard fortune*='moribus aut fortuna' (*Sal* 39.6).

927 *all maner havour of men*='quoiusque modi genus hominum' (*Sal* 39.6). 'havour' in this sense antedates 1st citation in *OED*, s.v. 'haviour', n., sense 2.

928 *that he trowed*. Not in *Sal*.

929–30 *the ambassatoures of Fraunce*. *Sal*: 'legatos Allobrogum' (40.1). Here as elsewhere *Con* simplifies via *Val*: 'Allobrogum: sunt populi galliæ transalpinæ' (sig. c4[v]).

931 *so sore oppressed*='oppressos' (*Sal* 40.1).

938–9 *in the place of comen resorte*='in foro' (*Sal* 40.2). Cf. e.g. 'cum forum commune sit', in Cicero, *Ad familiares* 5.15.2, in *Epistulae*, ed. Watt and Shackleton Bailey.

939–40 *of the state . . . of the Senate*='de statu ciuitatis' (*Sal* 40.2). *Con* misinterprets as discussion of Rome, unlike (for example) *Asc*, which explains correctly: 'de statu ciuitatis .s. allobrogum potius quam romanorum' (sig. d6[r]).

941 *so grete thraldome and sorowe*='tantis malis' (*Sal* 40.2).

944–5 *they loked for . . . mysery and wretchednes*. *Sal*: 'miseriis suis remedium mortem expectare' (40.3). *Con* contorts the sense, not realizing that 'miseriis suis' is dat.

947 *full of ioye . . . a grete hope*='in maxumam spem adducti' (*Sal* 40.4).

950 *of their thraldome and dett*='aere alieno' (*Sal* 40.4).

951–2 *nere to the comen place*='foro propinqua' (*Sal* 40.5). Cf. 938–9*n*.

952 *of his affynyte . . . thedyr of Sempronia*. *Sal*: 'neque aliena consili' (40.5). *Con* misunderstands the *alienus*+gen. construction, where 'neque aliena' means 'nor unfavourable' (cf. Ramsey, 170). *Con* instead interprets 'neque aliena' as meaning 'nor foreign/strange', hence 'of his affynyte'. 'by reson of . . . thedyr of Sempronia'='propter Semproniam' (*Sal* 40.5).

953 *at this tyme*='tum' (*Sal* 40.5), perhaps via *Val*: 'Tum: eo tempore' (sig. c4[v]).

954 *credens and auctoryte*='auctoritas' (*Sal* 40.6).

956 *bothe of noble and low degre*='quoiusque generis' (*Sal* 40.6), amplified via *Val*: 'Cuiusque: tam ordinis senatorii quam equestris' (sig. c4[v]). On these ranks, cf. 397–8*n*. On 'noble . . . degre' translating 'ordinis senatorii', cf. 906*n*.

957 *right innocent in the mater*='innoxios' (*Sal* 40.6), perhaps via *Val*: 'Innocuos innocentes' (sig. c4[v]).

957–8 *the Frenchmen*=‘legatis’ (*Sal* 40.6). Cf. 929–30*n*.

959 *helpe and diligence*=‘operam’ (*Sal* 40.6).

962 *dette and nedynes*=‘aes alienum’ (*Sal* 41.2).

963 *offers*. I.e. monetary offers;=‘merces’ (*Sal* 41.2).

964 *wise and stronge counseill*=‘tuta consilia’ (*Sal* 41.2).

964–5 *sewre truste and . . . puplisshe the treson*. ‘sewre truste and grete rewardes’= ‘certa praemia’ (*Sal* 41.2); the rest is interpolated.

966–7 *at the laste . . . our comen wele*=‘tandem uicit fortuna rei publicae’ (*Sal* 41.3), amplified via *Val*: ‘Fortuna rei p. ut rei publicæ magis quam fouerent coniuratoribus’ (sig. c5[r]).

968 *Zanga*. *Sal*: ‘Sangae’ (41.4). The **Z** spelling (*lectio difficilior*) first appears in *LaetT* (all imprints except **1493.1**) and is sustained in *BritT*. It was unusual enough that Parrasio, in his copy, corrects the **Z** to **S** on both instances that it appears (Cambridge, King’s College, Bryant.XV.3.3 [**1490**], sig. c5[r]); on Parrasio, cf. Introduction, p. xxxiv. All other incunabula also spell with initial **S**.

968–9 *the which had . . . all their sewites*=‘quoius patrocinio ciuitas plurumum utebatur’ (*Sal* 41.4).

970–1 *he incontinent gothe . . . of all thinges*=‘consilio cognito’ (*Sal* 41.5).

972–3 *dissimule and colour*=‘simulent’ (*Sal* 41.5).

976–7 *in the nerre . . . contrey of Fraunce*=‘in Gallia citeriore atque ulteriore’ (*Sal* 42.1), perhaps contextualized by some of *Val*: ‘in urbe citeriore: quæ est citra alpes. Vlteriore quæ est ultra alpes’ (sig. c5[r]). On ‘contrey’, cf. 435*n*.

977 *in the cite . . . lykewise in Appulia*. *Sal*: ‘item in agro Piceno Bruttio Apulia’ (42.1). ‘Bruttio’ not translated. Apulia is spelled ‘Appulia’ is most *LaetT* (incl. **1491**, **1493.3**), though as ‘Apulia’ in most earlier incunables.

979–80 *dyd all thinges at all adventures*=‘cuncta simul agebant’ (*Sal* 42.2). On ‘at all adventures’, cf. 865*n*.

980–1 *made metynges in . . . and grete besynes*. *Sal*: ‘nocturnis consiliis, armorum . . . portationibus, festinando agitando’ (42.2). *Con* translates as though each phrase were an abl. absol.; correctly, they are instrumental abl. modifying ‘effecerant’.

983 *into pryson*=‘in uincula’ (*Sal* 42.3), probably with the sense of ‘prison’ rather than (more generally) ‘forced confinement’, if *Con* follows *Val* here: ‘In uincula. in carcerem’ (sig. c5[r]). Cf. 1096–7*n*.

983–4 *of Catelynes fel`y'shippe*. *Sal*: ‘ex senatus consulto’ (42.3). *Con* translates ‘ex sociis’, which takes the place of ‘ex senatus consulto’ in *LaetT* (as also in *IncT* and *BritT*).

985–6 *had þe commyssion and auctoryte*=‘legatus praeerat’ (*Sal* 42.3). See Introduction, p. liii.

988 *whanne Catelyne they . . . a grete hooste*. *Sal*: ‘paratis ut uidebatur magnis copiis’ (43.1). A crux, since the abl. absol. makes it unclear who prepared the host; *Con* simply follows *Val*: ‘Paratis a catilina’ (sig. c5[r]).

990 *to Fesulas in Tuschan*=‘in agrum faesulanum’ (*Sal* 43.1), amplified via *Val*: ‘fesulanum: quæ est ciuitas hetruriæ’ (sig. c5[r]). On ‘Tuschan’, cf. 639–40*n*, 668. On ‘Fesulas’, cf. 589*n*.

992–3 *so noble and so faithfull a consull*=‘optumo’ (*Sal* 43.1).

996–7 *sondry and mooste mete places*=‘opportuna’ (43.2).

1000–1 *and lykewise every . . . bare malice vnto*=‘alius autem alium’ (*Sal* 43.2).

1009–10 *vpon the Senate in their counseill howse*=‘in curiam’ (*Sal* 43.3). Cf. 440–1*n*.

1010 *wylde and ferse*=‘ferox’ (43.4). ‘ferse’ here probably means ‘untamed’: cf. *Val*, ‘Ferox: indomitus natura’ (sig. c5[v]).

1016 *to haue home . . . to their contrey*=‘ad ciuis perferant’ (*Sal* 44.1).

1017 *their noble men*=‘eos’ (*Sal* 44.1).

1019 *sea`l'ed to their covenauntes*=‘dant’ (*Sal* 44.2). *Con* correctly grasps the sense from the previous sentence (‘ius iurandum’, 44.1).

But Cassius `a'unswerd . . . com theder hymsilff. *Sal*: ‘Cassius semet eo breui uenturum pollicetur’ (44.2). The sense is contorted by *Con*’s insertions of ‘But’ and ‘it nedyd not’ and by the strained translation of ‘pollicetur’ as ‘aunswerd’.

1020–1 *he wolde take . . . somwhat afore theim*. *Sal*: ‘paulo ante legatos ex urbe proficiscitur’ (44.2). ‘ex urbe’ not translated. ‘theim’=‘legatos’.

1021–2 *oone Titus Wolturcius*. *Sal*: ‘T. Volturcium quendam Crotoniensem’ (44.3). ‘Crotoniensem’ not translated, despite the word’s inclusion and explanation in *Val*: ‘Crotoniensem: de crotona ciuitate’ (sig. c5[v]).

1024 *to conferme and . . . amytie and frendshippe*=‘societatem confirmarent’ (*Sal* 44.3).

1024–5 *letters*. *Sal*: ‘litteras’ (44.4). Lat. pl. should more correctly be translated as Engl. sg. (cf. 811*n*).

1025–6 *Who I am*. *Sal*: ‘Qui sim’ (44.5). A crux, since ‘*quis* refers to the name and identification only, *qui* to the character of the writer’ (McGushin, 221); translating ‘qui’, Loeb gives ‘My present situation you will learn’, etc. All incunabula print ‘qui’. John Claymond apparently appreciated the *qui* vs *quis* distinction, emending to ‘Quis sim’ in his copy (Oxford, Corpus Christi College, *ф*.C.4.6(2) [**1492.2**], sig. c5[v]). *Con* simply follows *Val*: ‘Qui sim etc. Noluit ponere nomen suum ne si forte litteræ interceptæ fuissent nomen suum scriptum cognosceret’ (sig. c5[v]).

1026–9 *Now take hede . . . the lowiste degre. Sal*: 'Fac cogites in . . . etiam ab infumis' (44.5). *Con* translates an alternative version of the letter from Cicero, *In Catilinam*, 3.12 which *LaetT* had adopted in place of 'Fac cogites . . . ab infumis' (*BritT* does the same). **1491** reads: 'cura ut uir sis: et cogita quem in locum sis progressus: et uide quid iam tibi sit necesse: cura ut omnium tibi auxilia adiungas: etiam infimorum'. On the two versions of this letter, see Latte, 'Sallust: Diction and Sentence Structure', 44–5; Earl, *Political Thought of Sallust*, 94–5. Note that Parrasio, in his copy, substitutes the 'fac cogites' version in full here (Cambridge, King's College, Bryant.XV.3.3 [**1490**], sig. c6^{v}); on Parrasio, cf. Introduction, p. xxxiv.

1029 *Moreouer*='Ad hoc' (*Sal* 44.6), via *Val*: 'Ad hoc .i. prætcrca .i. præter has' (sig. c5^{v}).

1030 *that he mervelith*. Not in *Sal*; *Con* turns *Sal*'s direct question into an indirect statement.

1030–1 *the vile and banesshed men*='seruitia' (44.6). On vile, cf. 114, 598, 697, 712, 1030, 1064, 1176, 1573. The idea of *seruitia* as 'banesshed', which is unsupported by the Lat., may extrapolate from *Val*'s distinction between *servi* and Roman citizens: 'Quo consilio etc quia catilina repudiabat seruos ne uideretur contra dignitatem facere si uellet seruos ciuibus romanis immiscere' (sig. c5^{v}).

1031–2 *the Senate hathe . . . his honour there. Sal*: 'ab senatu hostis iudicatus sit' (44.6). 'from his honour' follows an idea in *Val*: 'ab senatu hostis: ob quam causam iam non potes tuam dignitatem tueri' (sig. c5^{v}).

1034–5 *whan the nyght . . . goyng to Catelyne*='constituta nocte qua proficiscerentur' (*Sal* 45.1), amplified via *Val*: 'Constituta: determinata diffinita nocte eundi ad catilinam' (sig. c5^{v}).

1037 *Pontinus. Sal*: 'Pomptino' (45.1). *LaetT* variants include 'Pōptino' (**1491**, **1492.2**), 'Promptinio' (**1493.1**), 'Pōptīo' (**1493.2**), 'Pomptino' (**1493.3**), 'promptino' (**1494**), 'prontino' (**1495.2**, **1497.5**), and 'prontini' (**1497.4**), but *Con*'s spelling probably arises from minim error in scribal transmission (**n** for **m**). The same name later appears in *Con* as 'Pomtinus' (cf. 1050*n*).

1037–8 *the brygge callid Milvius. Sal*: 'ponte Muluio' (45.1). Cf. 'ponte miluio' in, e.g., **1491** and **1493.3**.

1038 *the hole company of the Frenchmen*='Allobrogum comitatus' (*Sal* 45.1). Cf. 929–30*n*.

1040 *all thinges. Sal*: 'cetera' (45.1). *Con* misguidedly translates 'cetera' as though it comes after 'uti'.

1041 *He assigned to . . . men of armys. Sal*: 'permittit. Illi, homines militares' (45.1–2). *Con* follows the reading in most incunabula (incl. **1491**, **1493.3**), with no sentence break here and 'illis' (not 'illi') as the object of 'permittit'.

1047 *cheryd his company to fyght*='cohortatus ceteros' (*Sal* 45.4), amplified via *Val*:

'Cohortatus cæ. uidelicet ne timea[n]t: sed et ipsi fortiter dimicent cum hostium multitudine quæ obsederat eos' (sig. c5[v]).

1049–50 *made entrety and . . . for his lyffe*='multa . . . de salute sua . . . obtestatus' (*Sal* 45.4).

1050 *Pomtinus the pretor*. *Sal*: 'Pomptinum' (45.4). 'the pretor' is interpolated from *Val*: 'Prompti[n]um: hic promptinus prætor cognitus erat huic Volturcio' (sig. c5[v]). *Con*'s spelling probably derives from the variant 'Pomptinum', as given in several *LaetT* editions (**1490**, **1491**, **1492.2**, **1493.3**). Cf. 1037*n*.

1054 *to Cicero*='consuli' (*Sal* 46.1), via *Val*: 'consuli: ciceroni' (sig. c6[r]).

1055 *exceding charge and grete gladnes*='cura atque laetitia' (*Sal* 46.2).

1063 *Ceparius also, the which*. *Sal*: 'Caeparium Tarracinensem, qui' (46.3). Unlike other incunabula, no *LaetT* (except **1490** and **1491–2**) prints 'Caeparium' here; *Con* probably takes the name from *Val*, which glosses 'qui' as 'ceparius' (sig. c6[r]). 'Tarracinensem' is not translated, maybe because *Val* does not explain the word.

1064 *the vile people*='seruitia' (*Sal* 46.3). On 'vile', cf. 114, 598, 697, 712, 1030, 1176, 1573.

1066 *detectyng*. As vbl. n., antedates 1st citation in *OED*, s.v. 'detecting', n. Cf. 1138.

1068 *lad hym by the arme*. *Sal*: 'ipse manu tenens in senatum perducit' (46.5). 'in senatum' not translated, probably because om. in *LaetT* (as also in *BritT*).

1069–70 *convocacion howse of Concordia*='in aedem Concordiae' (*Sal* 46.5). Cf. 431–3*n*.

1070 *the congregacion of the Senate*='senatum' (*Sal* 46.6). Cf. 431–3*n*.

1072–3 *Flaccus, the* pretor vrbanus='Flaccum praetorem' (*Sal* 46.6), amplified via *Val*: 'Prætorem: urbanum' (sig. c6[r]). On different kinds of praetor, see Brennan and Lintott, 'praetor'.

1076 *who were the doers*. Misinterpreting 'qua de causa' (*Sal* 47.1).

1076–8 *Fyrst he aunswerd . . . rebellyon he dissimulid*. *Sal*: 'primo fingere alia, dissimulare de coniuratione' (47.1). 'of his iourney' follows the explanation in *Val*: 'Primo fingere: falso dicebat se iturum quidem fuisse extra urbem ad catilinam' (sig. c6[r]). 'all oder thinges' translates the *LaetT* variant 'alia omnia' (as also in *BritT*).

1078–9 *whan the Senate . . . shew the trothe*='ubi fide publica dicere iussus est' (*Sal* 47.1).

1083 *Antronius*. *Sal*: 'Autronium' (47.1). *Con* follows 'Antronium' (*lectio difficilior*), as given in most *LaetT* commentary editions (except **1495.2** and **1497.4**); the *lectio facilior* 'Antonium' is standard in *IncT*, most *ParisT*, and most *BritT*. On this name, cf. also 395, 418, 430, 1139.

Yla. *Sal*: 'Sullam' (47.1). See Introduction, pp. xxix–xxx.

Varguteius. *Sal*: 'Vargunteium' (47.1). Unless the medial **n** has been lost in scribal transmission, *Con* probably follows the reading 'Varguteium' as found in most *LaetT* commentary editions (all except **1493.1**, **1495.2**). All *IncT*, *ParisT*, and *BritT* instead have medial **n** or a macron over the **u**. Cf. 396*n*, 661*n*.

1085 *But*. *Sal*: 'ac' (47.2). *Con* translates 'at', the variant in almost all incunabula (incl. all *LaetT*).

denyed and colored all thinges='dissimulantem' (*Sal* 47.2).

1087 *howse of Cornelius*. I.e. the house of the Cornelii.

1090–1 *the augures had oftetymes aunswerd*. *Sal*: 'saepe ex prodigiis haruspices' (47.2). 'ex prodigiis' not clearly translated. On 'augures' see Introduction, p. lii.

1094 *afore the Senate*. Not in *Sal*, but suggested by *Val*'s gloss of 'omnes' (*Sal* 47.3) as 'senatores' (sig. c6[r]).

1095 *decreed*. *Sal*: 'decernit' (47.3). *Con* follows 'decreuit', the variant in all incunabula.

1096–7 *into honeste kepynge . . . to their honour*. *Sal*: 'in liberis custodiis' (47.3). I.e. not prison. *Con* ascertains the correct sense from *Val*: 'in custodiis quæ conueniant liberis hominibus ut non seruis: hoc est et domi seruarentur apud ciues romanas (sig. c6[r]). By extension, 'pryson' at 1187 and 1191 is probably also used in the (correct) sense of 'forced confinement', where the modern sense of 'prison' (=*carcer*) would be inaccurate.

1098 *of Lentulus Spinter*. *Sal*: 'P. Lentulo Spintheri' (47.4). 'P.' not translated.

1100–1 *fleing fro the cite*='ex fuga' (*Sal* 47.4), amplified via *Val*: 'quia ex urbe fugerat' (sig. c6[v]).

1101 *to Gneius Therencius*. *Sal*: 'Cn. Terentio senatori' (47.4). 'senatori' not translated.

1104 *mischevous purposis*='consilia' (*Sal* 48.1).

1105 *lyffte vp Cicero . . . to the hevyns*='Ciceronem ad caelum tollere' (*Sal* 48.1).

1106–7 *from tribute and bondage*='ex seruitute' (*Sal* 48.1). On 'bondage', see 518*n*.

1107–8 *Than they talkyd . . . vpon the bataill*. *Sal*: 'Namque alia belli . . . quam detrimento fore' (48.2). Several interpolations, contorting the sense of the Lat.

1110 *substaunce and lyving*='copiae' (*Sal* 48.2).

1111 *within the cite*. Not in *Sal*.

1112 *Affter that day*. Literal but inaccurate translation of 'Post eum diem' (*Sal* 48.3), which correctly means *postridie*.

1117 *in maner*='fere' (*Sal* 48.4). Cf. *MED*, s.v. 'maner(e', n., sense 2e(c).

1118–19 *of diuers noble men*='bonorum' (*Sal* 48.4).

1119 *of the appoyntment . . . with his hooste*='de itinere hostium' (*Sal* 48.4), amplified via *Val*, whose gloss takes the form of a purpose clause: 'De itinere hostium: ut catilina cum hostibus ad urbem ueniret' (sig. c6[v]). 'appoyntment', then, probably means 'purpose', which antedates the 1st citation of this sense of the noun in *OED*, s.v. 'appointment', n., sense 5.

1123 *thedyr*='ad urbem' (*Sal* 48.4).

1126 *of so grete myght and power*='summa potentia' (*Sal* 48.5).

1130–1 *gretly bounden*='obnoxii' (*Sal* 48.5), perhaps via *Val*: 'Obnoxii: obligati' (sig. c6[v]).

1131–3 *and askid of . . . in þe matere*='deque ea re postulant uti referatur' (*Sal* 48.5).

1132 *tryall*. Cf. 425–6*n*.

1135 *duraunce*. Antedates 1st citation in *OED*, s.v. 'durance', n. Cf. 1355.

1139 *by the dryffte of* ='a' (*Sal* 48.7). See Introduction, p. liv.

Antronius. *Sal*: 'Autronio' (48.7). *Con* follows 'Antronio', as in most *LaetT* commentary editions (**1491**, **1492.2**, **1493.1**, **1493.2**, **1493.3**); *IncT*, most *ParisT*, and most *BritT* give 'Antonio'. On the spelling, cf. also 395, 418, 430, 1083.

1141 *bolstred*. I.e. fortified, protected against. Antedates 1st citation in *OED*, s.v. 'bolster', v.

1141–2 *Oder men there . . . was Cicero doyng*. *Sal*: 'alii Tarquinium a Cicerone inmissum aiebant' (48.8). 'Tarquinium . . . inmissum' not translated, perhaps because the translator fails to parse the acc.–inf. correctly. An emendation to 'Ciceros doyng' or 'Cicero his doyng' is feasible, but *Con* or the scribe may also have been uncertain of how to form a gen. with this classical name, so it is left as written in the MS. Cf. also e.g. 'Manlius tentys' (765), not 'Manlius his tentys'.

1146 *wrongefull sclaunder*='contumeliam' (48.9).

1147 *Qvintus Catullus and . . . cheffe noble men*='Q. Catulus et C. Piso' (*Sal* 49.1), amplified via *Val*: 'Qu. catul. C. piso: nobilis[s]imi romani' (sig. d1[r]). On 'Catullus', cf. 810*n*.

1151–2 *condempned by his . . . all the parties*='oppugnatus in iudicio pecuniarum repetundarum' (*Sal* 49.2). The interpolation 'in the contreys' is based on material that follows in 49.2.

1153 *vpon oon of the Frenchmen*. *Sal*: 'quoiusdam Transpadani' (49.2). *Con* simplifies from *Val*: 'quendam gallum transpadanum' (sig. d1[r]).

1154–5 *Catullus vpon the . . . of their religion*='Catulus ex petitione pontificatus' (*Sal* 49.2), amplified via *Val*: 'Pontificatus .s. maximus: cum Catul. et cæsar competitores essent in pontificatu maximo: qui præerat omnibus templis sacris et etiam omnibus sacerdotibus' (sig. d1[r]). On 'Catullus', cf. 810*n*.

1158–9 *he by his . . . of the people*. *Sal*: 'quod is priuatim . . . grandem pecuniam debebat' (49.3). *Con* misses the point that Caesar owed money, perhaps being misled by *Val*: 'Egregia: excellenti quadam liberalitate animi muneribus maximis quæ populo distribuerat: Nam constat cæsarem populum romanum accepisse conuiuio' (sig. d1[r]).

1161 *the counseill howse*. Not in *Sal*.

1162 *with talys and lyes*='ementiundo' (*Sal* 49.4).

1163–4 *wherby they resyd . . . a grete plunge*='magnam illi inuidiam conflauerant' (*Sal* 49.4). On 'plunge', cf. 756*n*.

1164–6 *the garde of . . . temple of Concordia*. *Sal*: 'qui praesidi causa . . . circum aedem Concordiae' (49.4). 'garde of gentilmen'='equites Romani', echoing other translations of *eques* and *equestris* at 398, 453, 660. That these *equites* formed a 'garde' would have been clear from context and *Val*'s explanation: 'Circum locum stabant armati' (sig. d1[r]). 'Senate' and 'temple' also follow *Val*: 'Edem: templum concordiæ ubi senatus frequens habebatur' (sig. d1[r]). 'cum telis' not translated.

1167 *styrrid vpon a faithfull mynde*='animi mobilitate inpulsi' (*Sal* 49.4), except that 'vpon a faithfull mynde' follows the *LaetT* variant 'animi nobilitate' (as also in most *BritT*). 'nobilitate' is also the reading in *Val*'s lemma (sig. d1[r]). The unusual phrasing results from close translation of the Lat.

1169 *they wolde haue . . . had slayn hym*. *Sal*: 'gladio minitarentur' (49.4). 'weypons' pl. follows *Val*: 'Gladio: cum gladiis' (sig. d1[r]). 'had slayn hym' not in *Sal*.

1170–1 *yf Cicero asspying . . . into saffe places*. Not in *Sal* but translating *Val*: 'cicero periculum uidens saluti cæsaris complexus est eum . . . et hoc modo eum ex curia deduxit incolumem' (sig. d1[r]).

1172 *in doyng*. I.e. 'in the process of taking place'. This usage preceded in *MED*, s.v. 'doing(e', ger., sense 4a. Cf. 1683.

1173–4 *accordyng as the . . . alowid their shewinges*='conprobato eorum indicio' (*Sal* 50.1).

1174–5 *that were manymysid*='liberti' (*Sal* 50.1). Cf. Introduction, p. lii. Manumission was discussed, for example, in Reuchlin's *Vocabularius*: 'Manumissio . . . est datio libertatis . . . Et manumissus dicitur qui est liberatus a manu et potestate domini' (sig. o7[v]).

1176 *abowte the towne*. Not in *Sal*.

crafty men='opifices' (*Sal* 50.1), via *Val*: 'Opifices: dicuntur illi qui opere manuum suarum uitam substentant: et ab opere faciendo dicti sunt opifices' (sig. d1[r–v]).

1177 *in every of the lanes*='in uicis' (*Sal* 50.1).

1178 *of the sowgers*. Misleading interpretation of 'multitudinum' (*Sal* 50.1).

1180–1 *oper that he had done fore*. *Sal*: 'libertos suos, lectos' (50.2). *Con* follows *LaetT*'s variant 'libertos: electos suos' (or close variants thereof, and as also found in *BritT*). 'libertos' not translated.

1182 *beyng a multitude*='grege facto' (*Sal* 50.2), via *Val*: 'Grege facto .i. multitudine facta' (sig. d1[v]).

1184 *ordenyd grete watche and warde*='dispositis praesidiis' (*Sal* 50.3). On 'watche and warde', cf. 717*n*.

1187 *congregacion*='frequens senatus' (*Sal* 50.3). Cf. 431–3*n*.

1187–8 *that they had . . . the comen wele*='contra rem publicam fecisse' (*Sal* 50.3).

1189 *Decius*. *Sal*: 'D.' (50.4), standing for 'Decimus'. This praenomen was usually expanded as 'Decius', as e.g. in *Asc* (sig. e4[r]) and elsewhere in *Val* (sig. d2[v], glossing *Sal* 51.16). A classical glossary owned by Richard Bole similarly suggests, 'per d. decius' (Oxford, Balliol College, MS 121, f. iv[v]). Bole's Sallust commentaries further give 'Decium' as the correct acc. form of this name in the *BC* (Oxford, Balliol College, MS 123, ff. 124[r], 124[v], 145[r]). Cf. 1263*n*.

1189–90 *chosen to be . . . nexte yere folowyng*='consul designatus' (*Sal* 50.4), amplified with knowledge that could come from elsewhere in the translation: cf. 180–1*n*.

1192–3 *to suffre deth*. *Con* erases the potential ambiguity of *supplicium* (*Sal* 50.4; cf. Ramsey, 192), perhaps translating with an awareness of events described in *Sal* 52.

1194 *he yaue his . . . lett of tyme*. *Sal*: 'pedibus in sententiam . . . iturum' (50.4). The 'pedibus . . . iturum' idiom correctly means 'vote for', but *Con* works from *Val*: 'Itur pedibus in sententiam quia dicebat principes senatus cum duæ erant sententiæ uidelicet una suadens: alia dissuadens qui hanc suadentem sequitur et eat in dexteram: qui illam dissuadentem sequitur in sinistra: et ille qui in dexteram aut in sinistram iuisset pedibus ire in sententiam dicebatur. Nam quia erat maxima multitudo senatorum magnum spacium consumptum esset si singuli sententiam suam dixissent sed eo modo breuiter explebatur consultatio' (sig. d1[v]).

1195–6 *He said he . . . within the citee*. *Sal*: 'se dixit, qui . . . additis referundum censuerat' (50.4). In *Sal*, the antecedent of 'qui' is Tiberius Nero, where 'dixit' is a modern emendation. All incunabula give 'dixerat' (for 'dixit') and then 'quod' (not 'qui'). *Con* takes 'quod' as causal and, based on *LaetT*, legitimately assumes that 'He' refers to Silanus. *Con* misconstrues 'referendum' as 'revoke his sentence', probably to fit the interpretation that 'He' refers to Silanus rather than Tiberius Nero. 'bycause ther was . . . within the citee' misinterprets abl. absol. 'praesidiis additis'.

1200 *clene*. *Con*'s interpolation.

1202 *ner no maner man*. *Sal*: 'neque quisquam omnium' (51.2). *Con* follows 'neque hominum quisquam' or 'neque quisquam hominum', the variants in most incunabula (including all *LaetT*).

1205–6 *his reason is nothing worthe*. *Sal*: 'animus nihil ualet' (51.3). See Introduction, pp. xxx–xxxii. Parrasio in his copy also inserts this phrase (Cambridge, King's College, Bryant.XV.3.3 [1490], sig. d1^v^); on Parrasio, cf. Introduction, p. xxxiv.

1207 *I can wele . . . in many causis*. *Sal*: 'Magna mihi copia est memorandi, patres conscripti' (51.4). Here, as often in *Sal* 51 and 52, the vocative 'patres conscripti' is not translated (further instances are not noted).

1208 *hathe done many greate folys*='male consuluerint' (*Sal* 51.4).

1212 *riche*='magna atque magnifica' (*Sal* 51.5).

1213 *by vs*='populi Romani' (*Sal* 51.5).

1213–14 *ryght malicious and extreme ayenst vs*='infida atque aduorsa nobis' (*Sal* 51.5). 'extreme' as adv. antedates 1st citation in *OED*, s.v. 'extreme', adv. 'malicious'='infida'; cf. *MED*, s.v. 'malicious', adj., sense 1(c).

1220 *in all the . . . ayenst the* Pœnos='bellis Punicis omnibus' (*Sal* 51.6). Cf. e.g. Reuchlin, *Vocabularius*, s.v. 'Phaeniceon': 'cartaginenses dicti sunt pœni' (sig. f3^v^).
they='Carthaginienses' (*Sal* 51.6).

1223–4 *what should becomme . . . and theire honoure*='quid se dignum foret' (*Sal* 51.6), with 'honoure' suggested by *Val*'s gloss, 'quid ad dignitatem suam pertineret' (sig. d2^r^).

1225–6 *the grete and horrible dedys*='scelus' (*Sal* 51.7).

1227–8 *rather to youre . . . youre noble fame*. *Sal*: 'neu magis irae uostrae quam famae' (51.7). The sense is inverted in *Con*, perhaps because the translator accidentally misses the negative 'neu'.

1230–1 *to be done to a senatoure*. Not in *Sal*. *Con* is technically correct but misses the point that all Roman citizens, not just senators, were legally exempt from certain forms of punishment, as *Val* explains: 'nam leges non permittebant ciuem romanam uirgis cædi: nec capite puniri: sed si deprehensus esset: perpetuo carcere teneretur: sin autem extra urbem fuisset ita ut deprehendi non posset exularet' (sig. d2^r^).

1233 *may execute*. Not in *Sal*.

1239 *from theire moders brestes and slayne*='a parentum conplexu' (*Sal* 51.9). *Con* makes the gendered assumption that 'parentum' refers to 'moders', anticipating *Asc*'s gloss: 'a complexu parentum .s. vtrorunque sed præcipue matrum' (sig. e5^r^). 'and slayne' not in *Sal*.

1239–40 *to suffre by . . . the wykked lustis*='pati' (*Sal* 51.9), perhaps amplified via *Val*: 'Pati .s. stupra et adulteria' (sig. d2^r^).

1241 *the mordre `o'f the noble men*='caedem' (*Sal* 51.9).

1243 *overturnyd and vndone*='conpleri' (*Sal* 51.9).

1245 *vs*. *Sal*: 'uos' (51.10). Almost all incunabula (including all *LaetT*) give 'uos', so *Con* either misread 'uos' as 'nos' or thought that 'uos' was an error for 'nos'.
angry and ferse='infestos' (*Sal* 51.10).

1250–1 *private persones in . . . in hyd places*='Qui demissi in obscuro uitam habent' (*Sal* 51.12). *Con* probably translates **1491** 'agunt' (for 'habent'). 'demissi' is interpreted via *Val*: 'Dimissi in ob. .i. in humiles homines in humili et ignobili loco positi' (sig. d2[r]). Sg. verb ('ledith') despite pl. subject is odd: the mistake probably comes about because 'Qui', the Lat. subject, is the form for both masc. sg. and masc. pl.

1256 *in men of lowe degre*='apud alios' (*Sal* 51.14).

1256–7 *in the hye governoures*='in imperio' (*Sal* 51.14).

1260 *the extreme ende of all*. I.e. the punishment of execution, which misinterprets *Sal* (='postrema', 51.15) but follows *Val*: 'postrema .i. pœnas: nam primo dicitur de crimine deinde de supplicio agitur' (sig. d2[r–v]).

1260–1 *forgeting all theire . . . and horrible dedys*. *Sal*: 'in hominibus inpiis sceleris eorum obliti' (51.15). *Con* translates 'et omnibus impiis', the variant in all *LaetT* commentary editions (except **1493.1**), as is sometimes also found in *IncT*.

1262 *thowe after the sentence of divers*. Not in *Sal*.

1263 *Decius Sillanus*. *Sal*: 'D. Silanum' (51.16). Cf. 1189*n*.

1269–70 *elected to succede . . . dignite of consull*='consulem designatum' (*Sal* 51.18). Cf. 180–1*n*, 1189–90.

1270 *to iuge*='decernere' (*Sal* 51.18). 'iuge' is suggested by *Val*'s gloss, 'de nouo genere supplitii iudicare' (sig. d2[v]).

1270–1 *But to speke now of fere*. *Sal*: 'De timore . . . disserere' (51.19). *Con* follows 'De timore autem' etc., the variant in all *LaetT* (except **1494**, **1495.2**, **1497.4**, **1497.5**), as also *BritT*.

1273–4 *as the matere is in the selff*. Awkward translation of 'id quod res habet' (*Sal* 51.20). Cf. Loeb, 'in keeping with the facts of the matter'. Here, as often elsewhere, 'matere' translates 'res' (cf. e.g. 1683–4*n*).

1274 *deth is theire rest*. *Sal*: 'mortem aerumnarum requiem' (51.20). 'aerumnarum' not translated, perhaps due to misunderstanding of its function as an objective gen.

1278–9 *with sore strokys*='uerberibus' (*Sal* 51.21).

1279 *the lawe made by Porcius Cato*. *Sal*: 'lex Porcia' (51.22). *Con* follows *Val*, 'Lex portia: lex quam portius cato tulerat' (sig. d2[v]). Neither *Con* nor *Val* is accurate, however, because the three *leges Porciae* were instituted generally by members of the *gens Porciae*. The law referenced here seems to have 'abolished or restricted a magistrate's right to scourge a Roman citizen' (Ramsey, 199). Cf. 1345.

1280–1 *no senatour*. *Sal*: 'ciuibus' (51.22). Technically correct, but inaccurate as a translation of *Sal* and missing the point that all Roman citizens, not just senators, were exempt. Cf. 1230–1*n*.

1284 *yf thow thoughtest*. Not in *Sal*.

1285 *in a lesse . . . for their scourgyng*='in minore negotio' (*Sal* 51.24), amplified via *Val*: 'In minori neg .s. in uerberando' (sig. d2^{v}).

1286 *in a depper . . . iuge theim deth*='in maiore' (*Sal* 51.24), amplified via *Val*: 'In maiore .s. in necando' (sig. d2^{v}).

1287–8 *rebelles and conspirers*='parricidas' (*Sal* 51.25). Cf. 754*n*.

1289–90 *hir will*='lubido' (*Sal* 51.25), perhaps via *Val*: 'Libido: uoluntas' (sig. d2^{v}).

1291–2 *it is of ryght and deseruyd*='merito adcidet' (*Sal* 51.26).

1299 *xxx^{ti}*='triginta' (*Sal* 51.28). I.e. 30.

1305 *after their willis and appetitis*='lubidinose' (*Sal* 51.30).

1308–13 *whan Lvcius Sylla . . . and suche other*='uictor Sulla quom . . . creuerant, iugulari iussit' (*Sal* 51.32), amplified via *Val*: 'nota est discordia populi romani quæ fuit inter Syllam et marium qui fauorem preditorum ciuium factus est consul et syllam cum suis complicibus ex urbe depulit: et huius marii partes fouebat Danasippus quidem Romanus ciuis perditus: sed postquam Sylla recuperatis uiribus in urbem rediit hunc Danasippum et alios seditiosos ciues interfici iussit' (sig. d3^{r}). NB. also the spelling 'Danasippus' in *Val* (and e.g. **1491**), rather than 'Damasippus' as in modern editions.

1317 *or other goodes*. Not in *Sal*.

1318–19 *into the nombre . . . that were attented*='in proscriptorum numero' (*Sal* 51.33). On 'attented', cf. 884*n*; presumably this word also has the sense here of 'condemned to death', though note *Con*'s earlier misunderstanding of *proscriptio* (cf. 529*n*). Cf. *Val*: 'proscripti ciues erant hi qui cum nomina eorum in foro exposita essent interfici poterant a quocunque' (sig. d3^{r}).

1326 *power of armour*='exercitus' (*Sal* 51.36).

1328 *sworde of execusion*='gladium' (*Sal* 51.36), perhaps via *Val*: '[g]ladio ciues necare' (sig. d3^{r}).

1332 *good and behoffull*='proba' (*Sal* 51.37).

1333–4 *for our sowgers*. Not in *Sal*.

1338 *to invie and malice*=‘inuidere’ (*Sal* 51.38). ‘malice’ antedates 1st citation in *OED*, s.v. ‘malice’, v.

1340–2 *in theire mooste . . . scoureges and betenynges*. *Sal*: ‘uerberibus animaduortebant in . . . summum supplicium sumebant’ (51.39). *Con* misunderstands ‘summum supplicium’ (i.e. capital punishment), probably due to *Val*: ‘puniebant ciues uirgis tantummodo: non capitali pœna’ (sig. d3^{v}). ‘allonly’=‘tantummodo’.

1342 *waxed large and myghty*=‘adoleuit’ (*Sal* 51.40).

1344 *to deceve and oppresse*=‘circumueniri’ (*Sal* 51.40).

1345 *the lawes of Porcius*. *Sal*: ‘lex Porcia’ (51.40). *Con*, again, means ‘Porcius Cato’; cf. 1279*n*.

1346 *by the which*. *Sal*: ‘quibus legibus’ (51.40). ‘legibus’ not translated, probably because this word is om. in *LaetT* (as also in *BritT*).

1347 *banishment and exile*=‘exilium’ (*Sal* 51.40).

1350 *substaunce*. *Sal*: ‘opibus’ (51.42). *Con* probably translates ‘copiis’, the variant in *LaetT* (and also *BritT*).

1351 *so greate and so myghty*=‘tantum’ (*Sal* 51.42).

1356–7 *be of moste power and defence*=‘opibus ualent’ (*Sal* 51.43).

1369 *the go`d′dys and theire temples*=‘aris atque focis suis’ (*Sal* 52.3). *Con* guesses a translation of ‘focis’ (as at 1671, translating there as ‘sacrifices’) and uses ‘go`d′dys’ as metonym for *arae*; cf. e.g. Reuchlin, *Vocabularius*: ‘ara deorum’ (sig. c2^{r}).

1372–3 *But consull, what . . . trespasis ben done*. *Sal*: ‘Nam cetera maleficia . . . ubi facta sunt’ (52.4). ‘But consull, what standist þou thus’, not in *Sal*, translates from *Val*: ‘Consul quid stas: quasi dicat quis nescit coniuratores quos in uinculis tenemus esse necandos: et eos qui adhuc sunt in potestate sua uidelicet in exercitu catilinæ simili supplicio esse afficiendos’ (sig. d3^{v}). *Val*’s ‘Consul quid stas’ looks like a corrupted version of the immediately preceding sentence in *Sal* (‘quam quid in illos statuamus consultare’, 52.3). Beyond *Val*, the phrase does not appear in any *BC* text known to this editor. ‘pursew and ponish’=‘persequare’.

1375–6 *subdewed and taken*=‘capta’ (*Sal* 52.4).

1377–8 *youre fayre howsis, youre grete possessions*=‘domos uillas’ (*Sal* 52.5).

1378–9 *notable pictures and ryche ymages*. *Sal*: ‘signa tabulas’ (52.5). *Con* expands from *Val*: ‘Signa: statuas picturas’ (sig. d3^{v}).

1380 *loue and halse*=‘amplexamini’ (*Sal* 52.5).

1382 *for now it is nott*. *Sal*: ‘Non’ (52.6). *Con* translates ‘nam nunc non’, the variant in several *LaetT* (**1490**, **1491**, **1493.1**, **1494**, **1495.2**, **1497.4**, **1497.5**), as in some *BritT*.

of extorcion of the payment of sowgers='de uectigalibus' (*Sal* 52.6). The idea of 'extorcion' may be suggested by *BC*'s earlier use of *uectigal* with the sense of 'bribe' (cf. 482; *Sal* 20.7). 'payment of sowgers' (i.e. soldiers) is a new idea.

1384 *in dowte and ieopardy*='in dubio' (*Sal* 52.6).

1388–9 *that neuer pardoned . . . into any trespas*='Qui mihi atque . . . delicti gratiam fecissem' (*Sal* 52.8). Idiosyncratic reflexive use of 'pardoned', with the sense that Cato never granted (prospective) pardon either to himself or his 'mynde' (=*animus*) for future sins. Cf. Loeb, 'granted to myself, or to my impulse, indulgence'.

1391–2 *stronge and sewre*='firma' (*Sal* 52.9).

1399 *evill and wikked dedys*='malarum rerum' (*Sal* 52.11).

1401 *syrres*. Not in *Sal*.

1402–3 *the mooste erraunt . . . the comen hutche*='furibus aerari' (*Sal* 52.12), with 'comen' probably repeated from earlier (cf. 787*n*).

1407 *he be vexed and thinkes*='existumans' (*Sal* 52.13).

1408 *of hellys*. A literal, pl. for pl. translation of 'de inferis' (*Sal* 52.13). 'hellys' with sg. meaning is also seen in other early Tudor texts (cf. e.g. *STC* 19, 791, 1978, 14553, 16795, 16984, 20193.5, 24045, 24784).

1411 *in the strongeholdes from the cite*='per municipia' (*Sal* 52.14). Cf. 715*n*.

1415 *thorow all Italye . . . rounde abowte vs*='per totam Italiam' (*Sal* 52.15). 'the contreys rounde abowte vs', an interpolation, recalls the geographical sense of 'contreys' as at 376 and 868.

1418 *he*. Sc., Caesar.

1427 *impere*='rem publicam' (*Sal* 52.19).

1428 *moche more welthye*='pulcherrumam' (*Sal* 52.20).

of our felowis, of citezens. *Sal*: 'sociorum atque ciuium' (52.20). 'atque' not translated.

1431 *rightwese gouernaunce*='iustum imperium' (*Sal* 52.21), via *Val*: 'Iustum imp. uidelicet nullis iniuriis afficiendo socios' (sig. d4^{v}).

1432 *non oppression*. Not in *Sal*.

1433 *superfluouse lustis*='luxuriam' (*Sal* 52.22).

1434 *in the causes of the comen wele*='publice' (*Sal* 52.22).

1437 *f`l'ateryng requestes now occupieth*='ambitio possidet' (*Sal* 52.22), via *Val*: 'Ambitio ambire est blanditiis circumire' (sig. d4^{v}). Sg. 'occupieth' translates sg. 'possidet', even though *Con* has translated a sg. subject ('ambitio') with a pl. ('requestes'); see also 144*n*.

1438–9 *apetitis and plesures* = 'uoluptatibus' (52.23).

1440 *empty and naked*. *Sal*: 'uacuam' (52.23). 'naked' follows *Val*: 'Vacuam. desertam: quia res publica defensoribus nuda inuaditur a sceleratis hominibus' (sig. d4^{v}).

1441 *Here*. Engrossed in MS.

1448 *it was but . . . that blynded theim* = 'per ambitionem' (*Sal* 52.26).

1450–1 *to wret`c´hednes and mischeffe* = 'in miseriam' (*Sal* 52.27).

1451 *a sherpe and a dredfull* = 'aspera' (*Sal* 52.28).

1452 *lewdenes* = 'inertia' (*Sal* 52.28). I.e. laziness, which is closest to the meanings in *OED*, s.v. 'lewdness', n., sense 2; *MED*, s.v. 'leuednes(se', n., sense 1(d). Cf. e.g. Reuchlin, *Vocabularius*, s.v. 'iners': 'inertia . . . qua quis nescit quid facere debeat ex nimia pigritia' (sig. m5^{r}). *Val* specifically relates *inertia* here to physical laziness: 'Inertia: inertiam corporis' (sig. d4^{v}).

1453 *trewly trustyng* = 'confisi' (*Sal* 52.28).

1454–5 *in mooste perelles*. I.e. in the greatest dangers; = 'in maxumis periculis' (*Sal* 52.28).

1455 *helpe and strengith* = 'auxilia' (*Sal* 52.29).

1457 *welth and prosperite is obtenyd* = 'prospere omnia cedunt' (*Sal* 52.29). 'omnia' not translated.

1458–9 *they are angre and hate the* = 'irati infestique sunt' (*Sal* 52.29). 'the' (i.e. 'thee') is interpolated.

1462–3 *contrary to the . . . of his soueraigne* = 'contra imperium' (*Sal* 52.30).

1463–4 *for his noble—but in owterage—corage* = 'inmoderatae fortitudinis' (*Sal* 52.31).

1465 *rebelles ayenst theire contre* = 'parricidis' (*Sal* 52.31). Cf. 754*n*.

1467–8 *Trothe, spare . . . spared for* = 'parcite . . . pepercit' (*Sal* 52.32). *Con*, here as elsewhere, translates *parco* as 'spare' (cf. 345, 610, 1404), but the Lat. pun here is only imperfectly captured because *Con* must use 'spare' in two distinct senses: cf. *MED*, s.v. 'sparen', v., senses 1a(a), 2a(a); *OED*, s.v. 'spare', v.^{1}, senses I.1.a, III.10.a. 'Trothe' antedates *OED*, s.v. 'troth', adv. and interj.

1471–2 *Gabinius, Statilius, Ceparius*. *Sal*: 'Statilio, Gabinio, Caepario' (52.34). *Con* follows the order of names as given in all incunabula.

1472–3 *regarded or considred* = 'pensi' (*Sal* 52.34).

1474 *yf there were place to offende*. *Sal*: 'si mehercule peccato locus esset' (52.35). 'mehercule' not translated.

1476 *my wordes*. *Sal*: 'verba' (52.35). *Con* probably follows the *LaetT* variant 'mea uerba' (as also in *BritT* and most *IncT*).

1477–8 *is besy enforsyng . . . borders and passages*. *Sal*: 'faucibus urget' (52.35). *Con* follows the sense of *Val*, 'In faucibus italiæ: uidelicet in alpibus' (sig. d5^{r}), but in doing so fails to convey the threat's immediacy. Greater immediacy is suggested e.g. by Bole's Sallust commentaries, which give 'In faucibus .i. ante portas' (Oxford, Balliol College, MS 123, ff. 125^{v}, 146^{v}). Loeb prefers 'at our throats', taking *fauces* as a metaphor for throat, as also e.g. suggested by *Asc*: 'faucibus .s. ad deuorandum' (sig. f3^{r}).

1484 *of Wolturcius*. *Sal*: 'T. Volturci' (52.36). The praenomen 'T.' is not translated, probably because om. in *LaetT* (as also in *BritT* and most *IncT*).

1489 *had fynished his . . . was sett downe*='adsedit' (*Sal* 53.1), amplified via *Val*: 'Assedit .s. perorata oratione' (sig. d5^{r}).

1489–90 *all the honourable men*='consulares omnes' (*Sal* 53.1). *Con* could have been more accurate via *Val*, which glosses 'omnes consulares' as 'qui consulatum gesserant' (sig. d5^{r}).

1494 *that haue redde . . . and excellent actes*='multa legenti, multa audienti' (*Sal* 53.2).

1497–8 *menteine and beyre vppe*='sustinuisset' (*Sal* 53.2).

1498–9 *offte and many tymes*='saepenumero' (*Sal* 53.3).

1499 *the Romayns with a small strength*. *Sal*: 'parua manu' (53.3). *Con* translates 'populum romanum parua manu', the variant in all *LaetT* (as also most *IncT* and most *BritT*).

1501 *the mooste welthy and myghtiest*='opulentis' (*Sal* 53.3).

1502 *paciently suffer and ouerpasse*='tolerauisse' (*Sal* 53.3).

1507–8 *with superfluouse lustis and slothefull ease*='luxu atque desidia' (*Sal* 53.5), where 'superfluouse' follows *Val*: 'Luxu: luxuria superfluitate' (sig. d5^{v}).

1509–10 *lyke as she . . . baren and faderlesse*. *Sal*: 'sicuti †effeta parentum†' (53.5). A textual crux (cf. Ramsey, 213–14). *Con*'s interpretation follows *Val*: 'Sicuti effœta: diu inquit ciuitas parentibus quasi orba sine magnæ uirtutis ciuibus fuit' (sig. d5^{v}). 'she'='the comen wele' (1508; i.e. Rome).

1512 *diuers and contrary*='diuorsis' (*Sal* 53.6).

1517 *honour and glorye*='gloria' (*Sal* 54.1).

1519 *clene and perfyte*='integritate' (*Sal* 54.2).

1520 *notable and excellent*='clarus' (*Sal* 54.2).

1520–1 *faste and substanciall wey*=‘seueritas’ (*Sal* 54.2).

1522 *lightly foryeving offensis*=‘ignoscundo’ (*Sal* 54.3).

1524 *for men in perell and mysery*=‘miseris’ (*Sal* 54.3).

extreme execucion. I.e. the infliction of capital punishment (cf. *OED*, s.v. ‘execution’, n., sense 8.b). This is an inaccurate translation of ‘pernicies’ (*Sal* 54.3), but supported by the idea of death in *Val*’s (misleading) gloss, ‘Pernities: exitium’ (sig. d5^{v}). Cf. ‘extreme’ in the senses of death and capital punishment at 688, 1260.

1525 *gentilnes*=‘facilitas’ (*Sal* 54.3), via *Val*: ‘Facilitas quia faciles erat ad ignoscendum’ (sig. d5^{v}).

constancye and iustice=‘constantia’ (*Sal* 54.3).

1526–7 *contynuall watche and diligens*=‘uigilare’ (*Sal* 54.4).

1529–30 *a myghty hoste of sawgers*=‘exercitum’ (*Sal* 54.4).

1531 *laboure and study*=‘studium’ (*Sal* 54.5). *Con* mistakenly takes ‘studium’ as the nom. subject, missing or misinterpreting the *studium*+dat. construction.

1532 *sadnes and gravite*=‘seueritatis’ (*Sal* 54.5).

1533 *with a besy quarelous felowe*=‘cum factioso’ (*Sal* 54.6).

1533–4 *in vertew and valiauntnes*=‘uirtute’ (*Sal* 54.6).

1535 *in iustice and abstinence*=‘abstinentia’ (*Sal* 54.6).

1537 *happely*. Not in *Sal*. ‘happely’ in this sense (i.e. ‘happily’, ‘gladly’) antedates 1st citation in *OED*, s.v. ‘happily’, adv., sense 4.

1540 *doers of execucion*. *Sal*: ‘triumuiros’ (55.1). *Con* follows *Val*’s (essentially accurate) gloss, ‘Triumuiros: iudices rerum capitalium’ (sig. d5^{v}), but misinterprets ‘iudices’ as ‘doers’.

1545 *strongly wallid*=‘muniunt’ (*Sal* 55.4).

1545–6 *a chamber wowted of myghty ston*. *Sal*: ‘camera lapideis fornicibus iuncta’ (55.4). ‘fornicibus’ not translated.

1546–7 *fowle, deformyd, horrible . . . is right dredfull*. *Sal*: ‘incultu tenebris odore . . . eius facies est’ (55.4). *Con* follows the reading ‘inculta’ (i.e. a nom. sg. adj.) as printed in all incunabula. ‘deformyd’ follows *Val*: ‘Inculta: deformis’ (sig. d6^{r}).

1549 *this Lentulus*. *Sal*: ‘ille’ (55.6). *Con* follows the *LaetT* variant ‘ille Lentulus’ (as also in *BritT*).

1550–1 *the hye gouernaunce of the consull*=‘consulare imperium’ (*Sal* 55.6).

1555 *he resid and drew forthe*=‘adduxerat’ (*Sal* 56.1).

1556 *in his hoste*. Not in *Sal*.

1558 *into the felde* = 'in castra' (*Sal* 56.2), correctly assuming that the *castra* is in the field of battle: cf. *OED*, s.v. 'field', n.^{1}, sense I.ii.6.a. For other interpretations of *castra*, cf. 1566–7*n*, 1575*n*, 1587*n*.

1560 *to the mustre . . . and iij*^{xx}*horsemen*. I.e. 12,200 and 1,460. See Introduction, pp. xxxviii–xxxix.

1561 *ij M*^{l}. I.e. 2,000.

1562 *diffensible arraid* = 'instructa' (*Sal* 56.3).

1563–4 *at all adventures . . . but sharpe swordes* = 'ceteri, ut quemque . . . praeacutas sudis portare' (*Sal* 56.3). 'at all adventures' translates 'casus' via *Val*: 'Casus: sicut casu unicuique ad manus arma perue[n]erant' (sig. d6^r); on the Engl. idiom, cf. 865*n*. 'sperys or sithes' = 'sparos aut lanceas' (*Sal* 56.3), with 'sithes' suggested by *Val*: 'Sparus est genus teli quo utuntur rustici ad putandas arbores. et est oblongum et in extremo in curuum in modum pedis' (sig. d6^r). 'sharpe swordes' misinterprets *Sal* 'praeacutas sudis' (56.3); a later Tudor reader correctly glosses *sudes* as 'stakes' in a copy of a Paris 1504 edition (BodL, DD 20 Art., sig. f5^r), perhaps following *Asc*, 'sudes .i. hastilia non ferrata' (sigs. f4^v–f5^r). That said, *Con*'s addition of 'but' (adv.) correctly captures the sense of the Lat., that the soldiers are ill-equipped.

1566–7 *tentys and caryage* = 'castra' (*Sal* 56.4).

1569 *mischevous purposes* = 'incepta' (*Sal* 56.4).

1570 *bondemen and haskerdes* = 'seruitia' (*Sal* 56.5). As with other translations of words relating to Roman slavery, it is unclear to what extent *Con* is anachronistic (cf. e.g. 114*n*, 518*n*). 'bondemen', though, is at any rate a common early Tudor translation for such words. In Barclay's Sallust, 'bondmen' translates *servi*, *servitus*, and *servitia*, three times as part of a doublet ('seruauntes or bonde men', 'subgettes and bondmen'): see *Famous Cronycle*, 75, 78, 131, 189. The doublet 'seruant or bondman' also appears as a translation of *servus* in e.g. Udall, *Floures for Latine spekynge*, sig. R8^r. On the potential significance of such doublets, see Introduction, pp. l–li. On 'haskerdes', see Introduction, p. xliii.

1573–4 *vile men owtelawed* = 'cum seruis fugitiuis' (*Sal* 56.5). On 'vile', cf. 114, 598, 697, 712, 1030, 1064, 1176. 'owtelawed' recalls 'banesshed' as a description of 'vile men' (1030–1) but does not capture the full sense of 'fugitiuis': cf. e.g. Reuchlin, *Vocabularius*: 'fugitiuus recte nemo dicitur nisi qui fugit dominum' (sig. k7^r).

1575 *into their hooste* = 'in castra' (*Sal* 57.1).

1578–9 *fled faste into dyvers parties* = 'dilabuntur' (*Sal* 57.1), amplified via *Val*: 'Dilabuntur: in diuersas partes fugiunt' (sig. d6^r).

1580–1 *into þe felde . . . cite of Pistoie*. *Sal*: 'in agrum Pistoriensem' (57.1). 'cite' is introduced via 'cuiutas' in *Val*: 'Pistoriensem: pistorium ciuitas est hetruriæ' (sig. d6^r). Pistoria is also spelled 'Pistoie' in Lydgate, *Fall of Princes*, VI.3061.

1581 *by the strayte passages*='per tramites' (*Sal* 57.1), via *Val*: 'Tramites dicuntur angustiores semitæ' (sig. d6[r]).

1582 *into the hye . . . Fraunce callid* Transalpina='in Galliam Transalpinam' (*Sal* 57.1). For 'hye', which requires some geographical knowledge, cf. e.g. Reuchlin, *Vocabularius*: 'dicuntur alpes alti montes . . . Et ab alpes dicitur alpinus . . . Inde transalpinus .i. vltra alpes existens' (sig. b3[v]).

1585–6 *`to the entent' . . . and his company*='Catilinam agitare' (*Sal* 57.2).

1587 *hoste*='castra' (*Sal* 57.3).

1588 *satyld his company*='consedit' (*Sal* 57.3).

1590 *in the playnes*='locis aequioribus' (*Sal* 57.4), perhaps via *Val*: 'Aequioribus: planioribus' (sig. d6[v]).

1590–1 *in a redynes . . . folowe the chase*. *Sal*: 'expeditos in fuga sequeretur' (57.4). *Con* mistakes 'expeditos' as describing Antonius' men rather than, correctly, as the direct object of *sequor*. 'folowe the chase' (='in fuga sequeretur') introduces a contemporary hunting metaphor: cf. e.g. 'I folowe the chase as a hunter foloweth the chase of a wylde beest' (Palsgrave, *Lesclarcissement de la langue francoyse*, sig. III4[v]).

1599 *manlynes to men*='uirtutem' (*Sal* 58.1). 'to men' not in *Sal*.

1603 *it is folye for the to exhorte*='nequiquam hortere' (*Sal* 58.2). I.e. thee.

1604 *noyouse to be herd of*='auribus officit' (*Sal* 58.2). *Con* interprets the Lat. metaphorically when a more literal translation may have been preferable; cf. Loeb, 'obstructs his ears'.

1608–9 *while I abyde . . . goo into Fraunce*. *Sal*: 'dum ex urbe . . . Galliam proficisci nequiuerim' (58.4). Con's rendering in the present tense may reflect unfamiliarity with the classical construction of *dum*+present indicative.

1611 *yf oure mynde covetid*. *Sal*: 'si maxume animus ferat' (58.6). 'maxume' not translated, probably because this superlative is om. in all *LaetT* (except **1491–2**).

1613 *by handstrokys*='ferro' (*Sal* 58.7). 'handstrokys' antedates 1st citation in *OED* from an Engl. (rather than Scots) text, s.v. 'handstroke', n. Cf. 1684.

1618 *greate companyes abundantlye*='conmeatus abunde' (*Sal* 58.9). *Con* makes a reasonable but incorrect guess at translating 'conmeatus', perhaps because the word is not glossed in *Val*. Cf. the accurate gloss in *Asc*: 'conmeatus .i. victualia erunt nobis abunde' (sig. f6[r]). Failing to understand 'conmeatus' correctly, the translator can do no better than render 'abunde' very literally as 'abundantlye', which makes little sense in Engl.

inhabitantes in the citees='municipia' (*Sal* 58.9). Cf. 715*n*. Cf. perhaps Reuchlin, *Vocabularius*, s.v. 'municeps': 'Hoc enim nomine censentur castellani in municipio nati et permanentes. et etiam milites stipendiarii qui per custodiam municipii munera capiunt. Et etiam originales ciues. et in loco officium gerentes dicuntur sic. Et etiam quoddam genus romanorum ciuium olim dicebatur sic' (sig. p8[r]).

1619 *contrees vnder the iurisdiccion of Rome*. *Sal*: 'coloniae' (58.9). *Con* translates with the knowledge of a gloss such as, say, 'Colonia etiam dicebatur olim ciuitas vel regio capta a romanis' (Reuchlin, *Vocabularius*, sig. f6[r]).

1622 *dothe not defende*='non texerint' (*Sal* 58.10), perhaps via *Val*: 'Texerunt: defenderunt' (sig. d6[v]).

1626 *olde approved manlynes*='pristinae uirtutis' (*Sal* 58.12).

1629 *to vile and to grevouse*='foeda atque intoleranda' (*Sal* 58.14).

1630 *leve and ouercome*='relinquere' (*Sal* 58.15).

1642 *vnrevenged*='inulti' (*Sal* 58.21). Antedates 1st citation in *OED*, s.v. 'unrevenged', adj. *OED*'s 1st citation is Barclay's Sallust, where this adj. similarly translates 'inulti' (Barclay, *Famous Cronycle*, ed. Waite, 73; cf. *BJ* 31.2).

1648 *from the fotemen*. *Sal*: 'militibus' (59.1). *Con* translates the *LaetT* variant 'peditibus' (as also in *BritT*).

1649 *open perell*='exaequato periculo' (*Sal* 59.1), i.e. 'quasi dicit ipse pedes fuit et ita periculum exæquauit et cæteros audaciores reddidit', as explained by the ps.-Ognibene commentary (**1500.2**, sig. f2[v]). No equivalent gloss is offered in *Val*, hence perhaps *Con*'s inaccurate translation of *exaequatus* as 'open'.

1653–4 *.vj. cohortes, abowte . . . and xxij men*. I.e. six cohorts, 5,122 men. On this number, see Introduction, pp. xxxix–xl. The present edition assumes that 'cohortes' is intended as an Engl. noun here, but as untranslated Lat. at 1665 and 1679. Indeed, although *cohort* had already been used as an Engl. word by Caxton (cf. *OED*, s.v. 'cohort', n., sense 1), its foreignness had previously been a source of consternation (and comedy) for the author of *Knyghthode and Bataile* (1460): 'Cohorts the Latyn is, this regioun / Tenglish it fore, help vs, good Lord! Amen' (*Knyghthode and Bataile*, ed. Dyboski and Arend, lines 707–8).

1654 *banerrers and standers*. *Sal*: 'signa' (59.2), which should more accurately be treated as a metonym for 'reliquas cohortes' (see Ramsey, 223), as e.g. *Asc* explains: 'signa reliquarum .s. cohortum: aut reliquorum militum (sig. f6[v]).

1655 *the cheffe capytayns*='centuriones' (*Sal* 59.3). Sense would have been clear from *Val*, e.g. 'centuriones .s. qui præerant manipulis' (sig. e1[r]).

1656 *that belonged to the retynew of Rome*='euocatos' (*Sal* 59.3), via *Val*: 'Euocatos: euocati dicebantur qui scripti erant ex diuersis urbibus sociorum populi romani' (sig. e1[r]).

1658 *oon Fesulanus*. *Sal*: 'Faesulanum quendam' (59.3), i.e. 'a certain man from Faesulae' (Loeb), mistaken by *Con* as a person called 'Fesulanus'. Cf. 589*n*.

1659 *with his sonnys*. *Sal*: 'cum libertis' (59.3). *Con* translates the *LaetT* variant 'liberis' (as also in *BritT*).

1660–1 *in the bataill of Cymbris*='bello Cimbrico' (*Sal* 59.3). *Con* misinterprets because 'Cymbris' is not a place. 'Cimbrico' is more accurately glossed by *Val*: 'quod gessit contra cimbros' (sig. e1[r]).

1662–3 *sore diseasid in his leggys*='pedibus aeger' (*Sal* 59.4).

1664 *that grete capytayn*='legato' (*Sal* 59.4). This (correct) sense would have been clear from *Val*, e.g. 'Legati: qui legioni sex milium sexcentorum et sexaginta sex hominum præerant' (sig. e1[r]).

He. Sc., Petreius.

1665–6 *the garde of . . . to the forward*. *Sal*: 'cohortis ueteranas quas . . . conscripserat, in fronte' (59.5). *Con*'s translation of 'quas tumulti causa conscripserat' lacks accuracy; cf. e.g. Thomas Elyot's more accurate translation: 'He dyd set in the front of the battayle the bendes of olde souldiours, which he had gatheryd togither bycause of the sodayn commotion' (Elyot, *Bibliotheca Eliotae*, sig. I4[r] [s.v. 'Cohors']). '*cohortes veterane*' is underlined in the MS (cf. Introduction, p. xiv). The order of noun+adj. (i.e. '*cohortes veterane*') rather than adj.+noun was possible in contemporary Engl., especially when such combinations 'contain a borrowed adjective' and when the expression is 'a term going back to French or Latin' (Rissanen, 'Syntax', 208). In this edition, however, the phrase is treated as untranslated Latin, since it appears as part of a lexical gloss ('*veterane*' being understood as Lat. *veteranae*); see further Introduction, p. lv. On the off-chance that '*veterane*' was intended here as an English noun, it would antedate 1st citation in *OED*, s.v. 'veteran', n. Cf. 1684–5, where '*veterani*' also appears as untranslated Lat. together with another Engl. gloss. On 'cohortes', cf. 1653–4*n*.

1670 *onharnessid*. This sense antedates 1st citation in *OED*, s.v. 'unharnessed', adj.[1], sense 2.

1670–1 *for the temples and their sacrifices*. *Sal*: 'pro aris atque focis suis' (59.5). *Con* guesses a translation of 'focis' (cf. 1369) and takes 'temples' from *Val*: 'Pro aris et focis: pro templis et focis' (sig. e1[r]).

1672 *xxx[ti]*. I.e. 30.

1672–4 *in the hoste . . . the hole governaunce*='tribunus aut praefectus aut legatus aut praetor' (*Sal* 59.6). The idea of a 'depute' may follow Vegetius' suggestion that a *praefectus legionis* could serve as 'vicarius' to a legate (Vegetius, *Epitoma rei militaris*, ed. Reeve, 2.9.2). Cf. e.g. Reuchlin, *Vocabularius*, 'Vicarius . . . est qui uices alicuius gerit' (sig. y6[r]).

1677–8 *overlokyd and putt in a redynes*='exploratis' (*Sal* 60.1).

1678–9 *wardes of the hoste callid* coh\o/rtes='cohortis' (*Sal* 60.1). Cf. 1653–4*n*.

1681 *the light-harnessed men called* ferentarii='ferentariis' (*Sal* 60.2), amplified via *Val*: 'ferentarii dicuntur milites leuis armaturæ eo quod arma tantummodo ferebant' (sig. e1[r]). *Ferentarii* were 'skirmishers, who hurled missiles from a distance' (Ramsey, 226).

1683 *standers*. *Sal*: 'signis' (60.2). Better translated as a metonym for ranks of men; cf. 1654*n*.

gonnys and dartes='pila' (*Sal* 60.2). 'gonnys' is unlikely to mean an explosive weapon (*OED*, s.v. 'gun', n., sense I.1.a; *MED*, s.v. 'gonne', n., sense 2), since this would be a striking anachronism for a translation that typically resists anachronism, at least by the standards of other early Tudor translations (see further Introduction, pp. xliii–xliv, l–li). *Con* probably uses 'gonnys' in its next most common contemporary sense in *MED*, 'A siege engine that casts missiles' (sense 1; cf. *OED* sense I.2).

1683–4 *the mater is . . . swordes of handstrokes*='gladiis res geritur' (*Sal* 60.2). Here, as often elsewhere, 'matere' translates *res* (cf. e.g. 1273–4*n*). 'with swordes of handstrokes' may be a transposition error for 'with handstrokes of swordes', but *Con* may also have translated *Sal* 'gladiis' as 'with swordes', closely following the Lat., before adding 'of handstrokes' (not in *Sal*) as an afterthought. For 'in doyng', cf. 1172*n*. On 'handstrokes', cf. 1613*n*.

1684–5 *olde accustomed sowgers callyd* veterani='Ueterani' (*Sal* 60.3). '*veterani*' engrossed in MS. The idea that these soldiers are 'accustomed' (i.e. 'practised', 'experienced') picks up on the use of this adj. at 1666.

1685–6 *as well on . . . as ferder of*='comminus' (*Sal* 60.3).

1687–8 *among the feble-harnessed men*='cum expeditis' (*Sal* 60.4), via *Val*: 'Expeditis: leuis armaturæ' (sig. e1[r]).

1688–9 *that had the . . . fyght and labour*='laborantibus' (*Sal* 60.4).

GLOSSARY

Words are only glossed if they are obsolete in modern English, if their spelling may cause problems of identification, or if their sense differs from the standard one in modern English. In the alphabetical arrangement, consonantal **i** is treated as **j**, vocalic y is treated as **i**, and **u**, v, and **w** are ordered depending on whether the letter in question represents a vowel or a consonant. The ~ sign represents the headword in its most recently given form. The following abbreviations are used: *adj.* (adjective), *adv.* (adverb), *comp.* (comparative), *conj.* (conjunction), *imp.* (imperative), *impers.* (impersonal), *inf.* (infinitive), *interj.* (interjection), *intrans.* (intransitive), *n.* (noun), *pa.* (past tense), *pa. p.* (past participle), *pl.* (plural), *pr.* (present), *prep.* (preposition), *pron.* (pronoun), *pr. p.* (present participle), *refl.* (reflexive), *sg.* (singular), *subj.* (subjunctive), *superl.* (superlative), *trans.* (transitive), *vbl. n.* (verbal noun). Non-English nouns (e.g. *ferentarii*) are explained in the Explanatory Notes. A * next to the line reference indicates that the cited form is emended.

A

abyde *inf.* endure 129, 319, 456; **abyde** *pr. 1 sg.* await 1608

abowte *adv.* around 549, on the point (of doing) 1393, **aboute** 14, 634, around 1545, here and there 642, **went abowte** went about (doing something) 314, 644, 733, **was** ~ embarked on 1076, **were** ~ intended 1118; *see also* **besett, hale**

accloyed *pa. p.* oppressed 1201

accombred *pa. p.* overwhelmed 723, 1055

accompte *pr. 1 sg.* consider 79; **accompting** *vbl. n.* reckoning 1653

accustomed *pa. p.* habituated 681–2, 704, customary 552, practised, experienced 1684, ~ **vpon** familiar with 1666, **customed** customary 566

acorde *n.* harmony 222

adioyne *inf.* add 22

adventures *n. pl.* **at all** ~ no matter what 865, whatever the consequences 979–80, as it chanced 1563

advises *n. pl.* **by his** ~ under his direction, in compliance with his orders 458 (see n.)

advoutre *n.* adultery 315; **adwowtrees** *pl.* adultery 351 (see n.)

adwoutrer *n.* adulterer 329

aferde *adj.* afraid 1418, afraid of 1686

affyans *n.* (band of) confidence 338, 539

affinite *n.* fellowship 1569, **of his affynyte** part of his fellowship 952

afore *adv.* previously 142, 424, 463, etc.

afore *conj.* before 124, 318, 415, etc.

afore *prep.* to a higher degree than 1, in front of 440, 511, 691, etc.; ~ **that** before (*conj.*) 51, 761

aforehand *adv.* beforehand 762

aforetyme *adv.* previously 135, 459, 460, etc.

after *prep.* according to, in line with 11, 156, 320, etc., ~ **as** according to how 255, **aftyr** according to 466, **aftir** 81, 773, 1142; **after whan** after (*conj.*) 59, 159, 170, etc., ~ **that** 270, 656, 890, etc., ~ **þat** 1565, ~ **where** 595

agre *inf.* agree 1229; **agree me** *inf. refl.* consent, accede 106; **agrethe it** *pr. 3 sg. impers.* is it pleasing 1284; **agreed** *pa. p.* agreed 1034

agrevid *pa. p.* aggravated 1129; **aggreving** *vbl. n.* ~ **of** exaggerating 558

albeit *conj.* although 26, 463

all *adv.* entirely 476, 477

allonly *adv.* only 31, 81, 181, etc., **alonly** 7

alowid *pa. p.* certified 1174

ambassatoures *n. pl.* envoys 929–30, 938, 947, etc.

amonge *adv.* meanwhile 257

amonges *prep.* amongst 50, 105, 161, etc.

and *conj.* if 485, 914, 917, etc., ~ **yf** if (*in same sense*) 64, **as** ~ as though 371, 1106

angylles *n. pl.* corners 1176

anon *adv.* straightaway 278, 290, 340, etc.

anournyd *pa. pl.* adorned 301

apoyntment *n.* pact, agreement 430, **appoyntment** purpose 1119
appeching *vbl. n.* accusing 1483
appeling *vbl. n.* accusing 1139
applie *inf.* submit *958; **applie** *subj. pl.* attend 1227; **applied** *pa. 3 sg.* submitted 571; **applied** *pa. p.* consented 1537
appoynted *pa. 3 sg.* fitted out 836, arranged 989, 1665, ordered 1021; **appoynted** *pa. p.* agreed 440, set out 995
approvinge *pr. p.* confirming 5; **approved** *pa. p.* tried and tested 1626
armour *n.* arms, weaponry 168, 192, 193, etc., **armoure** 1429
arraid *see* **diffensible**
as *conj.* as though 896, 899, 940, ~ **for** as regards 96, 925, 1372
ascape *n.* mistake 28, **escape** possibility of escape 1254
assent *inf.* submit 599; **assent** *pa. p.* agreed 401, 858, **assente** 994, **assented** 555
asspying *pr. p.* perceiving 1170; **asspied** *pa. 3 sg.* perceived 343; **asspied** *pa. pl.* discovered 1335; **asspied** *pa. p.* detected 436, **aspied** caught sight of 938
astate *n.* formal pomp 837
attache *inf.* arrest 1038
atteynted *pa. p.* condemned to death 884 (see n.), **attented** 1319 (see n.), **attentyd** subject to attainder, forfeited 1355, 1410, **attaynted** 529 (see n.)
auctoryte *n.* power 684, 700, 790, etc., command, rulership 448, 519, 630, etc., official position, office 181, 434, 626, etc., position of authority, standing 177, political sanction 485, weight, influence 954, **auctorite** command, rulership 1583, good reputation (as an *auctor*) 6; **auctorytes** *pl.* commands, rulerships 907
auncetoures *n. pl.* ancestors 751, 1209
avaunce *inf.* promote 6; **avaunced** *pa. p.* improved, advanced 1213
aventure *inf.* take risks, venture 406, 636
awne *adj.* own 305, 357, 565, etc., **owne** 588, 1461, 1471, etc.
awne *pron.* private means 139, own situation, circumstances 863, own possessions 59, 131, **owne** 294, own situation, circumstances 1528, **of our awne** belonging to ourselves 502
aworthe *adv.* **takith well** ~ considers with indifference 97
ayen *adv.* again 115, 480, 650, etc., for a second time 1470
ayenst *prep.* against 77, 108, 161, etc., **ayenste** 1461

B

banerrers *n. pl.* standard-bearers 1654
bankettes *n. pl.* feasts 194, 280, 317
bawdre *n.* sexual immorality, debauchery 315, 329
be *prep.* by 573, among 1460
behalffes *n. pl.* matters, things 23
behoffe *n.* advantage 901
behovefull *adj.* useful 298, **behoffull** 1332
belongith *pr. 3. sg.* belongs 838; **belongith** *pr. 3. sg. impers.* is fitting 53
bequeith *pr. 1 sg.* commend, entrust 832
besett *inf.* besiege, surround 999, 1037; **besette** *pa. 3 sg.* surrounded 645; **besett** *pa. pl.* surrounded 1042; **bysett abowte** *pa. p.* assailed 755–6
bestyrre you *imp. refl.* stir yourselves up, rouse yourselves 509–10
bestys *n. pl.* animals, creatures 38, 43, 1643
bestowe *inf.* apply 10, **bestow** spend 111; **bestowing hymself in** *pr. p. refl.* applying himself to 1527; **bestowed** *pa. 3 sg.* stationed, arranged 1541, 1558; **bestowed theimselffes in** *pa. pl. refl.* applied themselves to 75
besy *adj.* busy, occupied 1477, 1687, meddlesome 1533
besynes *n.* task 10, 197, 929, event, affair 415, diligence, industry 660, zeal, application 973, action, work 981, plot, mischievous activity 634, 1539, **bysenes** 898, task 91, action, work 109
betenynges *n. pl.* beatings 1342
bethoght hym of *pa. 3 sg. refl.* reflected on 758
betwixt *prep.* between 567, 1023, **bytwixte** 913
bevayling *pr. p.* lamenting 940
byddith *pr. 3 sg.* invites, asks 1370
bydyng *vbl. n.* dwelling 152

bye *inf.* buy 251, 705; **by** *pr. pl.* buy 502
bolded *pa. p.* emboldened 474
bond *adj.* ~ . . . **man** serf, tenant (?) 712 (see n.)
bondage *n.* slavery, servitude (?) 518 (see n.), 1107, 1306, etc.
bondemen *n. pl.* men held in slavery or forced to work without payment (?) 1570 (see n.)
bounden *pa. p.* duty bound, obliged 1131
brayns *n. pl.* talent, ability 175, 211, **braynes** wits, intelligence 471
brake *pa. 3 sg.* put a stop to 444, broke 1549; **brake** *pa. pl.* violated 1221
brennyng *vbl. n.* burning 760
but *adv.* only 45, 88, 225, etc.
but *conj.* but 6, 16, 40, etc., and yet 384, 953, ~ **yf** unless 1470, **bvt** but 99, 110, 270, etc.
but *prep.* except 303, 309, 354, etc.

C

cam to *pa. 3 sg. impers.* came about 306
caryage *n.* baggage train 1567
caste *n.* cast (of dice), chance 1400
cause *n.* business, affair, matter 1137, 1144, 1265, etc., reason 358, 374, 1387, etc., concern, side espoused 822, 896, 1573; **causes** *pl.* cases, disputes 1200, matters of interest, affairs 1434, 1527
chamber *n.* room, dwelling place 502, room, enclosed space 1545
charge *n.* responsibility, duty 16, burden, hardship 1055, **his** ~ the accusation/charge against him 738, 1085–6, **yeueth in** ~ instructs 766; **charges** *pl.* luxury items, items of expense 324, expenditure 346
chase *n.* **folowe the** ~ go in pursuit 1591
chase *see* **chose**
chaunce *n.* outcome 886, luck, chance 1289, situation, circumstance 1584; **chaunces** *pl.* outcomes 271
cheryd *pa. 3 sg.* encouraged 1047
choyse *n.* decision 844
chose *inf.* encourage 514 (see n.); **chose** *pa. 3 sg.* selected 1655; **chase** *pa. pl.* chose 174; **chosen** *pa. p.* selected 382, 1189
cite *n.* city 150, 241, 697, etc., **citee** 125, 158, 326, etc., municipality (?) 707 (see n.), 977, **the cite** the city, Rome 137, 142, 145, etc., **the citee** 376, 393, 630, etc.; **citees** *pl.* cities 61, 203, 299, etc.
clene *adj.* morally upright 1200, 1519
clene *adv.* entirely, completely 258
clerely *adv.* entirely, completely 321, 789
clerkys *n. pl.* learned people 4, 31
coloure *inf.* misrepresent, distort 738, **colour** 973; **colored** *pa. 3 sg.* misrepresented, distorted 1085
coloure *n.* deceit, disguise 131, colour, shade 361, **colour** reasoning 899
comen wele *n.* state, country, commonweal 86, 100, 112, etc., **comyn wele** 380, 574, 878–9, etc., **comen welle** 136, **comen well** 901; *see also* **wele**
comyn *adj.* in common 42, public 823 (see n.), ~ **women** women who prostitute themselves for money 315, notorious, of low reputation 610, **comen** 329, 567, public, shared in common 938, 951; *see also* **comen wele, hutche**
comyns *n. pl.* the common people, plebeians 1656, **comens** 783, 900, **commyns** 866, **comons** lowly people 484
commyssion *n.* delegated authority, command 445, 986, 1154, **commission** 772, **commyssyon** delegation of power (i.e. consular elections) 584, **commyssion** 633
compas *n.* ingenuity, cunning 311
compassid *pa. p.* considered, pondered 392
competent *adj.* sufficient, adequate 201
compleyn *inf.* complain 942; **compleyned hym of** *pa. 3 sg. refl.* lamented 1005; **complenyd** *pa. p.* complained 1386
condicion *n.* state, situation 479, 524, 1352, etc., circumstance, manner 889; **condicions** *pl.* character, habits 124, 937, 1266
condytte *n.* guidance, watchfulness 1456
confusyons *n. pl.* commotions 67–8
coniuracion *n.* conspiracy 13, 36, 575–6
consciency *n.* conscience 361
contrary *adj.* contrasting, conflicting 723, 811, 1365, etc.
contrary *adv.* on the contrary 304
contraryly *adv.* in a contrary manner 1518

contrey *n.* province 446 (see n.), 448, 532, etc., region 1582, nation 969, homeland 168, 732, 775, etc., **contre** 950, 1465, 1487, etc.; **contreys** *pl.* regions 376, 381, 701, etc., territories around Rome 868, provinces 424, 435 (see n.), 907, etc., **contrees** 1619, nations 61, **contres** regions 152
convenyent *adj.* appropriate, suitable 10, 113, 642, etc., **convenient** 1419, 1513
correccion *n.* system for correcting errors 154
corsis *n. pl.* corpses 1242
counseill *inf.* take counsel, deliberate 1007, 1370, **cowncell with** consult, seek advice from 52; **counselid . . . with** *pa. pl.* took counsel, sought advice from 968; **counseld** *pa. p.* deliberated 1479
counseill *n.* scheme, secret plan 402, 409, 533, etc., council (i.e. Senate) 784, judgement, ability to advise 964, advice 1133, 1200, 1417, etc., ~ **house** building in which a council meets (i.e. the Senate House) 440–1, ~ **howse** 1009–10, 1161, **callid . . . to his** ~ brought into league with him 387–8, **callid . . . to their** ~ brought into their confidence 1081, **counsaill** advice, instruction 1137
cowrse *n.* **after the** ~ **of the lawis** in accordance with the laws 425
covenaunt *n.* mutual agreement 629; **covenauntes** *pl.* formal contracts, contracts under seal 1019
covenaunted *pa. 3 sg.* agreed, pledged 661
covetyse *n.* covetousness 143
cowardnes *n.* cowardice 1607, 1620, **cowerdnes** 1458
craftes *n. pl.* arts, practices 104, tricks, deeds 365, actions, conduct 615; **crafte** *sg.* trickery, wiliness 625
crafty *adj.* cunning, deceitful 130, 264, ~ **men** skilled labourers 1176
cryes *n. pl.* decrees 853
customed *see* **accustomed**

D

dartes *n. pl.* javelins 1683
dealyng *vbl. n.* behaviour 573
declare *inf.* tell, relate 92, 122, 897, etc., make known 1116; **declarith** *pr. 3 sg.* makes known, shows forth 2; **declarid** *pa. 3 sg.* revealed 1079; **declared** *pa. p.* related, told 14 (see n.), **declaryd** discussed 1407
degre *n.* rank, position in social hierarchy 394, 397, 400, etc.
deyntynes *n.* delightfulness, elegance 619
demenure *n.* behaviour 870
demure *adj.* grave, dignified 746 (see n.)
depper *adj. comp.* weightier, more serious 1286
derke *adj.* uninformed, obscure 32, dark 1546, **dyrke** 1409
deseytes *n. pl.* wiles, deceptions 265
desertes *n. pl.* good deeds 172, deeds 236, worthiness, merit 821, **theire** ~ what they deserve 1228, **their** ~ 1303; **the desert** *sg.* that which is deserved 1249, **the deserte** 1552
despaired *pa. pl.* despaired of 731
detectyng *vbl. n.* uncovering 1066, disclosure 1138
dew *adj.* proper, morally right 21, appropriate, correct 1647, **dewe** appropriate, sufficient 1132
dewty *n.* debt 826
diffensible *adv.* ~ **arraid** equipped for fighting 1562
dignyte *n.* office, rank, position 68, 535, 545, etc., **dignitie** 1154, 1253, **dignite** 419, 579, 1270, high office, high rank 103, 252, 308, high standing, high esteem 1189, **dygnyte** office, rank, position 581, high office, high rank 634; **dignities** *pl.* high offices 943, high officials 1334, **dignitees** 718, **dignyties** 685, offices 529, 827
diligens *n.* attentiveness 16, 1527, earnest effort 38, **diligence** 821, persistent effort 959
dischargith *pr. 3 sg.* releases 1275; **dischargyng** *vbl. n.* exculpation 332
discrete *adj.* discerning 1266, prudent, circumspect 1295
discretely *adv.* judiciously 1423
dispyte *n.* disdain 292
dispytefull *adj.* disdainful 538
displesure *n.* injury 356; **displeasures** *pl.* annoyances 536
disporte *n.* merry-making, merriment 619

disposicion *n.* temperament 65, 127, 250, etc., state, condition 940
dissimule *inf.* conceal, disguise 972, **dissemule** 745; **dissimulyng** *pr. p.* concealing, disguising 901; **dissimulid** *pa. 3 sg.* concealed, disguised 1078
distresse *n.* violence 1440, violence, hardship 1502, **make ~ vpon** attack 1009
doutefull *adj.* uncertain 912 (see n.), wavering 966, disputable 1200, **doutfull** undetermined 245, **dowtfull** dreadful 677
dowting *pr. p.* being afraid of 741, being uncertain 1057; **dowted** *pa. 3 sg.* was in doubt 5, 389, hesitated, was afraid 355, feared 659
drede *inf.* fear 728, 1285; **dredith** *pr. 3 sg.* fears 1417; **dredyng** *pr. p.* fearing 355; **dred** *pa. pl.* feared 282, **drad** 659; **drad** *pa. p.* feared 452
drede *n.* fear 119, 909, 1269, etc., **haue . . . in ~** fear 486, **~ of** fear to avoid 101, 1534
dredfull *adj.* terrifying 1409–10, terrible 1451, awful 1547, frightened 1051, **dredefull** terrifying 187
dredfully *adv.* fearsomely 571–2
dredfulnes *n.* fearfulness 1603
dryffte *n.* design, intention 1046, design, scheme 1139, **dryfte** 628
duraunce *n.* forced confinement 1135, **durans** 1355

E

ease *n.* idleness 245, 292, 406, etc., comfortable living 880, **with ~** easily 278
easely *adv.* easily 68, 622, 933, etc., readily, lightly 244, 1389, gradually 1679
effecte *n.* fruition, completion 635; **effectes** *pl.* essence, conditions 1407
egall *adj.* equal 93, 340, 1516
egally *adv.* equally 1558
egell *n.* eagle (i.e. a military standard) 1660
eyde *inf.* aid 164
eyde *n.* aid, assistance 1628; **aydes** *pl.* monetary contributions 784
eyder *see* **ethir**
eyn *n. pl.* eyes 362, 511
ellz *adv.* otherwise 741, 1415
emonxte *prep.* amongst 224, 248, 487, etc.
emperour *n.* emperor 838 (see n.); **improwrys** *pl.* emperors 64 (see n.)
endevour me/them/theim *inf. refl.* strive 22, 38, 974–5; **endevorith hym** *pr. 3 sg. refl.* strives 263; **endevour you** *imp. refl.* strive 1028
enforsyng *vbl. n.* reinforcing (his army) 1477
enowe *adv.* enough 825
entent *n.* plan, plot 548, 553, 667, purpose, intention 934, **intent** 29, 444, 1039, **to th'entent** for the purpose 554, **to the ~** 1585, **in this ~** for this purpose 1581; **ententys** *pl.* plans 1573
enterprysid *pa. pl.* ventured 526
entirmedle *inf.* mix together 1573, **intermedell** take part 631
entreprise *n.* **toke ~** strove 896; **enterprysis** *pl.* undertakings, tasks 85, **enterpryses** 1498
entrety *n.* **made ~** engaged in negotiation 1049
erraunt *adj.* notorious 1403
erst *adv.* sooner 1321
escape *see* **ascape**
esear *adj. comp.* easier 998
especiall *adj.* **in ~** especially 142
ethir *adv.* either 82, 176, 333, etc., **ether** 295, 1254, **edyr** 1149, 1601, **eyder** 1593
ethir *pron.* each 54, 80, **eyder** 1150, **ether** 1515, 1517
execucion *n.* infliction of punishment 1524, execution, capital punishment 231, 1153, 1315, etc., **execusion** 1320, 1328
exhorte *inf.* encourage 1603, 1638, **exorte** 465; **exhortyng** *pr. p.* encouraging 167, **exhorting** 1669; **exhortid** *pa. 3 sg.* encouraged 389; **exorted** *pa. p.* encouraged 647
extreme *adj.* exceedingly great 1150, severe 1340, **~ iugementes** capital punishment, execution 688, **~ ende** death, execution 1260, **~ execucion** infliction of capital punishment 1524
extreme *adv.* to an extreme degree 1214
extreme *n.* **in the ~ of it** finally, in the end 508

F

faculte *n.* field of knowledge 83
fayne *adj.* content 806, 1051
faynt *adj.* weak, cowardly 1453
fayre *adj.* ostensibly attractive, specious 974, beautiful 1378
fall *inf.* descend 182, 280, 1389, slide 339, turn attention 370; **fyll** *pa. 3 sg.* descended 615; **fyll** *pa. pl.* descended, sank 271, 672; **fallyn** *pa. p.* come to pass 469, **fallen** descended 480, splintered 789; **fallyng** *vbl. n.* descending 139
falle *n.* situation 829
false *adj.* untrue 98, 704, 740, etc., wicked 365, **falsse** erroneous 827, mendacious 1131, **commytted false wytnes** testified falsely 335
fame *n.* reputation 108, 749, 1228, etc., renown 199, 1252, 1253, general opinion 210, good standing 779
famyliar *adj.* closely associated 535
famyliaryte *n.* close association 337, 341, **famyliarite** fellowship 567
faste *adj.* resolute 1520
favour *n.* friendly regard 339, propitious regard 485, 1255, 1265, assistance, aid 767, 1030, goodwill, support 172, 420, 598, etc., partiality 1200
feble-harnessed *adj.* lightly-armoured 1688
felde *n.* field of battle 233, 915, 918, etc., belt of land surrounding a town, environs 835, 1580, 1583; **feldes** *pl.* fields 877
felyshippe *n.* company 375, 984
felle *adj.* severe 1262
felowe *n.* colleague 535, associate, accomplice 1140, person, chap 1533, 1600, **felawe** colleague 629; **felowis** *pl.* associates, accomplices 441, allies, loyal friends 305, 686, 1402, etc., **felawys** 1383
fenyd *pa. 3 sg.* feigned 1077
fense *n.* means of protection 1635
fensyd *pa. p.* fortified 204
fere hym *inf. refl.* be afraid 1122; **fere** *pr. 1 sg.* fear 1323; **fere me** *pr. 1 sg. refl.* am afraid 1449; **fere** *pr. pl.* fear 1452
ferforthe *adv.* **as ~ as** insofar as 1514
ferre *adj.* distant 152, 381, great, considerable 311
ferre *adv.* (by) far, considerably 4, 66, 331, etc., far (away) 112, 450, 466, etc., **fer** 170
ferse *adj.* fierce, cruel 138, untamed 1010 (see n.), violent 1245; **ferser** *adj. comp.* bolder, more courageous 1649
fersenes *n.* savagery 363, ferocity, rage 586
fersly *adv.* fiercely 1426, violently, forcefully 1682, 1685, **fersely** severely, sternly 1248
few *adj.* few 481, 691, 764, etc., small 1506, **fewe** 906
fyll *see* **fall**
fyre *inf.* to set on fire 1442
fyring *n.* setting of fire, fire-starting 1108, **fyryng** 1003; **fyringes** *pl.* setting of fires 1241, 1485
foly *n.* wantonness 314, foolishness, dullness 471, 653, 1005; **folys** *pl.* foolish things 1208
folye *adj.* foolish, unwise 1603
for *conj.* because, since 46, 51, 55, etc., on account of 15, 27, 175, etc., despite 459, 586, 734, etc., in place of 964
for *prep.* for 10, 17 (*bis*), etc., **fore** 1130, 1181, 1234, etc.; **for that** because, since (conj.) 26, 412, 525, etc.; **~ why** because, since (conj.) 313, 1109–10, 1428, **~ to** in order to 540, 1244
forder *adv.* further 973
forsothe *adv.* truly 1245, 1411, 1451
fortune *inf.* **It may ~** it may happen 1325; **fortuned** *pa. 3 sg.* chanced, happened 1065; **fortuned** *pa. p.* likely to happen 1374–5; **and it had fortuned Catelyne** *pa. p. impers.* if Catiline had chanced 914
fressh *adj.* stylish 282, vivid 503, cheerful, joyous 619, vigorous, not weary 1689; **fresshest** *adj. superl.* most stylish 312
fresshly *adv.* brilliantly 606
from *prep.* from 25, 32, 72, etc. away from 1411
full *adv.* very, exceedingly 26, 208, 266, etc.
fure *n.* fury 755

G

garnish *inf.* furnish 1556
gentill *adj.* courteous 250

gentilmen *n. pl.* gentry, knights (?) 1164–5 (see n.), **meane** ~ middle-rank citizens, gentry (?) 398 (see n.), 660, ~ **horsemen** knights, gentry knights (?) 453 (see n.)
gentilnes *n.* graciousness 273, kindness, generosity 801, 1397, 1525
gydyng *vbl. n.* conduct, behaviour 1295, **gyding** leadership 1658
gladded with *pa. pl.* found enjoyment with 1302
gladder *adj. comp.* more delightful 1337
gonnys *n. pl.* mangonels 1683 (see n.)
gouernaunce *n.* government, rule 911, 1431, power over, control 919, power, authority 1294, 1551, (military) command 844, 1529, 1664, **governaunce** 1674
governour *n.* commander 1599, **gouernoure** 1692; **governours** *pl.* rulers 181, **gouernours** 789, **governoures** 1257, 1509
grace *n.* favour, help 943
graunte *n.* permission 622, decree 784; **grauntes** *pl.* guarantees, privileges 528

H

habundaunce *n.* plenty 268, abundance 1126; **habundaunces** *pl.* abundance 498
hale *pr. pl.* ~ **abowte** hasten about (doing something) 505
halse *pr. pl.* embrace 1380
handstrokys *n. pl.* blows with handheld weapons 1613, **handstrokes** 1684
hange *inf.* depend 749; **hangith** *pr. 3 sg.* depend 483; **hynge vpon** *pa. 3 sg.* hangs over, threatened 665; **hynge** *pa. pl.* remained, were set 961
hard *adj.* harsh, tough 245, adverse, unlucky 926, difficult 949, **harde** 91, **herd** 609, **herde** harsh, difficult to traverse 1580, **herd chaunce** adverse fortune, bad luck 1584; **harder** *adj. comp.* more unlikely 508
hardy *adj.* resolute, courageous 130, presumptuous, foolhardy 234
hardynes *n.* bravery, courage 494, 766, 1416, etc.
harme *n.* harm, injury 683; **harmes** *pl.* harms, injuries 1107, **harmys** wrongdoings 1372
harnes *n.* arms, military equipment 696, 841, 1273, etc., **harnesse** 1449, 1621
harnessed *adj.* armed 663; *see also* **feble-harnessed, light-harnessed, onharnessed**
hasarder *n.* gambler, dice-player 329
haskerdes *n. pl.* people of low social rank 1570
hastardes *n. pl.* people of low social rank 873
hawnted *pa. pl.* frequented 348; **hauntyng** *vbl. n.* dwelling 952
haute *adj.* proud 428, 569
havour *n.* bearing, manner 927
hed *n.* ruler 154; **hedes** *pl.* heads 1445
hellys *n. pl.* hell, the Underworld 1408 (see n.)
herd, herde *see* **hard**
herein *adv.* in this matter 968
herkenyth *pr. 3 sg.* waits 1453
hyd *adj.* obscure, little known 1251
hym *pron.* him 2, 3, 7, etc.; **hym** *refl. pron.* himself 137, 217, 263, etc.; **hymselffe** 129, **hymselff** 184, 739, 770, etc., **hymsilff** 216, 1020, 1052, etc., **hymselfe** 331, 382, **hymsilffe** 646, 656, 750–1, etc., **hymself** 1527, **hymsilf** 1592, 1659; *see also* **them**
hynge *see* **hange**
hir *pron.* her 73, 207, 354, etc., **hyr** 572, 619; **hirsilff** *refl. pron.* herself 603
his *pron.* its 850, his 7, 11, 12, etc., **hys** 626
hystoryes *n. pl.* historical narrative, history 35, 116
hit *pron.* it 296, 464, 575, **it** 10, 16, 17, etc.
holdes *n. pl.* strongholds 715
hole *adj.* entire, whole 136, 784, 801, etc., uninjured 1689
holy *adv.* completely 1204
honour *n.* exalted rank, exalted office 106, 107, 115, etc., a woman's honour or reputation 609, reputation 829, moral virtue 1227, 1233, rank 1032, 1097, 1468, glory, fame, prestige 84, 87, 109, etc., **honoure** 897, rank 1224; **honoures** *pl.* offices of state 1156
hoorys *n. pl.* women who prostitute themselves for money, whores (derogatory) 194

hoste *n.* army 279, 454, 656, etc., **hooste** 275, 856, 988, etc.; **hostes** *pl.* armies 533
howbeit *adv.* nevertheless 74, 1146
howbeit *conj.* except that 263, 1561
hutche *n.* **comen** ~ public treasury 787, 1403

I

ymagenyd *pa. 3 sg.* feigned, invented 1137; **ymagenyd** *pa. p.* plotted 438, 650, contrived 1139
ymages *n. pl.* statues 281, 503, 1379
impere *n.* empire 62 (see n.), 259, 1394, etc., **impire** 235, 242, 1088, etc., **empire** 848; **imperys** *pl.* empires 72
improwrys *see* **emperour**
incontinent *adv.* immediately, at once 161, 665, 970, etc., **incontynent** 53, 1587
innocency *n.* innocence 291
instance *pr. pl.* entreat 793
instruccions *n. pl.* instructive examples 146
intermedell *see* **entirmedle**
interpreter *n.* translator 15
iwis *adv.* indeed 1414

J

iourney *n.* march 453, 1119, trip, journey 803, 1113, travel, travels 1075, 1077, **take his** ~ start on his travels, set out 1020, **toke his** ~ started on his travels, set out 764, 1566; **iourneys** *pl.* marches 1580
iuge *inf.* suppose, consider 61, judge 254, 609, judge appropriate 1270, ~ **theim** condemn them to 1286; **iugeth** *pr. 3 sg.* supposes, considers 97; **iuged** *pa. 3 sg.* judged, evaluated 726, supposed, considered 748, 1010, 1061, decided, decreed 1135, judged appropriate 1191, 1410; **iuged** *pa. pl.* regarded 245, supposed, considered 347, 853, 1109, etc.; **iuged** *pa. p.* adjudged 1031, 1187, 1287

K

kepe *inf.* keep (quiet) 564, maintain, keep 753, 1352, 1379; **kepte** *pa. 3 sg.* maintained, kept 574, 632; **kepte** *pa. pl.* kept, maintained 222, 907, 1305, owned, possessed 501; **kept** *pa. p.* maintained, kept 68, 667, 718, etc., **kepte** 221, 776, 1135, etc., treated 276; **kepe** *imp.* defend 1381; **kepyng** *vbl. n.* being kept (in custody) 1412
kepynge *n.* custody 1097
kynde *n.* kind, variety 33, tribe 153; **kyndes** *pl.* peoples, tribes 155
kynred *n.* family, ancestry 428
knoleage *n.* news, notice 665, **knolege** 1053, **knowleage** understanding 15, faculty of understanding 30, **yeue . . . knoleage** inform 855, **yaue . . .** ~ informed 971, **haue** ~ know 230, **had** ~ was informed, knew about 984, **yeven me in knolege** made known to me 831
knoleged *pa. pl.* confessed 1084

L

langere *inf.* hesitate 1425
lay *inf.* ~ **awey** discard, set aside 799, ~ **vnto** attribute to, set against 992; **lays** *pr. 3 sg.* positions 1667; **laye** *pa. 3 sg.* was encamped 1583, **laid on** added 753; **laid** *pa. pl.* hid, concealed 1042, ~ **to** added to, set against 1085, **layde awey** discarded 731, **laid . . . abowte** struck on all sides 1685; **laid** *pa. p.* set out 882, set against 1440, **layd** established 1196, **laid by** set aside 25, ~ **to** attributed to, set against 738, ~ **vnto** 1146, 1150, **laied by** 583
ledith *pr. 3 sg.* leads 1250 (see n.), 1647; **ledde** *pa. 3 sg.* led 454; **ledde** *pa. pl.* led 874; **ladde** *pa. p.* led 58, **led** 748, 1627, **ledde** 934
lefull *adj.* legal 689
leyser *n.* available time 425
lernyd *adj.* educated 24, 86, 605
lernyd *pa. 3 sg.* taught 365, discovered 1035; **lernyd** *pa. pl.* learned 192; **lernyd** *pa. p.* discovered 150
lessyth *pr. 3 sg.* diminishes 269; **lessid** *pa. 3 sg.* diminished 586, 906; **lessid** *pa. p.* diminished 885
leste *adj. superl.* least 222, 1254
lett *inf.* prevent 1331, obstruct, block 1611
lett *inf.* grant 1640; **lett** *imp.* let, allow 1401, 1402

lett *n.* hindrance 657, 1194
levyd *adj.* lascivious 329
lewdnes *n.* poor conduct 1392, **lewdenes** lack of initiative 1452
lycens *n.* freedom of action 277
lyght *adj.* easy 327, **light** empty 471; **lighter** *adj. comp.* less severe 1284
light-harnessed *adj.* lightly armed 1681
lightly *adv.* easily, readily 96, 157, 413, etc., **lyghtly** 322, 1017
lyke *adj.* equivalent, the same 90, 296, 341, etc., similar 1517, **in ~ wise** in the same way 263, 698, 1084, etc., **in ~ maner** 476
lyke *conj.* like 39, 76, 258, etc., ~ **as** as though 602, 739, 1509–10
lyked beste *pa. pl.* decided 967
lynage *n.* family, ancestry 125
lystith *pr. 3 sg. impers.* **it ~ vs** we decide 1613; **lysted** *pa. pl.* desired 276, **lustyd** 617
logeinges *n. pl.* dwellings 960
love *n.* lust, sexual desire 280, 353
lowly *adj.* humble 745
lowly *adv.* humbly 730, obediently 799
luste *n.* inclination 319; **lustis** *pl.* sexually wilful appetites 71, 143, 308, etc., **lustys** 293
lusty *adj.* vigorous 493

M

maistre *n.* superiority 1533
malice *inf.* regard with malice 1338
malice *n.* hatred 95, 410, 557, etc., malicious action 778; **malices** *pl.* hostile acts 223
malicious *adj.* hateful 360, 753, 1443, wickedly cunning, crafty 1214
manere *n.* way, method, fashion 182, 402, 995, etc., custom, habitual practice 277, 861, kind, style (of) 624, **maner** 45, 252, 285, etc., custom, habitual practice 299, 476, way, method, fashion 312, 467, 551, bearing, behaviour 617, 1266, **in ~** to some degree 1117; **maners** *pl.* customs, morals 19, 72, 107, etc.
manhode *n.* valour, courage 1399, 1685
manymysid *pa. p.* manumitted 1175
manlynes *n.* boldness, bravery 50, 184, 468, etc., **Manlynesse** 228
marchesse *n.* borderland 707; **marchesses** *pl.* borderlands 640
marveyle *n.* surprise 1437
matere *n.* affair, business 98, 123, 388, etc., situation 1157, 1366, 1427, etc., substance 249, subject, topic 205, 460, **mater** 33, affair, business 436, 469, 957, etc., subject, topic 27, 1513; **maters** *pl.* things, affairs 368, 516, 636, etc., circumstances 682, 1584, **matters** affairs 392
may *pr. 3 sg. intrans.* prevail, fare 1416
meane *adj.* unremarkable 310; *see also* **gentilmen**
medelyng *vbl. n.* getting involved 112, involvement 1358
melodies *n. pl.* musical performances 1646
memoryall *n.* renown, reputation 46
mesemyth *see* **semyth**
mesure *inf.* control, regulate 1329
mesure *n.* moderation 134, 227, 268, etc.
mete *adj.* suitable, appropriate 357, 587, 646, etc., agreeable 384, 469, ready 598, 926, 1591, etc.; *see also* **vnmete**
mete *n.* food 75
metely *adv.* moderately, fairly 133
methynkith *pr. 3 sg. impers.* it seems to me 122, 1367, **methinkyth** 312, **methinkith** 1268; **methoughte** *pa. 3 sg. impers.* it seemed to me 848
myndes *pr. pl.* think 37
mynysshed *pa. p.* diminished 889
myscheffe *n.* wickedness 102, **in ~** in (their) time of distress 1003; **mischevis** *pl.* wicked deeds 336–7
mischevous *adj.* wicked 271, 328, 548, etc., **myschevous** 374, **mischevouse** 449, 1390, 1404, etc., **myschevouse** 870, **myscheuose** 1482
mystrustyng *pr. p.* suspecting 1018, **mystrusting** fearing for 1051
mo *adv.* ~ **and** ~ increasingly 753
mony *n.* money 251, 1439, **money** 421, 588, 594, etc.
more *adj. comp.* greater, larger 403, 579

N

nay *interj.* no 1354, 1455
ne *conj.* nor 268, 456, 521, etc.

necessite *n.* poverty 337, 777, difficult circumstance 393, hardship, destitution 785, requirement 796, need, unavoidable circumstances 1622, 1638, **necessitie** 513, hardship, destitution 403, 540; **necessities** *pl.* the state of needing things, hardship, destitution 489, difficult circumstances 536
nede *n.* hardship, destitution 616, **hathe** ~ has a requirement (to do something) 54–5
nedyd *pa. 3 sg. impers.* was necessary 606, 1019
ner *conj.* nor 16, 360, 372, etc.
nether *conj.* neither 515, 564, 565, etc., **nethir** 268, 273, 297, etc., **nethire** 1330, **nedyr** 1602, **neyder** 1621, **nother** 1276
nether *pron.* neither of 758
nygh *adv.* almost 1516
non *adj.* no, not any 195, 315, 885, etc.
non *adv.* not, not at all 319, 917, 1415, etc.
noyouse *adj.* offensive, displeasing 1604

O

obeysant *adj.* obedient, submissive 40, 74, **obesaunt** 243, 346
obteyne *inf.* obtain 30, 541, 581; **obtenyd** *pa. p.* secured 892, 1457; **obtenyd** *pa. p. intrans.* been successful 413, 917; **obtenyng** *vbl. n.* obtaining 50
occupy *inf.* make use of 687; **occupieth** *pr. 3 sg.* exercises, makes use of 81, take possession of 1437 (see n.); **occupy** *pr. pl.* enjoy 45; **occupied** *pa. 3 sg.* kept busy 260; **occupied** *pa. pl.* exercised, made use of 255; **occupied** *pa. p.* held, possessed 314, 1156, 1550, kept busy 382, seized 434
of *adv.* off 1570, 1686
offense *n.* crime 1433, wrongdoing 459, **offence** 1467; **offensis** *pl.* wrongdoings 94, 807, 843, etc., **offencis** 140, **offensys** 316
onharnessid *adj.* unarmed 1670
onys *adv.* once 289, 912
onlyke *adj.* different 155
onsaciable *adj.* insatiable 268
onto *see* **vnto**
open *inf.* make known 1605; **openyth** *pr. 3 sg.* reveals, makes known 1039; **openyd** *pa. pl.* revealed, made known 969; **openyd** *pa. p.* revealed, made known 552, 1056
opyn *adj.* publicly known 185, 421, 975, readily perceived 336, brazen, notorious 1487, **open** unobstructed 243, 1619, obvious 1649
opynyon *n.* belief, view 828, plan, plot 925
oppression *n.* acting oppressively, acting tyrannically 272, oppressive acts, tyrannical acts 307, 1432, extortion 293; **oppressyons** *pl.* oppressive acts by rulers 460
ordynaunce *n.* decree 699
owte *adj.* outer, distant 1356
owterage *n.* **in** ~ rashly excessive 1464
owteward *adv.* externally, abroad 507, **owtewarde** 1431
ouercome *inf.* surpass, exceed 506, prevail over 1630, **ouercom** 625; **ouercame** *pa. 3 sg. trans.* prevailed over 1506–7; **ouercamme** *pa. 3 sg. intrans.* triumphed 967; **ouercomen** *pa. p.* defeated 285–6, 1376, **overcomme** 1238
overlokyd *pa. p.* surveyed, supervised 1677
overpasse *inf.* pass by, skip over 1513–14, **ouerpasse** endure 1502; **ouerpassed** *pa. pl.* passed through, lived through 76; **overpassed** *pa. p.* passed by, missed 1006
overrunne *inf.* go through superficially (?) 17 (see n.); **overrynne** *pr. pl.* go through superficially 38
oweth *pr. 3 sg.* ought 1289

P

payne *n.* punishment 1261, 1273, **payn** 1228, **pyne** physical torture 1275; **paynes** *pl.* punishments 1307, ~ **of dethe** the death penalty 1464
pardoned *pa. 3 sg. refl.* granted pardon to 1388 (see n.)
parell *see* **perell**
partetakynges *n. pl.* events, actions 119
party *n.* region 640, faction 887, **partye** 767, **toke partie** took up arms 1309, **Off the odere** ~ on the other side 1662; **parties** *pl.* factions 631, 903,

1045, etc., regions 701, 986, 1356, etc., persons involved in a dispute 1152

peas *n.* peace 65, 87, 146, etc., **pease** 408, 726; **peasis** *pl.* periods of peace 1221

peasable *adj.* peaceful 384

peasably *adv.* peacefully 911

peasid *pa. p.* stilled, calmed 360, appeased 1129

peradventure *adv.* perhaps 517, 1496

perell *n.* jeopardy 574, 1140, danger 664, 709, 776, etc., **parell** 123; **perelles** *pl.* dangerous situations 63, dangerous situation 1366, dangers 110, 165, 171, etc., **perellz** 245, 1057, **parelles** 1603, **perelles of** possibility of danger from 1417–18

perfeccion *n.* morally perfect living 352

perlowse *adj.* dangerous 1414, **perelouse** 866

pictures *n. pl.* statues 281, paintings 502, 1378

pyne *see* **payne**

plate *n.* vessels, utensils 282, 1317

pleasure *n.* source of gratification 78, whim, desire 1218, **plesure** self-gratification 1433; **pleasures** *pl.* enticements 340, gratifications 140, 323, 499, etc., **plesures** 308–9, 1439, **playsures** 731

plunge *n.* **putt to a** ~ put in a critical situation 756, **put . . . to a grete** ~ 1164

polecy *n.* prudent conduct of life 187, **polycye** guile 625, **police** practical wisdom 678, **pollice** good government 1431

pompouse *adj.* magnificent 498

pompously *adv.* magnificently 406

pompowsnes *n.* magnificent living 103 (see n.), 324

poour *n.* power 290, 688, **power** 11, 56, 159, etc., **powere** 410, 451, 1624

porte *n.* hometown 400

possibylite *n.* effort, ability 40, **possibilitie** 896

prayes *n. pl.* spoils, booty 530, 675, 1107, etc., **prayers** 378

prayse *n.* praise 83, 200, 862, etc., **prayes** value 522; **prayses** *pl.* praises 9, 1105

prevente *inf.* anticipate 762, 1538, **prevent** 320; **preventid** *pa. p.* acted prematurely 439

prevy *adj.* covert, secret 637, 644, concealed 646, ~ **to** acquainted with 628, **prevey to** 920

prykkyd *pa. p.* ~ **of** distressed by 336

prynce *n.* ruler 413; **prynces** *pl.* monarchs 482

pryson *n.* prison 983 (see n.), 1542, 1543, forced confinement, custody 1187, 1191, **prison** 1135

pryvely *adv.* secretly 283, 1042

prodygally *adj.* extravagantly 277, 323–4, 378

pronosticates *n. pl.* omens 695

prove *inf.* try, test 1595; **provyd** *pa. pl.* turned out 637; **provid** *pa. p.* revealed 814, found guilty 1283

pumppe *n.* bilge well 872

puplisshe *inf.* make publicly known 965; **puplisshed** *pa. 3 sg.* published 743, **pupplisshed** made publicly known 710; **puplished** *pa. p.* made publicly known 349, **pupplisshed** 1102, **publisshed** 1576

purpose *n.* plan 29, 206, 436, etc., evil intent 444, intention 679; **purposes** *pl.* plans 994, 1569, **purposis** 1104

putt *inf.* award 578, subject, expose 775, put 1605, **putte** 183, **putt to dethe** execute 1300; **puttith** *pr. 3 sg.* puts 1657; **putt** *pr. pl.* impose 796; **putt** *pa. pl.* put 909; **putt** *pa. p.* secured 1355, put 40, 614, 844, etc., **putte** 191, **putte forthe** put to the service of 100, **putte by** deprived 702, **put by** prohibited (from) 423, 1608, **putt by** taken away 1648, ~ **fro** deprived of 670, **put** (. . .) **from** 792, 1032, taken away from 1295, **putt to deth** executed 1281; **puttyng . . . to deth** *vbl. n.* executing 1321; *see also* **plunge**

Q

quarell *n.* dispute, contention 809, ~ **of bataill** armed combat 61

quyete *n.* **in** ~ at peace 523, 808, 908

quykke *adj.* lively 1600

quyteth *pr. 3 sg.* rescues 787

R

rappe *inf.* ~ **and rynde** get by any means 330–1 (see n.)
rate *n.* quality 1650, **after the ~ of** in proportion to 716
ravishment *n.* rape 1238, **ravisshment** 127–8; **ravishmentes** *pl.* rapes 351
reason *n.* intellectual faculty 44, 52, 81, etc., **reson** 104, 1204, cause 1030, **reason** good sense 134, **by ~ of** on account of 524, 1152, **by reson of** 935, 952; **reasons** *pl.* intellectual faculties 286
recouer *inf.* recover from 540; **recoveryd** *pa. p.* restored to strength 1311
redeme *inf.* get rid of by payment 785; **redemyng** *vbl. n.* making good 331
reders *n. pl.* teachers, people who read and expound to pupils or students 24
reducith *pr. 3 sg.* transforms 32
reyse *inf.* mobilize 709, stir up 1064, 1176; **reysid** *pa. 3 sg.* stirred up 668
rekenyd *pa. pl.* ~ **vp** listed, enumerated 1236
rekkyst *pr. 2 sg.* care, heed 1286; **rekkyd** *pa. pl.* cared, heeded 296
renowme *n.* fame 82, **renome** 1518
requyre *inf.* demand 547, 746, **require** 798; **requyrith** *pr. 3 sg.* demands, requires 144; **it requyrith the** *pr. 3 sg. impers.* you must 52; **require** *pr. pl.* demand 1229; **required** *pa. 3 sg.* required 736; **requyred** *pa. pl.* demanded 1014, 1184
rerewarde *n.* part of army behind the main body 1667
residew *n.* remainder, the rest 496, 1542, 1654
resonyng *n.* studying, reflection, the action of reason 53, 57
rewle *n.* governance, rulership, power 60, 178, 239, etc., command 41, 275, authority 56, 887, good governance 262, control 1205, **taken in ~** taken command of 136; **rewles** *pl.* dominions 908
richesse *n.* wealth 103, 199, 201, etc.
right *n.* what is correct, what is morally right 254, 1224, correct, morally right 1195, **ryght** 43, what is deserved 1303, **the ~** what is correct, what is morally right 1202, **of ~** deserved 1291, **ryghte** moral right 1219, **the right** 208; **of ryght** (*adv.*) properly 6, correctly 1313
ryghtwes *adj.* righteous, morally correct 259, **rightwese** 1431
rightwesly *adv.* righteously 1210
rygure *n.* severity 1265
rynde *see* **rappe**
rypyng *vbl. n.* ripening 358
rowme *n.* situation, post 821, **rome** space 1655
rude *adj.* ignorant, uneducated 32, **rewde** rural, rustic 153 (see n.)
rumour *n.* hearsay, unsubstantiated report 681, noisiness 1042

S

saffegarde *n.* security, safety 847, 1272–3, 1634, **savegarde** 630, 1196; **saffegardes** *pl.* defensive precautions 1541, **sauegardes** 734
satyld *pa. 3 sg.* settled, arranged 1588
sawiour *n.* soldier 515, **sowger** 1691; **sowgers** *pl.* soldiers 279, 762, 1178, etc., **saugers** 284, **sawgeorus** 377, **sawgers** 1530
sawtes *n. pl.* attacks 645, 759, 768, etc.
saying *n.* oration, speech 744, 1244, 1246, etc., talk 954, testimony 1134; **sayinges** *pl.* reports 556, comments, remarks 93, 547, 1086, orations, speeches 1386, oration, speech 1489
scant *adv.* scarcely 287
scastye *n.* scarcity 268
science *n.* academic knowledge, book-learning 31, 83
sclaunder *n.* calumny 1146; **sclaundres** *pl.* calumnies 820
scorne *n.* mockery 312; **scornys** *pl.* insults 491
scrye *n.* uproar, outcry 1045
sealed *pa. pl.* set seal, swore 1019
season *n.* moment of time 592, **seson** period of time 1302; **seasons** *pl.* opportunities 1006
secondare *adj.* second-rank 718
see *n.* sea 73, 318, 904; **sees** *pl.* seas 242, 311, 499, etc.
seke *adj.* weak 625
semyth *pr. 3 sg. impers.* seems 91, ~ **me** seems to me 43, **mesemyth** 358, **semeth me** 1267; **semyd** *pa. 3 sg.*

seemed 159; **semyd me** *pa. 3 sg. impers.* seemed to me 117–18
sentence *n.* opinion 1190, 1194, 1196, etc., **yeue . . . ~ of** pass judgement on 1422
serche *inf.* strive 43
sett *inf.* set 214, 251, 280, etc., **sette** 321, 894, 1247, **sett vpon** embark on 474, 495, 537, attack 1000; **settyth** *pr. 3 sg.* sets 208, **settith** 478, arranges, draws up 1654; **sett** *pr. pl.* set 504; **sett** *pa. 3 sg.* set 368, 1675, ~ **vpon** attacked 197–8, ~ **forward** began to move 1566, ~ **forthe** 1587; **sett** *pa. pl.* set 294, ~ **forward** began to move 167, **sette vpon** attacked 458; **sett** *pa. p.* set 136, 511, 1213, etc., arranged, drawn up 1165, 1590, 1647, inlaid 281, ~ **vpon** 544, attacked 1169, ~ **vppon** embarked on 1578, ~ **by** esteemed 184, 290–1, ~ **fore** anticipated, awaited in an ambush 1474, **evill** ~ set on evil 858, **sette vpon** intent on 82; **sett on** *imp.* attack 1625
sewre *adj.* certain 800, 1262, reliable 964, secure 1392, **sewer** certain 1606, secure 1617
sewrly *adv.* surely 77, 207, 286, etc., **sewre** 1268, **sewrely** 1417
seurty *n.* security 1165
sewte *n.* petition 1357, candidacy 545, **seute** 634; **sewites** *n. pl.* petitions 969
shewynge *n.* testimony 20; **shewinges** *pl.* testimonies 1174
shrewed *adj.* wicked 127
sight *n.* appearance 720, 1547
signes *n. pl.* banners, standards 233, signatures 366, portents 695, badges, insignia 837, 1334
syngler *adj.* special 451, **singler** 969
synnes *conj.* since 442, 1090
syrris *n. pl.* sirs 1377, 1622, **syrres** 1401, **syrrs** 1606
sythen *conj.* since 480, **sithen** 755
sithes *n. pl.* scythes 1564
so *adv.* such 105, 189, 410, etc.
so *conj.* so long as 1403
socour *n.* protection, refuge 795, 1524, aid 802, reinforcement 1608, **socoure** 1594, 1655
socourerd *pa. 3 sg.* aided 1688
softe *adj.* soft-hearted, lacking in courage 279, supple 342
sondry *see* **sundry**
sore *adj.* painful 1278, intense 1318, fierce 1689, 1693; **sorer** *adj. comp.* more painful 1282
sore *adv.* badly 143, 361, 376, etc., extensively 1386
sore *n.* disease 857
space *n.* time, interval 25, 181, 422, etc.
sparis *pr. pl.* refrain 1403; **sparid** *pa. 3 sg.* dispensed, used up 610, refrained 356, **sparyd** 576, **sparid (. . .) for** avoided incurring 345–6, **spared for** held back on account of 1468; **spared** *pa. pl.* refrained 283, **sparid** avoided 315; **spare** *imp.* leave intact 1468; **sparyng** *vbl. n.* refraining from killing 1404
speche *n.* oration, speech 514, 746, 1599, talk 1194
speciall *adv.* especially 1255, 1531
specially *adv.* especially 804
spede *inf.* prosper, meet with success 496
spoylid *pa. pl.* pillaged 283; **spoyled** *pa. p.* deprived 779; *see also* **dispoyled**
spoylinges *n. pl.* spoils 675
stabelissh *inf.* establish 1024
stand *inf.* stand in an election 621; **standist** *pr. 2 sg.* stand still, do nothing 1372; **standith** *pr. 3 sg.* stands 1659; **stonde** *pr. pl.* stand 1466; **standyng** *pr. p.* standing in an election 422; **stode** *pa. 3 sg.* was underpinned 50, stood (in an election) 382, 534; **stode** *pa. pl.* were standing 392, 542, 842, stood 724, rested, was founded 1110; **stant** *pa. p.* arranged in battle formation 1562
standers *n. pl.* standard-bearers 1646, 1654, 1683
styrre *inf.* stir up, incite 514, 893; **styrred** *pa. 3 sg.* stirred up, incited 578; **styrred** *pa. pl.* stirred up 429; **styrred** *pa. p.* stirred up 139, 1181, 1193, **styrrid** 1167, 1208
stomake *n.* spirit, courage 126, 130, 372, etc.; **stomakes** *pl.* spirits 279, 1123, 1517, etc.
strayte *adj.* narrow 1581, **straite** 1655
straytnes *n.* narrowness 1639
straunge *adj.* unfamiliar 26, unusual 572, ~ **from** alien to 1268
straungers *n. pl.* travellers, wanderers 77, foreigners 456, 1332, outsiders 466

streight *adv.* straight away 191, 1053, 1595
strengith *inf.* strengthen 767
strengith *n.* force 195, 381, 410, etc., support 1455, military force 846, 996, 1413, **strength** 1499; **strenghthis** *pl.* forces 1042
stryffe *n.* struggle 197, contest 225, dispute, contention 902, 913, **striffe** 49; **stryves** *pl.* disputes, contentions 128, conflicts 791, civil discord 865
stryke *inf.* strike 1010; **stroke** *pa. 3 sg.* struck 585; **stryken** *pa. p.* struck 165, fallen 1003, **strekyn** afflicted 680
study *n.* academic study 115, 216, **studye** 11, diligent effort 1531
substanciall *adj.* reliable 1521
substaunce *n.* means of subsistence 322, 378, 1110, foundation, basis in fact 521, material wealth 716, 824, 861, etc.
suffre *inf.* endure 129, 244, 789, etc., permit 497, 1060, 1612, **suffer** tolerate 1389, permit 1475, endure 456, 1502, 1629, **suffre deth** be killed 1193; **suffred** *pa. 3 sg.* permitted 959; **suffred** *pa. pl.* suffered 421, 1464, ~ . . . **deth** were killed 559; **suffred** *pa. p.* tolerated 276, permitted 1143, 1357, **sufferd** endured 460, permitted 1281, 1346
sundry *adj.* various 156, **sondry** 996
surmyse *n.* allegation 1134
swete *adj.* agreeable 278, 618

T

tarye *pr. pl.* delay, procrastinate 1445; **taryed** *pa. pl.* delayed 232; **tarying** *vbl. n.* procrastinating, delaying 835, 937, 1065, etc.
temptyd *pa. 3 sg.* enticed 388
tendre *adj.* youthful 29, 99, 748, etc.
tentys *n. pl.* camp 191, 765, 1566
than *adv.* at that time 58, 67, 180, etc., thereupon 62, 171, 183, etc., **then** 552, at that time 673
that *pron.* who 37, 62, 82, etc., which 32, 45, 96, etc., ~ **their** whose 334, 884
thederward *adv.* thither 1021, **thedirward** 1033
thedyr *adv.* thither 952, 1065, 1070, etc., **thether** 394, 433, **theder** 1020, 1039, **thedir** 955
them *pron.* them 25, 28, 54, etc., **theim** 79, 163 (*bis*), etc., **þem** 237, **thaim** 240, 495; **theimselffes** *refl. pron.* themselves 75, 221, 229, etc., **themselffes** 170–1, 225, 235, etc., **themselfes** 37, **theirselffis** 729, **theirsellffes** 731, **theim** 57, 61, 165, **them** 38, 167, 311, etc., **hym** 1122
then *conj.* than 193, 407, **than** 44, 173, 186, etc.
thense *adv.* thence 233, **thens** 856
therin *adv.* in that 128, 426, 661
therof *adv.* in relation to that 681, 695, 1286, as a result of that 110, 258, of that 713, 940, from that 24, 550, of itself 1509, of it 857, **þerof** 260
therto *adv.* to that purpose 319, 1018, moreover 375
therunto *adv.* unto that place 740, unto that matter 290, 403, **thervnto** 389, 1540, unto that place 1204, **theronto** unto that matter 139, unto that thing 622
thyder *adv.* thither 981
thorow *prep.* throughout 717, 1415, through 1171, 1579, on account of 446, 558, 704, etc., **thorowe** 1271, 1361
thowe *conj.* although 522, 581, 819, etc., **though** 90, 104, 1127, **thowgh** 1390, **as thowe** as though 1413
thraldome *n.* servitude, slavery 518 (see n.), subjugation, wretchedness 777, 849, 941, etc.
thryes *adv.* thrice 1087
thryst *n.* thirst 319
to *adv.* too 205, 260, 277, etc.
trayties *see* **treatise**
translatyd *pa. p.* carried across, conveyed 72
treatise *n.* narrative, account 12, **trayties** 124
treson *n.* civil strife 127, treason 710, 736, 855, etc.
tryall *n.* evidence, proof 425, legal examination 1132
trothe *adv.* truly 1467
trowe *pr. 1 sg.* believe 1246, 1348, 1466, **trow** 1407; **trowed** *pa. 3 sg.* believed 928
truste *inf.* confidently expect 525, ~ **vnto** rely on 521, ~ **to** believe in 967; **truste** *pr. 1 sg.* believe 516; **trustyng** *pr. p.*

confidently expecting 621, 1632, believing 1453, ~ **to** relying on 1571, 1628; **trusted** *pa. 3 sg.* confidently expected 534, 875, **trustid** 1568; **trusted** *pa. pl.* confidently expected 557, 941; **trusted** *pa. p.* believed 412; **trustyng** *vbl. n.* hoping 30

U

vnclene *adj.* morally blemished, sinful 359
vndiscretly *adv.* injudiciously 746–7, 979
vnlernyd *adj.* uneducated 76, 1294
vnmete *adj.* unsuitable 1296
vnpurveid *adj.* unprepared 663
vnthrifftynes *adj.* wastefulness 869
vnto *prep.* unto 26, 61, 185, **onto** unto 832
vse *n.* exercise 192
vtterly *adv.* forthrightly 972

V

vagaboundes *n. pl.* dissolute people 671–2, homeless wanderers 870
varye *inf.* waver 631
verrey *adj.* actual, true 249, 1634
verrey *adv.* extremely 226, 535
vertew *n.* excellence, courage, moral virtue 47, 73, 95, etc., **vertu** 74; **vertewis** *pl.* courage, moral virtues 102, **vertuys** 290
vertewis *adj.* virtuous, pertaining to virtue 250, **vertuouse** 64–5
vicious *adj.* morally corrupt 149, 287, 327, etc., **viciouse** 868
viciousnes *n.* immorality 315, 594, 674, etc.
vile *adj.* lowly, servile 114, low-born 484, contemptible, dishonourable 490, 705, foul 1629, **the** ~ morally flawed people 186, ~ (. . .) **men** commoners, low-class people (?) 598 (see n.), 1030–1 (see n.), 1573 (see n.), ~ **persones** 697 (see n.), ~ **people** 1064 (see n.), 1176, ~ **man** servile person (?) 712 (see n.)
visage *n.* looks, appearance 363
vytaill *n.* food supplies 1612
voyde *adj.* worthless 470, 1271, 1375, etc.

W

wanne *see* **wynne**
warde *n.* watchfulness 717, 1184; **wardes** *pl.* divisions, sections (of an army) 1556, 1559, 1647, etc.
warded *pa. p.* fortified 204
ware *pa. 3 sg.* wore 646
warke *n.* work, effort 1318; **warkys** *pl.* resources, means 44, **werkys** works, writings 11
warly *adj.* warlike 193, 933, 1562
warnyng *n.* signal 1678
watche *n.* keeping awake 129, 360, 649, vigilance 717, 1184, 1527; **watches** *pl.* lookouts, vigilance 760
watched *pa. 3 sg.* kept awake 648
waye *pr. 1 sg.* evaluate 1636; **way** *subj. pl.* weigh 1226
wele *n.* state 1383; *see also* **comen wele**
welth *n.* riches 292, 1213, prosperity 286, 1457, **welthe** 875, riches 46
welthy *adj.* valuable 530, rich 1501, prosperous 160, **welthye** 1428
wex *inf.* grow 243; **waxed** *pa. 3 sg.* grew, became 568, 1342
what *adv.* why 1372
where *conj.* when 28, 595, 664, etc., at which 1014, in which place 192, 758, 800, etc., **wher** 1596, when 14 (see n.)
whereas *conj.* seeing that 70, 106, 659, etc., although 1220, when 1421, **wheras** 1316
wherfore *adv.* on account of which 43, 509, 583, etc.
wherto *conj.* wherever 1203, 1244
wheruppon *adv.* consequently 162, 699, 1596
wheruppon *conj.* as a consequence of which 816, 845, 971, etc., **whervppon** 681
wilde *adj.* uncivilized, savage 240, agitated, disturbed 361, **wylde** untamed, undomesticated 43, untamed, violent 1010
wilfulnes *n.* high-spiritedness 288, 530–1, obstinacy 789, purpose, resolve 1296, eagerness, inclination 1303, impulsiveness 1204–5, 1390, **wilfulnesse** 71, obstinacy 180
willed *pa. 3 sg.* desired 973, **willid** 1079
wynne *inf.* win 44, 84, 86, etc., ~ **theim** obtain their acquiescence 346; **wyne** *pr.*

pl. win 480; **wanne** *pa. 3 sg.* won 1521; **wanne** *pa. pl.* won 543; **wonne** *pa. p.* won 69, 420, 594, etc.

wise *see* **lyke**

withoute *conj.* unless 217, 479, 517, etc., **withowte** 1136

witt *n.* intelligence, mind 76, 616

wode *adj.* mad 244

wolgare *adj.* vernacular 13

wonne *see* **wynne**

wonte *pa. p.* accustomed 572, 694, 728, etc., **wont** 1086

worshipfull *adj.* honourable 401, 705, 1239

worshippe *n.* honour 511, 1616, high office 582, social standing 828–9

wounde hym *pa. 3 sg. refl.* made his way 757

wowted *pa. p.* vaulted 1545

Y

ye *adv.* ~ **and** indeed 87, 283, 370–1, etc.

ye *interj.* yes, indeed 1411, 1438, 1439, etc.

yere *n.* year 181, 621, 1090, etc.; **yeris** *pl.* life 350, years, time 1289, years 890, 1510, age 493, 494, 595, etc., **yerys** 344, **yeres** years, lifespan 111

yernyd *pa. pl.* earned 877

INDEX OF PROPER NOUNS

Spellings from MS Nn.3.6 are in bold. Where known, life dates are given for individuals who were not contemporary with Catiline's conspiracy. Roman names are ordered alphabetically by *nomen*. Biographical information is largely based on Ramsey.